THE ULTIM
SOUTHERN
CYCLING GUIDE
LOIRE TO MEDITERRANEAN

Richard Peace

EXCELLENT BOOKS

EXCELLENT BOOKS
94 BRADFORD ROAD
WAKEFIELD
WEST YORKSHIRE WF1 2AE
TEL / FAX: (01924) 315147
Website : www.excellentbooks.co.uk
Printed 2008

ISBN 978-1-901464-20-7

Whilst the author has researched the routes for the purposes of this guide, no responsibility can be accepted for any unforeseen circumstances encountered whilst following them. The publisher would, however, welcome any information regarding any material changes and any problems encountered.

Front cover photos (clockwise from top left): Beach at Port-la-Nouvelle, south of Narbonne along the Canal de la Robine; Town cycling in Dijon; On the Luberon Cycleway near Forcalquier
Rear cover photo: Lake Annecy's cycle path amidst the Alps
Frontispiece: Cycling the Rhône-Sète Canal alongside the Mediterranean

Printed by
www.beamreachuk.co.uk (Yorkshire)

Contents

Introduction

THE ROUTES

If you have always fancied taking in the sights of Southern France on two wheels away from any traffic but wondered where the best routes are this is the guide for you. Since 1997 a French organisation called AF3V has been promoting the development of a network of waymarked cycle routes and greenways.
This growing traffic-free network, with many routes based on old railways and canal towpaths and known as *voies vertes,* gives you access to stunning French landscapes, be it the splendour of Alpine lakes and peaks, miles of Atlantic beach, the World Heritage Site of the Canal du Midi or the exotic Côte d'Azur. There are also longer signed touring routes known as *véloroutes* linking the most interesting sights in an area using a mixture of minor roads and traffic-free tracks and paths. For the majority of the routes in the book a touring or mountain bike would be more than adequate and the broad tarmac of many routes will also suit racing bikes. Indeed many *voies vertes* are used not only by family and leisure cyclists but by groups of racers making them of the widest possible appeal to all groups of cyclist.

CYCLING IN FRANCE

It is simply a pleasure. France is a cycling nation and accords cyclists status on the road and some great facilities, from wonderful off-road riding to city centre automated bike hire. If you're unfamiliar with cycling in France here are a few handy tips.

You will no doubt know to ride on the right hand side of the road, path or track you are on. However, you should also be aware of an old rule of the road called priority from the right which is still a consideration. In the absence of all other road signs this rule still applies - effectively it means traffic joining from the right has priority - even if on a seemingly minor road. If, though, your road has yellow diamond on white background signs you have priority, until you come to one with a black line through. Side roads in the main have stop or give way markings and roundabouts also usually have give way systems so this rule won't apply here. However, this is not always so and in any case it's wise to make a habit of treating traffic coming from the right with extra caution as some drivers may still adhere to the old law, even if road markings say otherwise!.
In France traffic lights go directly from red to green but do go to amber between green and red. A red light accompanied by an amber flashing arrow pointing to the right means you can turn right as long as you give way to other vehicles. A green light replaced by a flashing yellow light means you may proceed but have to give way to crossing traffic and pedestrians.
Where a cycle path is indicated by a white bicycle on a circular blue background, it is obligatory to use it in preference to the road. Where it is on a rectangular background, it is optional.

Symbols on road signage will normally be familiar. Accompanying text includes:

Cédez le passage – Give way
Obligatoire - compulsory
Route barrée – road closed (although not necessarily to cyclists)
Sauf livraisons – Except deliveries
Sens interdit – No entry
Sortie de camions – Lorries entering/leaving
Vous n'avez pas la priorité – You do not have priority
Chausée déformée – uneven surface
Rappel – Restriction / advice still applies
Sauf riverains – Except residents
Sens unique – One way
Route partagé - Shared route (i.e cycles mix with motor traffic)

Note that many of these text instructions, especially on *véloroutes*, don't apply to bicycles. For example the *Loire à Vélo* route (part of EuroVelo 6 across the whole of France) uses many sections of virtually traffic-free road marked *sauf riverains*.

ROADS, PATHS & TRACKS

A brief glossary:

E roads European roads **A roads** Autoroutes **N roads** National routes

D roads Departmental roads **C roads** Minor country roads (often not signed)

Don't be surprised if road numbers on the ground do not correspond to what's on your map. A large scale renumbering exercise has been under way.

Itinéraire / parcours Route **Bande cyclable** Cycle lane

Piste cyclable Cycle path *or* cycle lane

Voies vertes Totally traffic routes. They tend to be at least two or three metres wide, flat, well surfaced and suitable not only for cyclists but also for walkers and often for rollerbladers, wheelchair users and horseriders.

Chemin de halage Towpath **Vélo tout terrain (VTT)** Mountain bike

Vélo tout chemin (VTC) Hybrid or conventional bike (i.e. thicker tyres than racers)

Vélo de course is normally a racing bike.

For detailed information on bicycle riding advice see www.fubicy.org (French only - they also publish a handy French language booklet full of practical riding advice)

Different routes and areas have different signing systems although very often official cycle routes are signed in green and white. There is a national system of Grandes Randonnées (GR), long distance routes for hikers (and sometimes cyclists), all of which are on the IGN map 903. Marked on the ground by red and white stripes, they are often suitable for cycling, although a mountain bike may be needed, so these are largely outside the scope of this book. Petites randonnées, more local paths, are also often cycleable by mountain bike. There are plenty of French-language guides on GRs and PRs (and a fair number of English language ones too).

The white cyclist on a green background is extremely common in signage, often incorporated into the particular route sign style. The slightly non-standard signing pattern at bottom left is used around La Rochelle.

Cycling in towns and cities is pretty common but cycling levels, like the conventions and rules that govern local cycling conditions, vary quite a lot. In some places it can be the norm to cycle freely in pedestrian precincts, but not in others, although there's usually signage to tell you what actually should be. As in the UK, cyclist behaviour at traffic lights can be unpredictable. It seems to be fairly normal for cyclists to treat one way streets as two way, even if there is no signage.

GETTING THERE AND AWAY

Taking a bike along with your car, caravan or motorhome is obviously one popular option and is much the same experience as in the UK. However, if you are planning to go with bike alone it's definitely worth knowing a bit in advance about bikes and other forms of transport in France.

TRAINS

Getting your bike to France and taking it on trains when there is not normally a problem, especially if you are reasonably prepared, for example organising tickets in advance or simply collecting a stack of timetables.
Both Eurostar and the French railways (SNCF) will carry, free and as normal luggage, folding bicycles and bicycles dismantled and in a bike bag. Eurostar say this should be no bigger than a normal suitcase and SNCF say 120cm x 90cm maximum. If you're happy to travel with your bike only from Folkestone to Calais, Eurotunnel is a lot cheaper and will carry your bike on the same train as you (you load the bike onto a bespoke trailer then hop in the vehicle that tows the trailer which drives onto the train!). If you're taking bikes by motor on Eurotunnel, see their website for further information.
If you want to take a fully assembled bike, this will go on Eurostar via the registered baggage service at a charge and it will arrive within 24 hours of registration. Many French trains will carry fully assembled bikes:
TGV – many services between Paris and the east of France accept bikes but there is a charge and reservation is needed. The new Duplex (two deck) TGV services do not accept bikes. To get between stations, crossing Paris by bike is not that bad, especially with the aid of a map showing cycle routes – find Carte des itinéraires cyclables on **www.paris.fr** to download one.
Other services – consult the timetables. Trains which will carry bikes are identified with a bicycle logo on both paper and on-line timetables (although the absence of a logo doesn't always mean that they won't - check locally for specific services). On local trains there is no charge but on long distance journeys there is and reservation is required (these longer distance inter-regional trains are known as Corail).
When buying Eurostar travel tickets, you don't need to do anything about your bike. Just make sure you have your tickets or booking reference to hand when taking it in to the baggage office. If you want to be sure that your bike will be there when you arrive, take it in 24 hours before your own arrival time. At the time of writing Eurostar were reported to be implementing a system that would allow your bike to go on the same train as you - enquire about this.
French rail tickets can be booked online from the UK but to get a bicycle space reservation, very inconveniently, you need to ring SNCF in France when you've bought your travel ticket. Rail Europe can give you details of the current system of doing this from the UK and can also sell you your train tickets direct. When buying tickets at a French railway station, do allow plenty of time – you can often be faced with a queue and a long wait.
www.sncf.com is the website for French trains. **www.sncf.co.uk** and **www.raileurope.co.uk** offer similar online booking services. Rail Europe can be contacted on 08708 371 371 or in person Monday to Saturday at 178, Piccadilly, London. Eurostar is on www.eurostar.com or telephone 08705 186 186 (£5.00 fee for telephone bookings). Eurotunnel is on **www.eurotunnel.com** or telephone 01303 282201.

On the train:
TGV (High speed services) Bicycles travel in a separate compartment to which you may not have access during the journey.
Corail Téoz (luxurious inter-city services) wall racks (hook type) in a spacious cycle compartment. Your seat is normally in a carriage next to the one where your bike is.
Corail Lunéa (overnight inter-city services). Most Lunéa trains have a separate cycle compartment with wall racks (hook type).
Corail Intercité No specific cycle facilities.
TER (local trains) Some trains have racks, others don't. There's normally a bicycle logo by the doors where you should load your bicycle.
Car If on a timetable a service is by car, or autocar, this is a road journey by bus and is not supposed to carry bicycles. You may find a friendly driver with a quiet bus who will accept your bike but if you do want to get where you're going, don't rely on this happening.

There's an excellent little map book of the French railway system, Le Train en France, showing all the lines and all the stations. Available online from **www.iterritoires.com**

FERRY

Taking bikes on the ferry is usually a lot simpler than by train. If you're going as a foot passenger, you usually have to board with the motor vehicles and lash your bike to the deck side or elsewhere as directed by crew. When booking you should include your bike (which needs booking on even if there's no charge for it). If you're taking bikes by motor vehicle it's worth checking the rules and charges, partricularly for total dimensions and particularly if you want them on the roof.

EUROPEAN BIKE EXPRESS

Easy and efficient travel designed specifically for cyclists. Air conditioned coaches with reclining seats pulling a purpose-built trailer capable of carrying all manner of bikes and bike trailers. Runs throughout the summer serving western France on an Atlantic route and central, Alpine and Mediterranean France (and even into Spain) on other routes. Single or return journeys. Great for touring - you can go out on one route and return on another. UK pick-up points down the eastern side of England between North Yorkshire and Kent, with M62 / M6 feeder service on certain dates.
www.bike-express.co.uk 3, Newfield Lane, South Cave. HU15 2JW Tel: 01430 422111

AIR

A wide range of departure points and destinations can make this worth considering. Bikes need to have the handlebars flush with the frame and the pedals flush or removed. They should also be boxed or bagged, which gives you the problem of what to do with a box particularly at the other end.

NB When travelling as a group by any form of public transport always contact the carrier in advance to see that they can accommodate you.

There are occasional bus services with bike racks (e.g. some of the services between Nantes and Noirmoutier) but these are extremely rare.

ACCOMMODATION

More plentiful and cheaper than in the UK. Hotels, guest houses and hostels are usually very welcoming to cyclists and even if they don't have dedicated cycle storage will generally have somewhere secure for bikes. Tourist offices are plentiful and tremendously helpful in sourcing accommodation. Chambres d'hôte are often billed as the equivalent of bed and breakfast and often are, but sometimes they are more like small hotels. Logis de France is a hotel chain with many Logis Vélo hotels where you are offered such help as luggage transfer, weather forecast, cycle washing facilities, local route information and of course secure storage. Youth hostel information can be found on **www.fuaj.org** and indicates which hostels have cycle storage. Gîtes d'étape can be similar to a hostel or more like bunkhouses where you'll get basic dormitory facilities but need a sleeping bag - see **www.gites-de-france.com** or **www.gites-refuge.com** for more info. If you're wanting to hire a gîte rural, (a holiday home - usually self-catering) see **www.gites-de-france.com** again or local tourist authority sites. Clévacances are flats, chalets and houses for holiday hire - **www.clevacances.com** is a good starting point. Camping sites are generally very good whether you've got a small tent on a bike or several bikes on a motorhome - websites and publications on this abound - **www.campingfrance.com** is good.

VÉLORAILS

Vélorails are lengths of disused railway with the track intact and used now to carry pedal-powered railcarts. The usual arrangement is two people pedalling with a bench behind for two or three passengers. There are one or two vélorails near cycle routes described in this book, for example at Hyères on the Côte d'Azur route and at Confolens in the Charente. For a list and location map, see **www.velorail24.com**. They are at: Fédération des Vélos-Rail de France, Gare de Labaurie 24800 Eyzerac

WITHOUT YOUR BIKE

French cycle holiday companies abound - sometimes they're aiming to explore a particular area or theme, sometimes guided, sometimes self-guided with back-up available, sometimes touring, sometimes fixed base. They can offer baggage transfer and deliver you into the lap of luxury each evening or they can be fairly minimalist affairs relying more on camping or basic accommodation. A good start point for investigating is **www.frenchentree.com/france-cycling-holiday** If avoiding holiday companies and needing a bike, bike hire is reasonably common and you should enquire locally. Cities such as Orléans, Lyon and Toulouse have city-wide automated cycle hire suitable for short hops across town.

MAPS

The majority of maps in this guide are based on Michelin 1:200,000 maps - usually sufficient outside urban areas. In larger towns and in cities you should pick up a street map (a cycle map if possible) from the tourist office. Specific cycle maps and guides for a particular route or area are listed under the *Route Info* section of a chapter under *Maps, guides and websites*. Where a route is not yet fully signed or simply to give an overview of an area the guide also uses 1:1,000,000 million mapping and tells you where more detailed mapping is available.

Should you want even more detailed information on an area IGN 1:100,000 maps are excellent, showing the majority of minor roads and many tracks in an area as well as having cycle tracks traced in red. See **www.ign.fr** for more details.

WEATHER

Without a doubt Southern France is a sunny place and it's possible to have an enjoyable cycling break at just about any time of year if you plump for the sunniest locations such as Languedoc-Roussillon or the Côte d'Azur, both areas enjoying famously mild and dry winters. Perhaps surprisingly the Alps also receive some of the sunniest weather year round, although cycling the higher passes is likely to be out because of permanent snow at any time between November to May. Also bear in mind mid-summer can be just too hot for cycling, especially for longer tours if you want to be cycling during the middle of the day when temperatures are at their maximum. Even as far north as the Loire Valley the average July daily maximum temperature is around 26 Celcius, only a couple of degrees lower than the average for Nice. The further east and inland you go the more 'continental' becomes the climate with extremes of heat in summer and cold in winter - though within the area covered by this guide the 'continental' climate pattern only really applies to northern parts of the Alps and Franche-Comté.

Perhaps as much a factor for cyclists as the question of rain or sun is the question of wind or no wind. Most feared of all is the Mistral which tends to blow south down the Rhône Valley for almost a third of the year, being commonest in spring.

Strong winds can also blow along the Canal du Midi and out to the Med. However, it would be a pity to let fear of wind stop you cycling - you are more likely, statistically speaking, not to encounter excessive winds and even if you do, hopefully you will have allowed a few days off the bike - so now is the time to take them! Also be aware that the Atlantic coast can be subject to storms at just about any time of year. A good generalisation is that spring and autumn often hold the best cycling weather and let you avoid the worst of the mid-July to end of August holiday crowds and the associated high prices (it's also wise to avoid Easter holidays for similar reasons).

For a forecast one of the most useful sites is **www.meteofrance.com**

FURTHER CONTACTS

The AF3V national office can be found at:

AF3V Association Française de Développement des Véloroutes et Voies Vertes.

www.af3v.org

AF3V chez Association Vélo 5, avenue F. Collignon, 31200 Toulouse

Telephone 05 34 30 05 59

The website for AF3V gives much information and has a route search facility for well over 200 véloroutes and voies vertes and an expanding English language version. There is a biennally published guide book, the "Guide Touristique des Véloroutes et Voies Vertes de France" listing 150 or more routes and available from AF3V or **www.cartovelo.com** or join AF3V as a member to receive one free.

Tandem riding on a beautiful, high quality greenway section between Dole and Besançon on EuroVelo 6 - see pages 48-65

The Camargue & The Rhône-Sète Canal

Route Info

Camargue & Rhône - Sète Canal
Whilst this is the only long distance route in the guide that is not an 'official' signed route it's simply too good to miss. The first leg of the journey picks up the very broad track along the lagoon-surrounded Rhône - Sète Canal. It's then a mixture of minor roads and tracks through the watery Camargue, visiting the extraordinary towns of Saintes-Maries-de-la-Mer and Aigues-Mortes before finishing in Arles with its monumental Roman amphitheatre.

Grade EASY

Start / finish Sète / Arles

Route length 83 miles / 132km. A there-and-back excursion to Montpellier will add a further 14 miles / 23 km. Alternatively heading east when you reach the Rhône - Sète Canal to end at Beaucaire gives a shorter journey option of 67 miles / 108km

Total height climbed 351ft
Total height descended 259ft
(Reverse the figures if biking east - west)
Average climb - Sète to Arles 4.2 ft per mile
Average climb - Arles to Sète 3.1 ft per mile

Route advice A largely flat route through some amazing scenery.
NOTE: The track between Mas de Cacherel and Méjanes is stony and rutted in places. Bikes with front suspension advised though not essential. The Rhône-Sète Canal towpath can be stony in places but generally is a better quality surface than the track above, which is certainly best avoided in wet weather.

Train access TGV service to Sète and Arles. TGV trains run to the north of the route through Nîmes and Montpellier.

Nearby routes
Canal du Midi - 20 miles / 32km on mainly minor roads (link route pg39)

Maps, guides and websites
No detailed route info available at the time of writing.

Don't Miss

Horse & Bull Culture in the Camargue

One of the most iconic images in all France is that of wild horses splashing through the salt marshes of the Camargue, that area where the Rhône delta mingles its waters with those of the Mediterranean. Whilst most horses you'll see here today are at best semi-wild (many are stabled and used for riding tours of the marshes) they are still a strikingly beautiful feature of this eerily and seemingly empty landscape. Seemingly empty that is until you start to notice the striking plants and animals that have found a niche in this unique salty world. The unusual birdlife includes night herons and nesting pink flamingoes.
You are also likely to see the native small black bulls here (don't worry, they are fenced off from major public rights of way). Used in the local version of bullfighting, they are not killed in the contest and it's usually the bullfighters who come off worst.

A Bit of Roman Entertainment

Resembling a weirdly out of place alien spaceship made of stone, the first century Roman amphitheatre known as Les Arènes, totally dominates its immediate town centre surroundings in the lovely town of Arles. Today houses and shops encircle it but in medieval times the arches themselves in this vast circular structure housed around two hundred dwellings and three churches - now all gone.
As well as an incredible sight from the outside you can wander around the inside or use one of its 25,000 seats to watch a bullfight, play or concert.

Suggested Day Rides on the Route

Into the Camargue from Arles or Saintes-Maries-de-la-Mer Pg15
19 miles return ride from Saintes-Maries-de-la-Mer to Domaine de Méjanes. 25 miles return ride from Arles to Domaine de Méjanes.
The shorter option here uses the road heading north-east out of Saintes-Maries-de-la-Mer for around 2 miles before heading right onto an unmarked track that skirts the Étangs of Malagroy and Vaccares. It rejoins tarmac at the Domaine de Méjanes where there is a small tourist railway, restaurant, information point, bullring and riding stables. There are walks and rides (on horse and mountain bike) from here out into the wildest parts of the marshes.
The route from Arles uses quiet minor roads as shown on the map (more main roads in the Camargue can get very busy in holiday season).

Saintes-Maries-de-la-Mer is touristy but has retained its character

Montpellier - Isle of Maguelone Pg13
24 miles return ride from the extremely elegant heart of Montpellier to the unusual wine-producing island of Maguelone, with a once important cathedral, now largely ignored, and some restored typical fisherman's huts on the north shore. You'll need a town map of Montpellier where you find your way to the impressive new development called the Antigone. Here cycle down the main pedestrianised avenue to the River Lez. A signed route (signs often discrete, for 'Les Plages') takes you south along the river to a cycletrack alongside the road to Perols and Carnon. There are all the usual seaside attractions at Carnon Plage if you want them, but for a really unusual ride head west on the Rhône-Sète Canal towpath (south side) to the cathedral island of Maguelone. If you want more seaside attractions and funky 60s architecture visit Palavas-les-Flots, just to the south of the canal between Maguelone and Carnon-Plage. An optional return route uses a rougher track, as shown on the map.

Traffic-free cycling by Montpellier's River Lez

MONTPELLIER

A truly beautiful city, Montpellier's highlight is the vast, light, central square of Place de la Comédie, bounded by an extravagant theatre at one end and the large park known as the Champs de Mars at the other. To add to a great selection of longstanding museums a new aquarium and zoo are now on the city's attractions list.

The bike route between the historic centre and the River Lez passes through the huge modern development known as the Antigone - like much of the old centre of Montpellier it is car-free and its broad, main avenue, classically inspired, is one of the most unusual developments you will see. The final section of the link route into and out of the city follows the broad banks of the River Lez. An extremely worthwhile detour from the main route.

MONTPELLIER

15 MILE RETURN DETOUR *i*

15 MILES *i*

Palavas-les-Flots

Maguelone

13 MILES *i*

4 MILES *i*

Frontignan

0 MILES *i*

Sète

Montpellier has its very own mini-version of Paris's Arc de Triomphe

AIGUES-MORTES

Translated, the town's name means 'dead waters' - originally intended as a major medieval port it silted up. This means its thirteenth century fortifications and street plan have been well-preserved and despite the heavy concentration of tourist shops it's a great place to stroll around. Look out for the Tower of the Salted Burgundians - the name gives away the fate of the unlucky soldiers killed in a battle here!

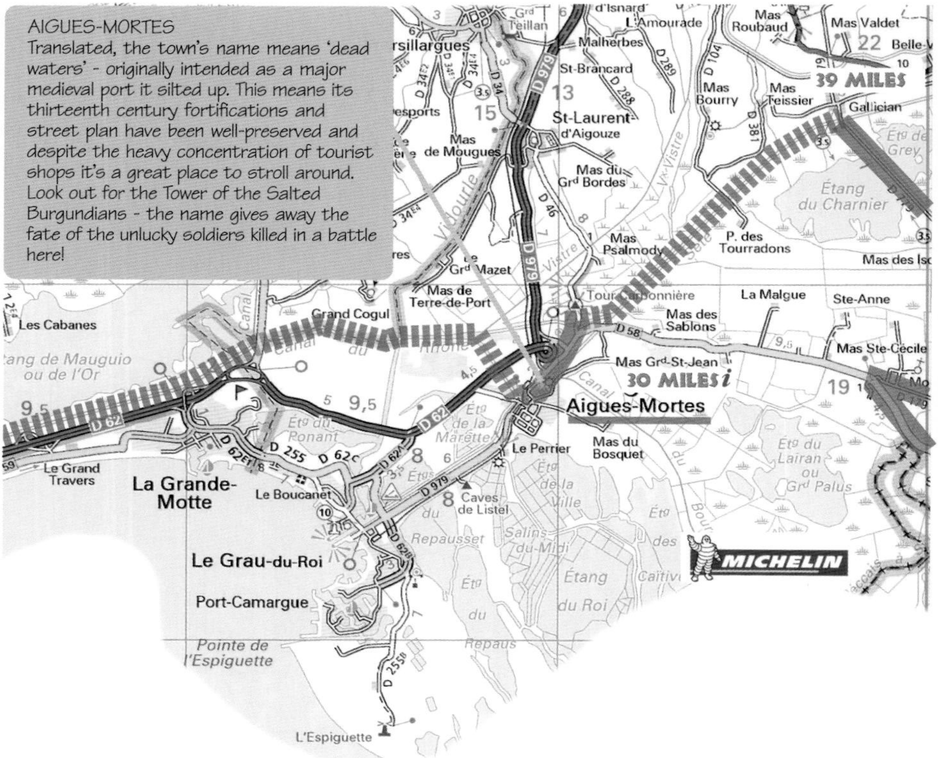

The ancient walled town of Aigues-Mortes

ARLES

Whilst the brilliantly preserved Roman amphitheatre is the main draw here (see Don't Miss pg11) Arles is also a very pleasant city in its own right, especially the area around the Place de la République, housing the cathedral and town hall.

Van Gogh lived a period of his life in Arles and the Fondation Van Gogh houses work of modern artists he inspired.

As well as the Roman Amphitheatre (known as Les Arènes) other remains include an ancient Roman theatre, excavated sections of a chariot racetrack and a Roman burial ground.

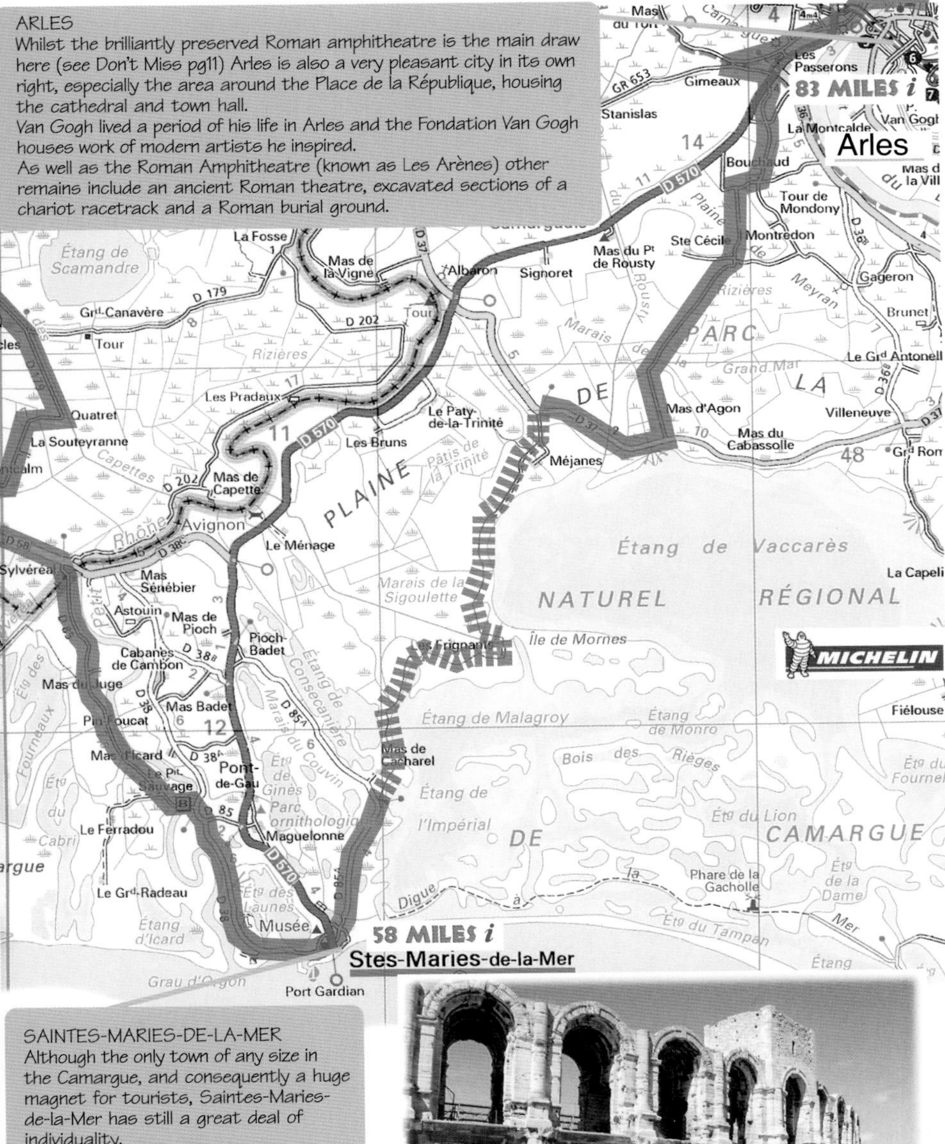

SAINTES-MARIES-DE-LA-MER

Although the only town of any size in the Camargue, and consequently a huge magnet for tourists, Saintes-Maries-de-la-Mer has still a great deal of individuality.

Amongst the regular trappings of seaside resorts typical of the area are a couple of highly individual attractions. There is the lovely and ancient Romanesque church (it houses a statue of Sarah, patron saint of the gypsies which is carried to the sea during the gypsy pilgrimage at the end of May). The Baroncelli Museum details Camargue traditions and wildlife.

Just part of the huge Roman amphitheatre at Arles

Around the Luberon

Route Info

Luberon Cycleway
Though graded difficult, this route isn't as difficult as you might imagine as it follows the base of the Luberon mountains. There are, however, several extended and reasonably steep climbs on the eastern section, especially after the pretty town of Reillanne.

Grade DIFFICULT

Start / finish Attractive market town Cavaillon is your start and finish point.

Route length 147 miles / 237 km

Total height climbed 17,500ft
Average climb - 119ft per mile

Route advice This véloroute is well signed in both directions. Uses mainly decent quality minor roads.

Train access North-south TGV service to Avignon and a local line along the eastern edge of the route with stations at Manosque, Pertuis and La Brillane.

Nearby routes
Forcalquier Loop & Les Ocres Loop
Both link to the Luberon. See overleaf and pgs 68-69 for more detail.
There are some spectacular but difficult signed road routes in the Var region to the south-east of the Luberon. See pgs 70-71.

Maps, guides and websites
www.veloloisirluberon.com
Under review at the time of writing - the old version has useful information on the Luberon Cycleway and links to basic information on the Forcalquier and Les Ocres Loops. Includes accommodation and cycle hire along the way. Leaflets showing services and a basic map from local tourist offices.

Don't Miss

Hilltop Villages

If you head clockwise around the Luberon massif you will soon encounter a lovely string of hilltop villages; although many now house a good proportion of holiday homes (no doubt helped by the fact they are the main subject of Peter Mayle's bestseller *A Year in Provence)* they have still, by and large, kept their character and cycling between them is an ideal way to take in their varied charms.
Oppède le Vieux is undoubtedly one of the most beautiful of all the hilltop villages featuring a ruined castle and is worth the extra riding up the valley side to visit its centre. Ménerbres, sitting atop a long ridge, has one of the most dramatic outlines whilst Lacoste and Bonnieux hold some of the most dramatic views. It's certainly worth allowing yourself plenty of time on this section of the route to explore these lovely villages.

The Dry South

The hotter, drier southern side of the Luberon massif features much fewer villages - no doubt in part because it failed to recover from the devastating events of 1545
when the area between Lourmarin and Mérindol saw the massacre of some 3,000 residents suspected of being protestants. The crumbling ruins at Mérindol remain today as a haunting reminder of the terrible event.

For details of Mont Ventoux see pgs 68-69

Signage

Luberon By Bike is signed in both directions - generally very well signed. White detailing signs the route clockwise and orange takes you counter clockwise. There are also occasional information boards (left).

Suggested Day Rides on the Route

Cavaillon to Oppède le Vieux Pg 18
17 miles return ride. Pick up the signs in front of Cavaillon station and follow the route clockwise (white detailing) through the flatlands before starting to climb through a series of villages on the north-eastern slopes of the *Petit-Luberon* as the mountain chain is known west of the main pass. Taillades, Robion and Maubec are all very characterful villages but the real highlight of the ride comes as you start to climb up the edge of the Luberon to lovely Oppède le Vieux. It tumbles down the hillside, with the more modern houses at the bottom and an ancient crumbling castle at the top. Visitors by car have to leave their vehicles further down the slope and walk up to the village, further enhancing the special atmosphere here. Look out for the viewpoint and ceramic sign that attractively maps out the landscape between here and Mont Ventoux, some 30 miles to the north. Restaurants and café in Oppède.

Reillanne to St. Michel l'Observatoire pg19
18 miles return ride. This is where the hills become more serious and the terrain more alpine in character and so you'll need to be prepared to tackle the long steady climb out of Reillanne and to climb steeply away from the River Large towards St Michel. The nearby domes you see approaching the charming village of St Michel are indeed an observatory as the name suggests although night-time viewings for the public are rare events sadly.
Reillanne is based around a large square overlooked by a hilltop church. There are plenty of shops and cafes here so you can stock up on goodies and drink coffee before the ride. St Michel is smaller but still has cafes and shops.

Apt to Bonnieux Pgs 18, 17
14 miles return ride. From the pleasant town of Apt on the River Calavon you head anti-clockwise on the route (orange detailing) to climb steadily to lovely hilltop village of Bonnieux. It overlooks the Calavon plain, Lacoste village and Mont Ventoux and is sited on the Lourmarin pass, the only metalled road across the Luberon range. Its tourist trappings today don't give much of a clue to its historical importance. It was accorded important privileges by Count Raymond of Toulouse and was a Knights Templar base. Today there's a rather classy restaurant on Place Carnot and a museum of breadmaking. If you want to make this into a circular ride you can head north out of Bonnieux on the D149 to the lovely old bridge known as Pont Julien and pick up the high quality tarmac greenway here that heads back towards Apt. Note, however, that at the time of writing construction work was ongoing on the final section into Apt.

There are also two signed loops off the Luberon route - *Les Ocres a Vélo* (32 miles / 50km) and the much, much hillier *Pays de Fourcalquier a Vélo* (48.5 miles / 78km). Both make excellent longer day rides, though the Fourcalquier loop is only for the fit and experienced to ride in a day. See pgs 68-69 for more details.

North of Reillanne lie glorious views of the Alps

HILLTOP VILLAGES
Riding clockwise round the route you will head through the following beautiful villages, each with cafes and restaurants:

* Oppède le Vieux - some lovely houses and a couple of cafes in the lower part of the village then crumbling village ruins lead up to an ancient château.
* Ménerbes - superbly located on a high ridge
* Bonnieux - atmospheric village with great views and a museum of baking.

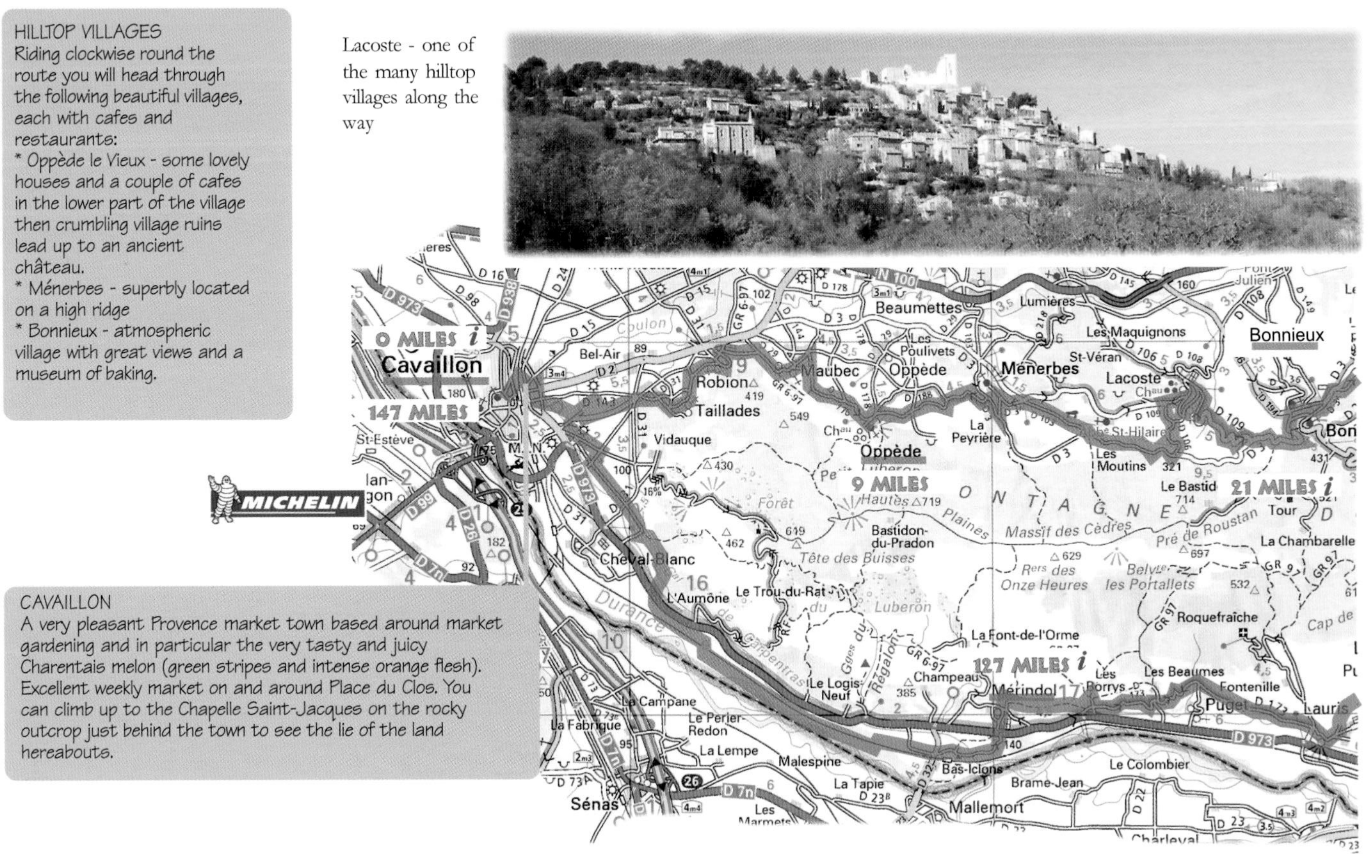

Lacoste - one of the many hilltop villages along the way

CAVAILLON
A very pleasant Provence market town based around market gardening and in particular the very tasty and juicy Charentais melon (green stripes and intense orange flesh). Excellent weekly market on and around Place du Clos. You can climb up to the Chapelle Saint-Jacques on the rocky outcrop just behind the town to see the lie of the land hereabouts.

LOURMARIN
Another quite rich village, known principally for its sixteenth century château, now owned by the University of Aix, though it is open for guided tours.
The existentialist writer Albert Camus is buried here.

ST-MICHEL-L'OBSERVATOIRE
The village here is named after the nearby observatory, which was located here as the area reputedly has the clearest skies and least pollution in all France.
If you arrive in mid-summer enquire locally to see if any nighttime viewings are available at the observatory.

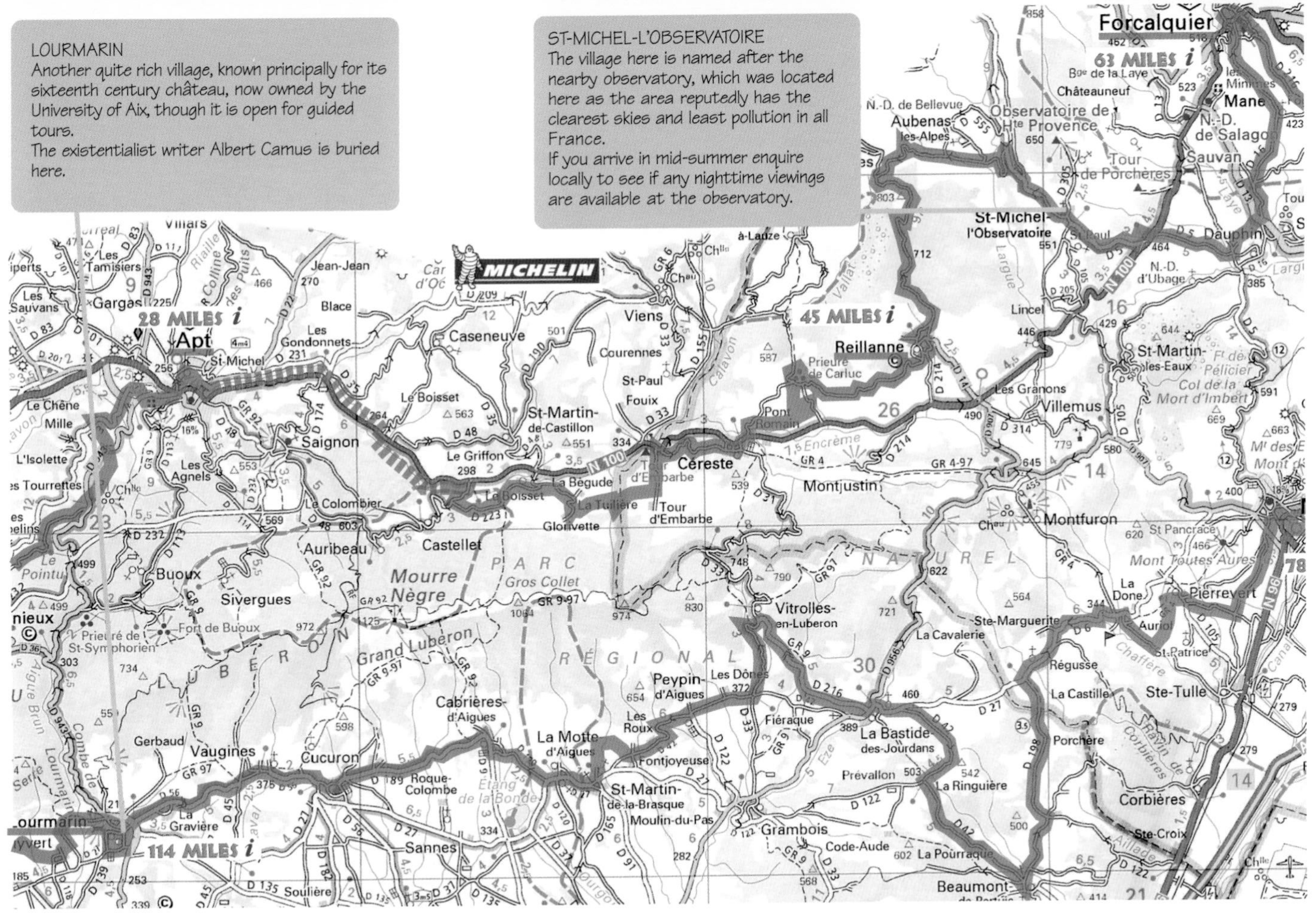

FORCALQUIER
A rather isolated and ancient settlement; it was hugely important in medieval times but has since become a quiet backwater, leaving its many fine buildings and monuments best appreciated in quiet contemplation.
It also has a lovely setting on a small wooded hill, something you really appreciate as you cycle in and out of the town on the Luberon Cycleway.

Forcalquier

MANOSQUE
Despite its rather unattractive outskirts this town has a lovely old centre, accessed via the old city gates.
It was home to famous Provence author Jean Giono and also houses an incredible work of art in the Fondation Carzou by an artist of the same name. Called the Apocalypse, it adorns the walls of the Fondation Carzou building and is most definitely worth searching out.

Old Manosque

Across Volcano Country

Route Info

Across Volcano Country
The topography of the Auvergne, dotted with the remains of extinct volcanoes, is always going to be pretty tough cycling country - especially if you want to sample the unusual, incredible views from the volcanoes themselves and the surrounding gorges. This véloroute passes one of the most famous volcanic summits, Puy Mary.

Grade Difficult

Start / finish Port d'Agres / Blesle

Route length 96 miles / 154km
Total height climbed 14,750ft
Total height descended 13,660ft
(Reverse the figures if biking east - west)
Av. climb: Port d'Agres - Blesle 152 ft per mile
Av: climb - Blesle - Port d'Agres 140 ft per mile

Route Advice Whilst you are on pretty quiet roads for most of the route there is one very long, sustained but spectacular climb up to Puy Mary. Add to this several lesser but still steep climbs and you have the most demanding long distance ride in the guide. Plan to do it between May and October - otherwise snow may block the route.

Train access Aubin station lies about 6 miles south of Port d'Agres on the line between Rodez and Figeac. You can also access the route further north at Maurs on the same line which heads north-east to Aurillac and Murat.

Nearby routes
Eventually the véloroute will link to the Lot valley route (pg 138-143) and will be crossed by the véloroute Dordogne.

Maps, guides and websites
www.cantaltourisme.com has basic area info in English and downloadable cycle brochures in French.
No 15 in the IGN *Cyclo Guide* series details 25 routes on minor roads in the area (Le Cantal à Vélo - Cantal by Bike).

Don't Miss

Volcanoes of the Cantal

The route takes you across the southern part of the *Parc Naturel Régional des Volcans d'Auvergne* and over some of the oldest volcanoes in the whole park. Don't worry though - volcanic activity ceased around 6,000 years ago and today you can travel through a rugged and often strangely eroded landscape, with many of the villages made up of distinctive grey volcanic rock. This particular area, the Monts du Cantal, is actually the remnants of France's largest extinct volcano, though somewhat cut down to size and sliced into with ice-age valleys. Today the most heated geolithic activity in the area is provided by spa towns where you can still 'take the waters'.
The Parc's wildlife includes Mouflon (mountain sheep), marmots, chamoix and rock thrushes.

Extinct volcanoes make a fine backdrop

Near Puy Mary

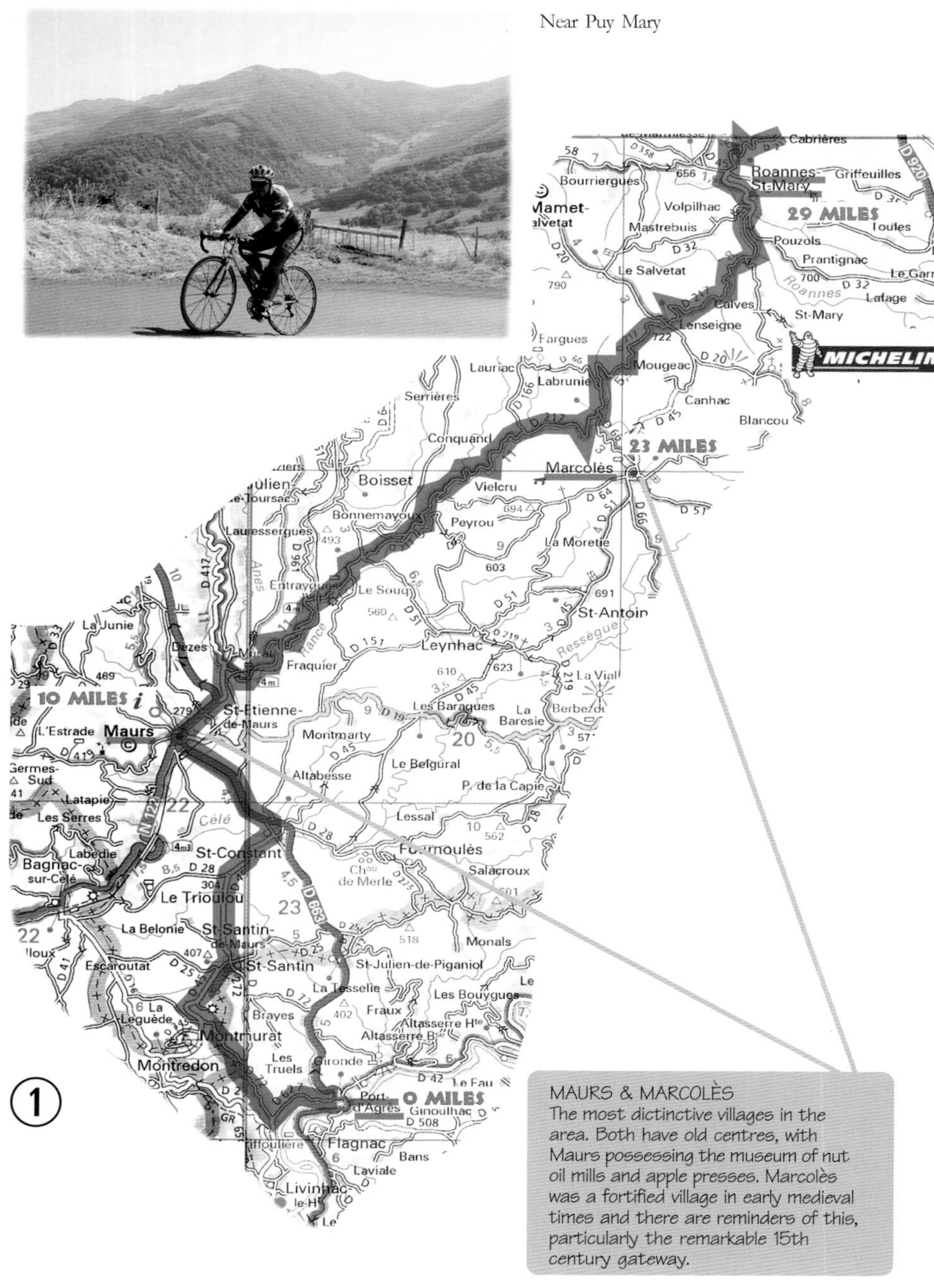

LE PUY MARY
Leave the route at the Col du Pas de Peyrol and it's a short walk to the 1787 metre summit of the pyramid shape of onetime volcano Le Puy Mary. There are dramatic views along the valleys and ridges which radiate from the mountain but you're unlikely to be on your own - it's one of the most visited places in the area. Visitor centre.

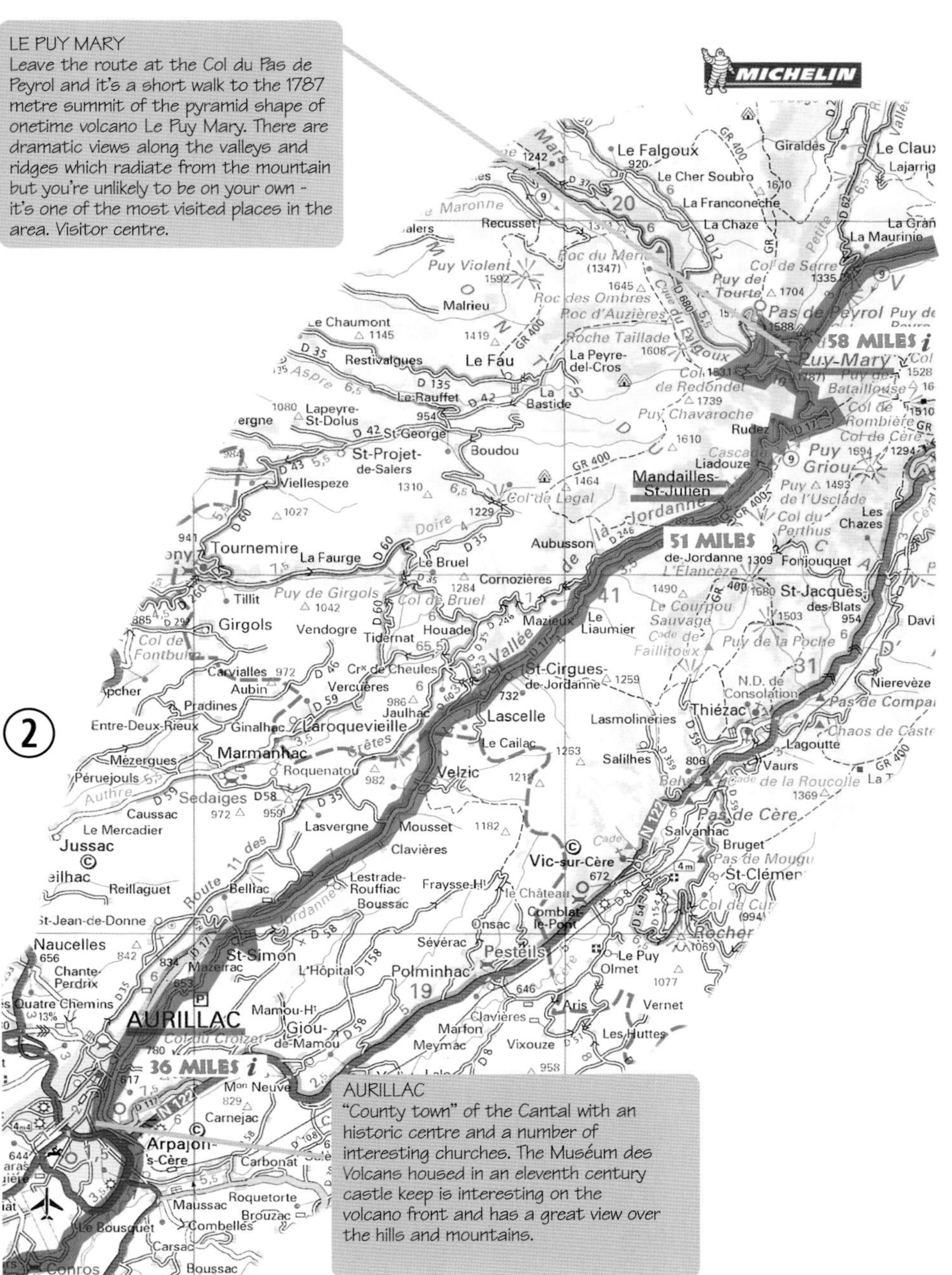

AURILLAC
"County town" of the Cantal with an historic centre and a number of interesting churches. The Muséum des Volcans housed in an eleventh century castle keep is interesting on the volcano front and has a great view over the hills and mountains.

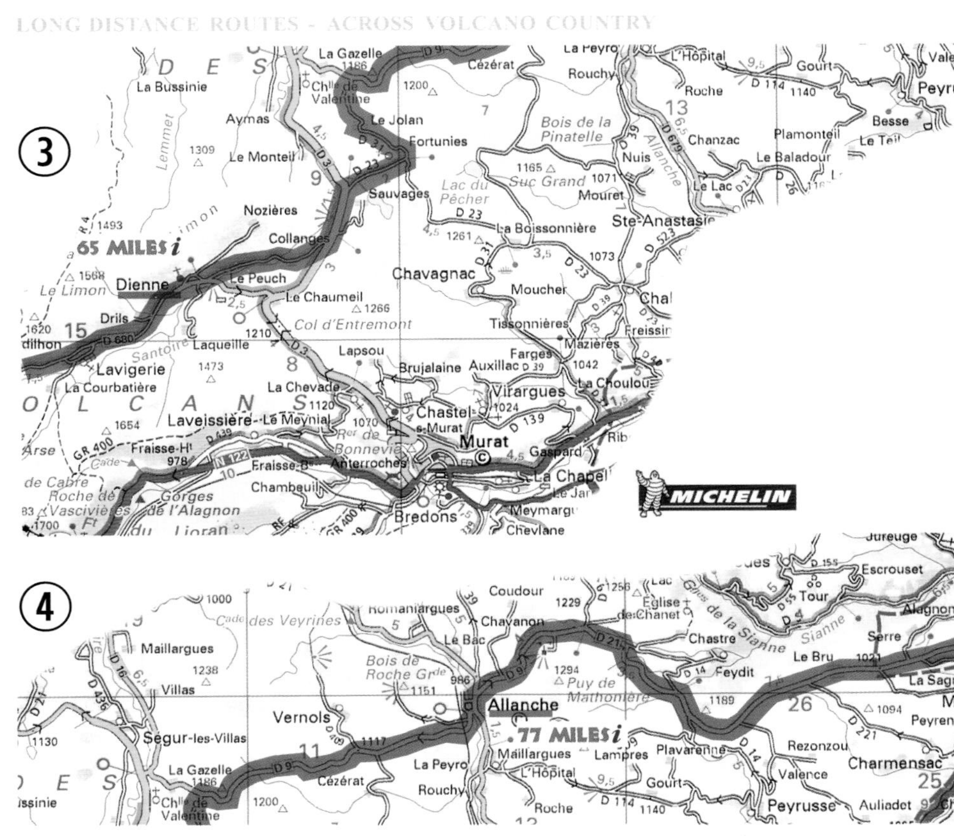

96 MILES
Blesle

BLESLE
Medieval Blesle has ancient stone towers, timbered houses, a Romanesque church and the remains of a Benedictine abbey.

5

CYCLING FODDER AUVERGNE CHEESES

This route passes through the south-west of the Auvergne, a region known for the quality of its cheeses; out of 34 cheeses with the prestigious Apellation d'Origine Contrôlée rating (AOC) 5 are from the Auvergne. Names to look out for here include bleu d'auvergne, cantal, fourme d'ambert, st. nectaire and salers. Of these salers is the only one still occasionally produced in the traditional small-scale manner, in *burons*, small huts of volcanic stone. Only 10 *burons* remain active, whilst more than 1000 are disused.

The Garonne Valley

Route Info

The Garonne Valley
This is largely a towpath route along the Canal Latéral à la Garonne but the western part, between Bordeaux and La Réole, uses the excellent Roger Lapébie cycle track and minor roads. It's mainly a flat, traffic-free route, ideal for exploring at a steady pace. Whilst the canal architecture may not be as spectacular as its neighbour, the Canal du Midi, the greener countryside, often filled with fruit orchards and maize is a delightful contrast to the Midi's drier, more Mediterranean surroundings. What's more, it visits Bordeaux and Toulouse, two of the south's great cities. Moissac is an architectural highlight and towns like Agen and Montauban (on a branch canal option) are very pleasant stop-offs with their own more local charms. In time it's planned to link the Garonne Valley route with the Canal du Midi and extend it west to the Atlantic, to form an official véloroute called 'Entre Deux Mers' - between the two seas. There's nothing at all to stop you cycling from Atlantic to Med right now on a course very similar to the planned final, fully signed and officially promoted route.

Grade EASY

Start / finish Bordeaux / Toulouse

Route length 159 miles / 256km. A there-and-back excursion to Montauban will add a further 14 miles / 23 km.

Total height climbed 351ft
Total height descended 259ft
(Reverse the figures if biking west - east)
Av. climb - Bordeaux to Toulouse 40 ft per mile
Av. climb - Toulouse to Bordeaux 37 ft per mile

Route advice The vast majority of this route is on excellent traffic-free surfaces and is flat or on gentle gradients. The Roger Lapébie cycle track is excellently surfaced and north of Montech you are more often than not on a recently laid, extremely cycle-friendly surface.

Train access The lovely Corail Téoz trains, with their excellent bike carriage space, run between Bordeaux and Toulouse which are linked with each other and with Paris via a TGV service.

Nearby routes
Canal du Midi - direct link. Pgs 34-39
Atlantic Coast Route - direct link. Pgs 40-47
Lot Valley Véloroute - 4 miles from Damazan on the Garonne Canal to Aiguillon using minor roads Pgs 138-143

Maps, guides and websites
The French language guide *Bordeaux-Toulouse à vélo le long du canal de Garonne* costs 6 euros and is well worth having even for non- French speakers as it lists accommodation and other useful information. By Julien Savary. Available locally or from www.cartovelo.com

Signage

Eventually the Garonne route will be well-surfaced along its entire length and, when joined with the Canaldu Midi route, will be known as *La Voie Verte Entre Deux Mers* - Between Two Seas Greenway At the moment, like the Canal du Midi signing, it is all rather variable. Despite this the canal towpath north of Montech is now very well-surfaced as far as Meilhan-sur-Garonne and there are a number of signing schemes along the way, athough the line of the high quality bike route is usually pretty obvious.
The largely tarmac Roger Lapébie cycle trackinto Bordeaux is not only well surfaced but well signed with both signs indicating it's a cycle track and large information boards full of local points of interest - see opposite. Roger Lapébie won the 1937 Tour de France and lived for part of his life in Bordeaux.

Suggested Day Rides on the Route

Bordeaux to Créon Pg27
About 20 miles return ride. Start from the eastern side of the Pont de Pierre in Bordeaux and follow the riverside road (keeping the Garonne on your right) until meeting the Roger Lapébie cycle track on your right. Well-signed, this contra-flow cycle lane soon becomes a fully-fledged traffic-free trail through some lovely lush countyside. The old stations at Latresne and Lignan are now cafe-bistros and at Créon try the excellent pancake house in the main square. Bike hire at the 'Station Vélo' in Créon, right next to the cycle track.

Agen to Marmande Pgs 30-29
38 miles one way. Train return. Leaving Agen to the west you cross the mightily impressive River Garonne with great views back across the bridge to the town, backed by craggy green hills. There is then a very idyllic countryside section of route bringing you to Buzet-sur-Baïse, a major marina with a tourist information office. You'll then pass through Damazan (old 'bastide' town - i.e. fortified - with an ancient fortress and a wine museum) to the very attractive village of Le Mas-d'Agenais. The local church houses a world-renowned Rembrandt and there is a superb viewpoint over the Garonne valley. From Montpouillan use minor roads into Marmande, the regional market town. Look out for the nude statue in the central Place Clemenceau clutching a tomato - once thought to be an aphrodisiac!

Agen to Montauban Pgs 31-32
47 miles one way. Train return. A lengthy but truly spectacular ride, visiting the UNESCO world heritage site monastery at Moissac and the beautiful town of Montauban. Simply head south-east out of Agen on the superbly-surfaced towpath. At Valence you can use the D11 to make a detour south to the pretty village of Auvillar. Montech (home of the weird and wonderful 'pente-d'eau' or waterlift which can be used instead of the five locks here) you head off up the Montech canal to sample the delights of Montauban. If you don't fancy doing the whole distance there are several stations nearby the canal before Castelarrasin from where you can hop on a train back to Agen.

Moissac's ancient abbey houses its famous cloister

Don't Miss

City of Elegance
Whilst Bordeaux lacks internationally famous highlights in the mould of Paris's Eiffel Tower it certainly equals the country's capital for the overall elegance of its buildings and open spaces. And it's a pretty cycle and pedestrian friendly place too, meaning you can soak up its atmosphere at your ease.Its eighteenth century centre is made up largely of light grey stone that give its wider pedestrian thoroughfares an airy, relaxed feel.
The area fronting the west bank of the Garonne has some fine residences and imposing official buildings, all blending harmoniously together.

A Medieval Wonder
The medieval cloister at Moissac is hugely famous within both France and the wider world of medieval architecture. The abbey that houses it itself is hugely impressive, parts of it dating back to the 11th century (for example its incredibly decorated south porch).
The cloister is based around 76 marble columns with the arches bearing all manner of carvings. It is still pretty much as when it was built - it was completed back in 1100. Since then it has proved a massive influence on all manner of ecclesiastical buildings and has escaped threats from a flood that destroyed much of the rest of the town, a new railway line very close by and several wars.

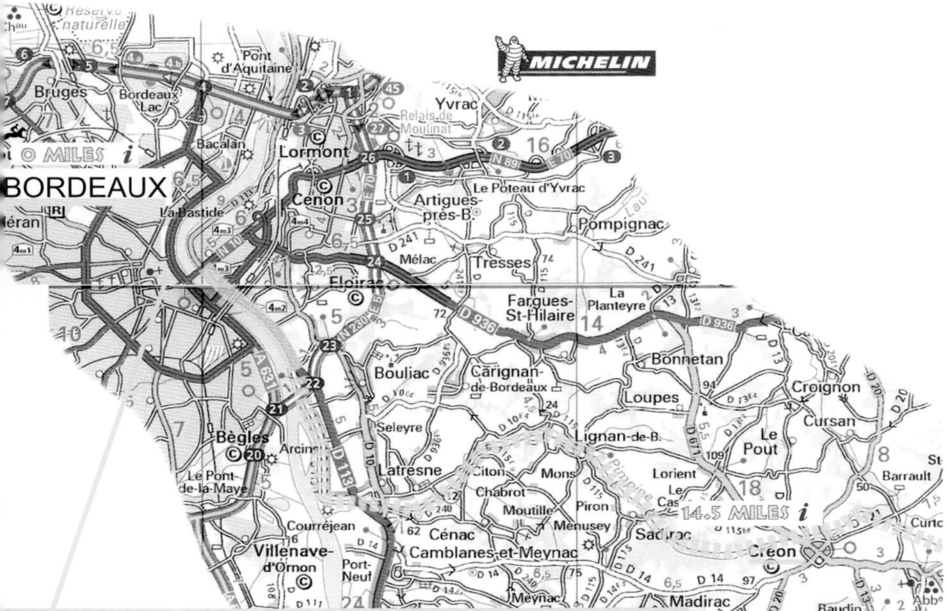

BORDEAUX

One of France's most beautiful cities, Bordeaux's riverfront is described in the Atlantic Coast Route on page 47. You certainly shouldn't miss the charms of the Place de la Bourse, the Customs Museum and the 'mist fountain'.

The city's heart is around the intersection of Cours de L'Intendance, a lovely wide avenue of a street and the north-south pedestrian axis of Rue Sainte Catherine, with its vast range of cheap eateries. If you are searching for a hotel try the streets around Place Gambetta.

There is a fine list of attractions in Bordeaux itself including the Museums of Fine Art and of Aquitaine but the greatest pleasure here is to stroll and take in the different styles of the different quarters - all fashioned to a large degree with the same type of light grey stone but all purposely designed to be different yet to complement each other. The *Chartrons* or quays alongside the Garonne are a case in point.

The route leaves Bordeaux near the very grand riverside area

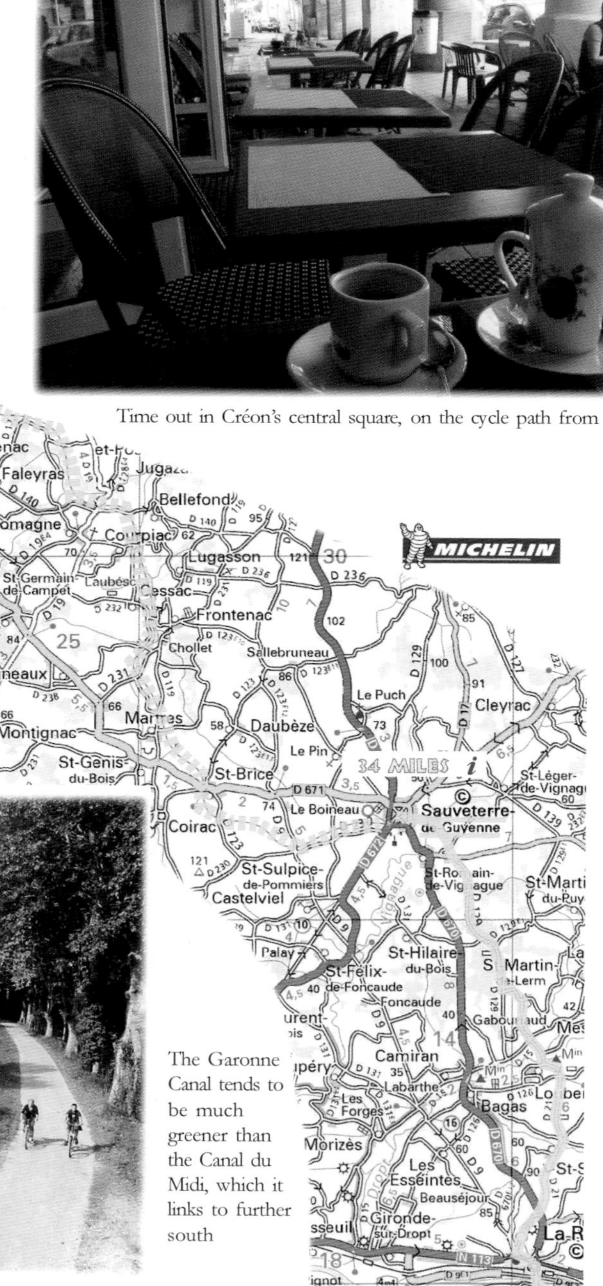

Time out in Créon's central square, on the cycle path from Bordeaux

The Garonne Canal tends to be much greener than the Canal du Midi, which it links to further south

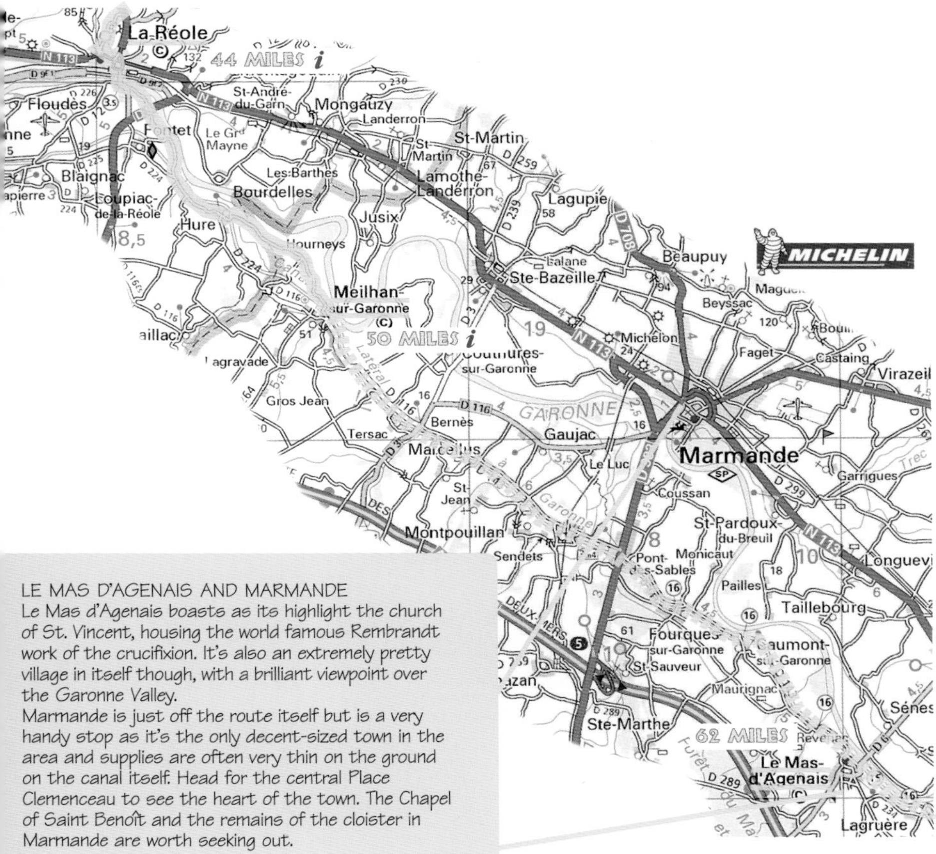

LE MAS D'AGENAIS AND MARMANDE

Le Mas d'Agenais boasts as its highlight the church of St. Vincent, housing the world famous Rembrandt work of the crucifixion. It's also an extremely pretty village in itself though, with a brilliant viewpoint over the Garonne Valley.

Marmande is just off the route itself but is a very handy stop as it's the only decent-sized town in the area and supplies are often very thin on the ground on the canal itself. Head for the central Place Clemenceau to see the heart of the town. The Chapel of Saint Benoît and the remains of the cloister in Marmande are worth seeking out.

Many sections of the canal towpath are well-surfaced

Agen canal bridge

AGEN

In a lovely setting, backed by craggy, green cliffs and on a fine stretch of the Garonne, Agen has few highlights but is a nice place for a stopover with its many pleasant corners. The Théâtre Ducorneau and the Hôtel de Ville are worth keeping an eye out for. There is a lovely view of the town as you cross the canal bridge over the Garonne, with the church of Notre Dame being the highpoint of the view, quite literally. The Museum of Fine Arts here houses several works by Goya.

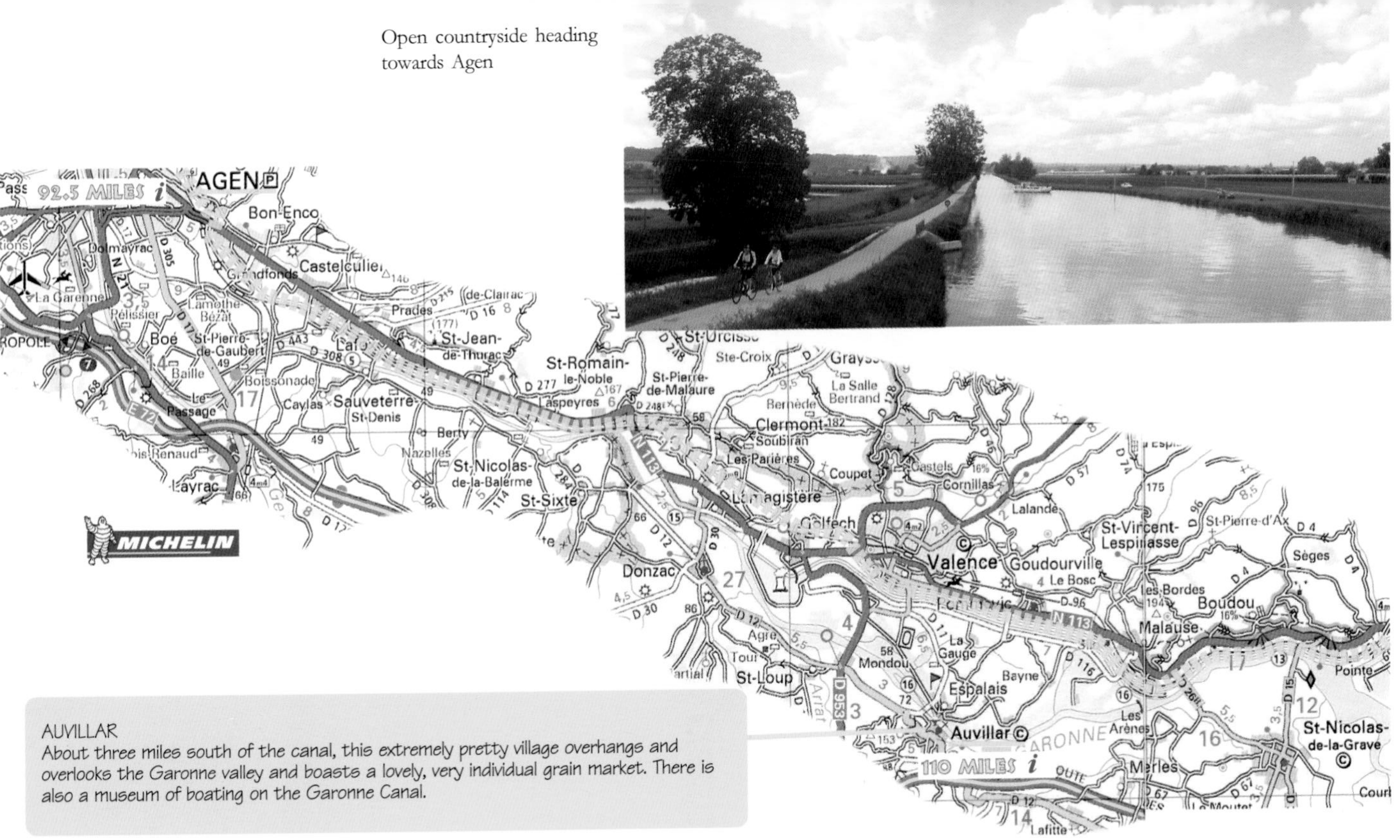

Open countryside heading towards Agen

AUVILLAR
About three miles south of the canal, this extremely pretty village overhangs and overlooks the Garonne valley and boasts a lovely, very individual grain market. There is also a museum of boating on the Garonne Canal.

MOISSAC
The very impressive abbey here is described in 'Don't Miss' on page 26. The abbey and town are worth a day's exploration and there is a very pleasant area to wander around where the canal passes through Moissac. Just south-east of the town the canal passes over the river Tarn, just before it enters the Garonne on a spectcular brick aqueduct.

MONTAUBAN
This 14 mile detour up a branch canal from Montech makes an ideal stop-off from biking. Its long history has left a town centre that's a pleasure to stroll round, with its many fine pink brick houses. The centre of life here and an outstanding attraction is the Place Nationale, surrounded on all sides by arched arcades. Also look out for the Place du Coq and the Ingres museum, housing examples of his work in the former Bishop's Palace.
At Montech there is an impressive *pente d'eau* or water slope - in effect it carries boats around the series of locks here using a 'slice' of water and hauling engines.

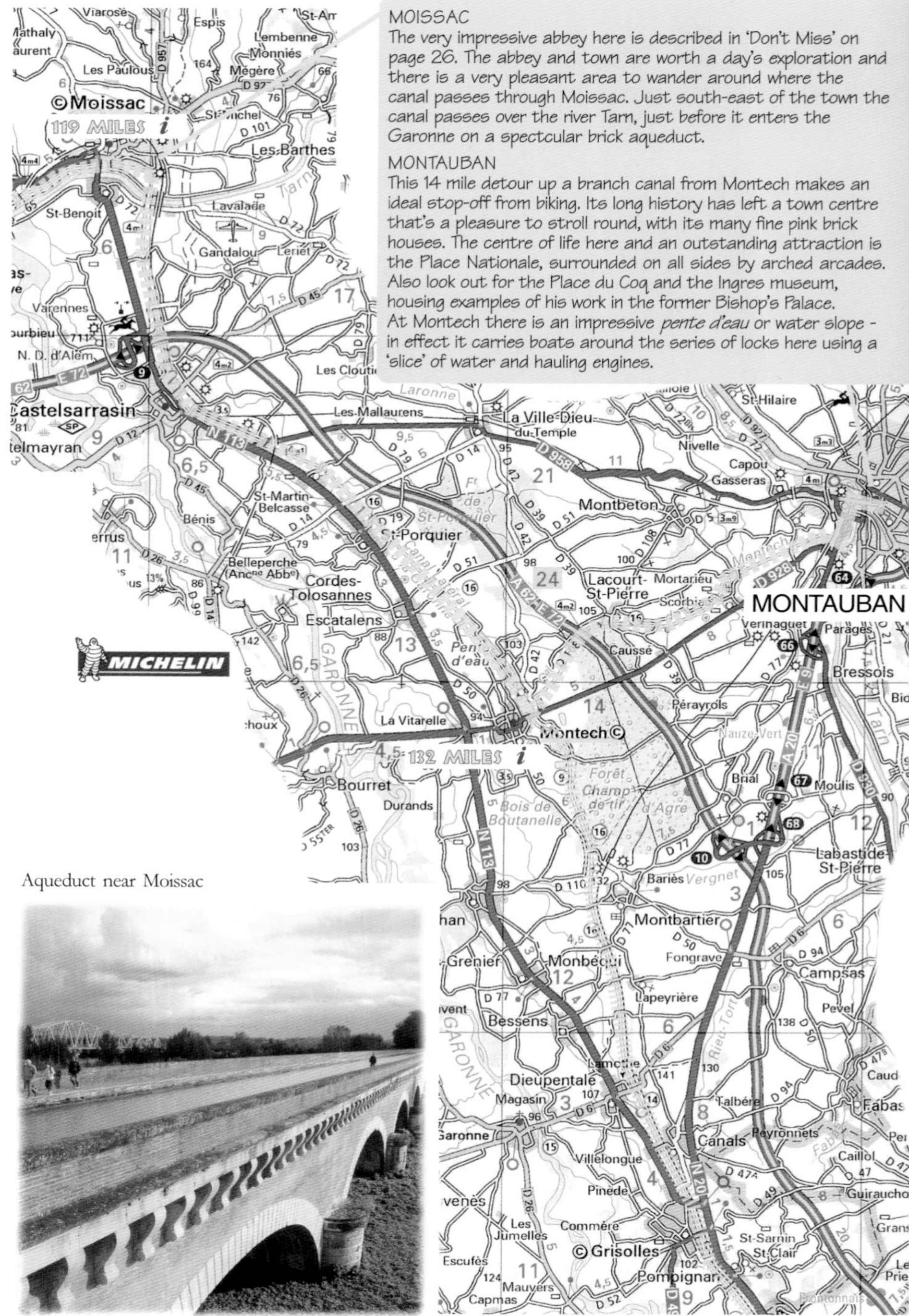

Aqueduct near Moissac

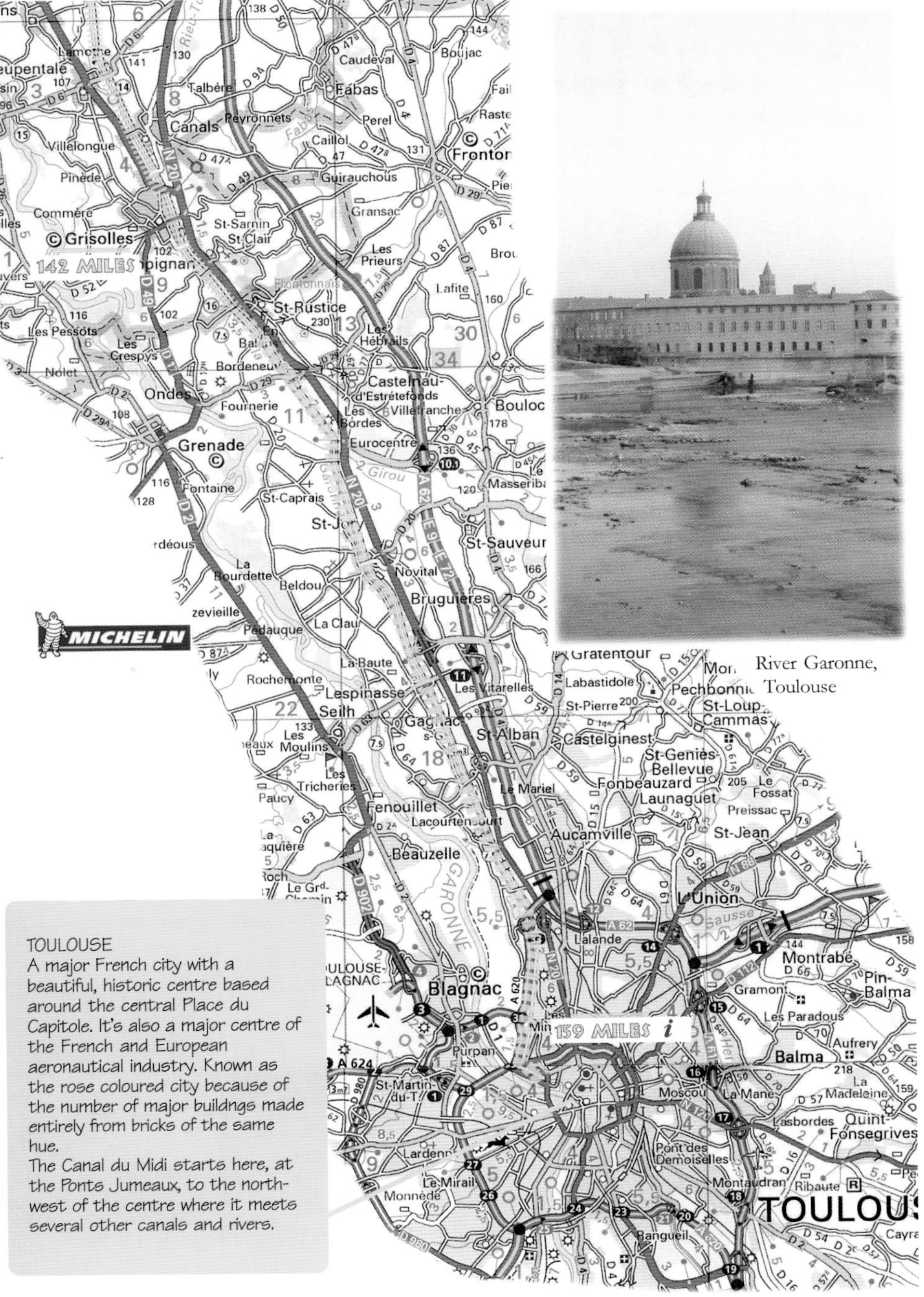

River Garonne, Toulouse

TOULOUSE
A major French city with a beautiful, historic centre based around the central Place du Capitole. It's also a major centre of the French and European aeronautical industry. Known as the rose coloured city because of the number of major buildngs made entirely from bricks of the same hue.
The Canal du Midi starts here, at the Ponts Jumeaux, to the north-west of the centre where it meets several other canals and rivers.

Canal Du Midi

Route Info

Canal Du Midi

Simply one of the most popular cycle routes in France and for good reason - it follows the course of a UNESCO World Heritage Site (the canal itself). Sumptuous bridges and enormous locks are all accessible along a towpath running for over ninety per cent of the length of the canal. The canal threads through some the finest cities and towns in the south of France, such as Toulouse, medieval Carcassonne and cliff-top Béziers. Others such as Narbonne are nearby. It links to the Canal Latéral à Garonne to the west in Toulouse and the Rhône-Sète canal (accessed through the lagoon known as the Bassin de Thau) at its eastern end. Link all three and add the traffic-free trail linking Bordeaux to the Atlantic and you have the prospect of a mammoth 470 mile virtually traffic-free and virtually flat ride.

Grade EASY

Start / finish Toulouse / Marseillan.

Route length 146 miles / 235km. A there-and-back excursion to Port-la-Nouvelle adds 42 miles / 67 km.

Total height climbed 3630ft
Total height descended 4064ft
(Reverse the figures if biking east - west)
Average climb - Toulouse to Thau 25 ft per mile
Average climb - Thau to Toulouse 28 ft per mile

Route advice There are several high quality tarmac sections as shown on the map. The vast majority of the rest of the route is on good quality towpath.

Train access Lots of stops along the length of the route. Served by TGV, Corail Téoz and local trains.

Nearby routes
Garonne Valley - direct link pgs 25-33
Tarn to Midi - direct link pgs 144-148
Rhône - Sète Canal - around 20 miles away using roads around the north side of Thau lagoon. pgs 11-15

Maps, guides and websites
Two French language guidebooks are available locally: *Le Canal du Midi* by Phillippe Calas. Pub: Édisud. 12 euros. Full colour guide with decent route section maps. *Toulouse - Sète à Vélo le long du Canal du Midi* Of the two this is probably the more useful. It features accommodation listings and street level town. Mainly black & white. www.canalmidi.com A great source of English language info on the canal, with accommodation and cycling advice.

Signage

Although you'll see many unsigned sections along the entire length of the towpath naturally navigation is not difficult - the course of the main towpath is normally very obvious. There is usually signage on the sections that are smoothly surfaced and managed - namely west of Toulouse and west of Béziers; both sections have information boards along the way, sometimes featuring a more detailed map of the area. Eventually the whole route will be surfaced and signed to an equally high standard (along with the Garonne Valley route as far as Bordeaux) and known as *La Voie Verte Entre Deux Mers* - Between Two Seas Greenway. At the moment it is all rather variable and ad hoc - this shouldn't spoil your enjoyment of riding the actual route though, which is largely good quality and with virtually no access barriers.
Some signs, like that opposite, show recommended routes to nearby attractions, for example to the beaches of Valras-Plage and Sérignan-Plage east of Béziers. The example on the far right is in Carcassonne.

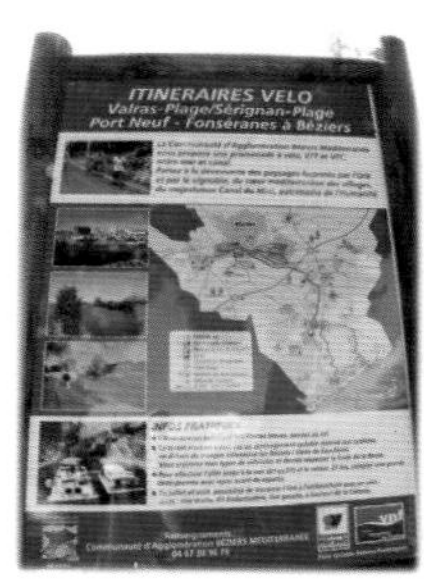

Suggested Day Rides on the Route

Toulouse to Castelnaudary Pg36
39 miles one way. Train return. Follow the Canal du Midi from Ponts Jumeaux across the northern edge of Toulouse's centre then head along the good quality canalside cycle path out of the city and into very pleasant countryside. Look out for small scale canal features like the 'lavoir' or old laundry at Montgiscard before passing through the area known as the Lauragais. Villefranche, Avignonet and Port all bear the suffix and all are near enough the canal to take a quick break. Near Naurouze there is a monument to the 'father' of the canal Paul Riquet. Finally at Castelnaudary seek out the incredible basin, built to act as a reservoir to feed the canal.

Carcassonne to Trèbes Pg37
18 miles return ride. A relatively short but very beautiful ride from the medieval splendour of Carcassonne to the small, attractive village of Trèbes. On the way you'll get great views of the citadel of Carcassonne and chance to see the impressive canal bridge and locks at Fresquel.

Béziers to the Oppidum d'Ensérune Pg39
17 miles return. The shortest but most spectacular day ride and crammed with interest. Heading west on the canal out of Béziers you cross the monumental canal bridge and head onto the huge chain of canal locks at Fonserannes, one of the most popular spots on the canal. At the pleasant port of Colombiers you can break for lunch as there are several eating opportunities at the marina by the canal. Head off the canal at Malpas tunnel (visitor centre here) then follow signs on minor roads to make the steep climb to the archaeological hilltop site known as the Oppidum d'Ensérune. There are amazing views from here of the Étang de Montady, an ancient lake, now drained to leave an incredible field pattern. If you're very keen on the ancient past, the town of Nissan-lez-Ensérune houses an archaeology museum and is a short detour to the south of the canal.

Béziers to Agde Pg39
19 miles with train return. The main reason for this ride is to visit the unusual town of Agde and to detour down to the Mediterranean (a signed route takes you to the extensive beach at Portiragnes Plage). Agde itself is made of dark volcanic rock and is a very atmospheric place to stroll and take a food break.

Don't Miss

Carcassonne's Cité

Seeing Carcassonne's hilltop citadel for the first time, especially lit up at night, is a jawdropping moment. However, its looks can deceive - its seeming medieval perfection is partly the product of a nineteenth century restoration - the trick works and it's quite easy to imagine a whole host of medieval characters trekking up the hill to the safety of its immense walls and countless turrets. Inside it's a different matter, with much of the space given over to rather tacky tourist businesses selling everything from plastic swords to burgers and ice-cream. Despite all this there are all sorts of buildings inside, including genuine medieval ones and a gruesome Museum of Torture that most kids will just love! Caracassonne's citadel really is a different world - in more ways than one.

Toulouse - The Pink City

Toulouse's epithet as *La Ville Rose* almost fails to do it justice - it refers to the pink colour its buildings become when hit by strong morning or evening light. Enormous swathes of its historic heart are made of ancient, beautifully worn brick, including vast churches, an abbatoir, bridges and an observatory. The effect is quite overwhelming at times as you move between the huge main square called the *Capitole,* its surrounding mix of broad, elegant shopping streets and much older, narrow twisting alleys.

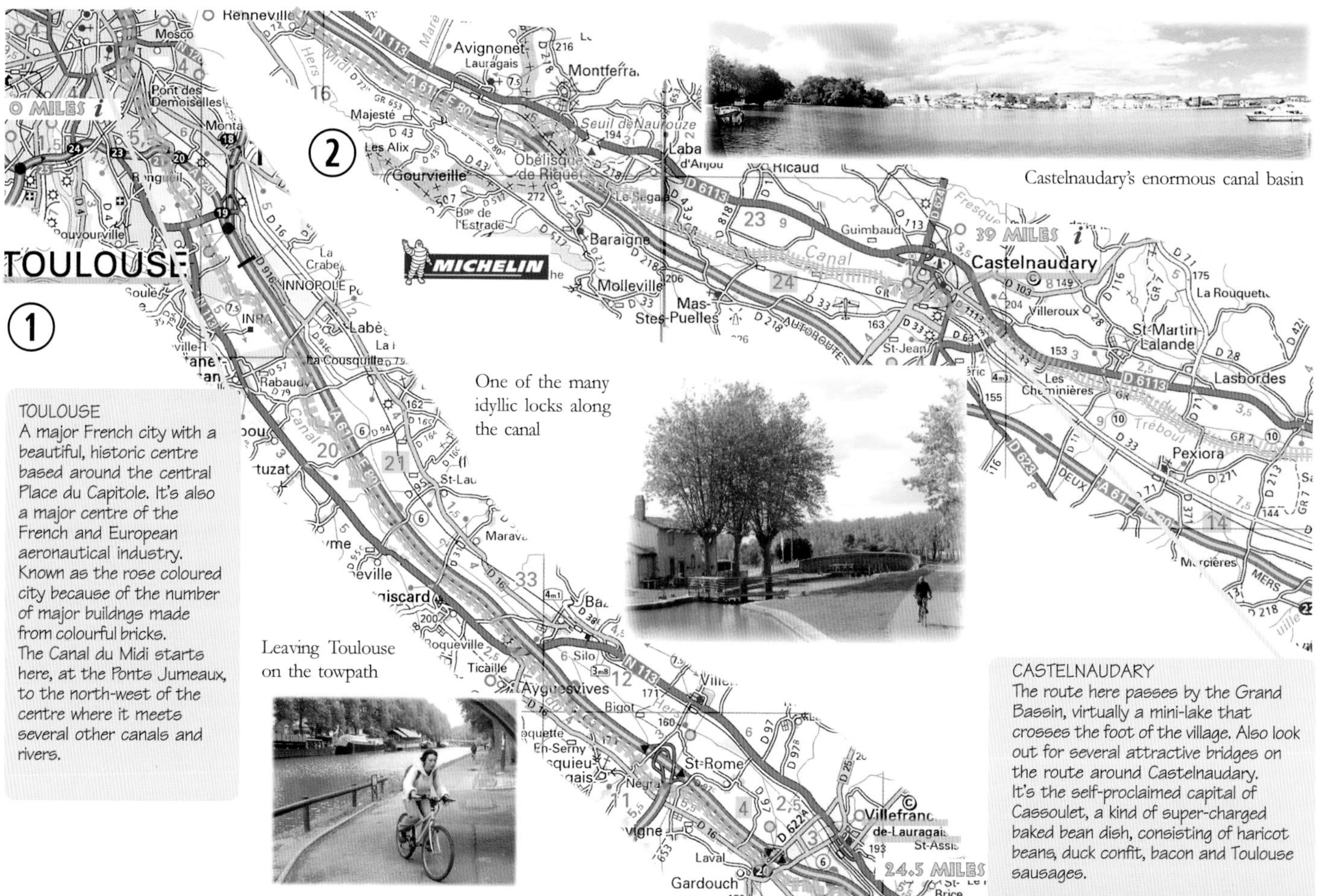

Castelnaudary's enormous canal basin

One of the many idyllic locks along the canal

Leaving Toulouse on the towpath

TOULOUSE
A major French city with a beautiful, historic centre based around the central Place du Capitole. It's also a major centre of the French and European aeronautical industry.
Known as the rose coloured city because of the number of major buildngs made from colourful bricks.
The Canal du Midi starts here, at the Ponts Jumeaux, to the north-west of the centre where it meets several other canals and rivers.

CASTELNAUDARY
The route here passes by the Grand Bassin, virtually a mini-lake that crosses the foot of the village. Also look out for several attractive bridges on the route around Castelnaudary.
It's the self-proclaimed capital of Cassoulet, a kind of super-charged baked bean dish, consisting of haricot beans, duck confit, bacon and Toulouse sausages.

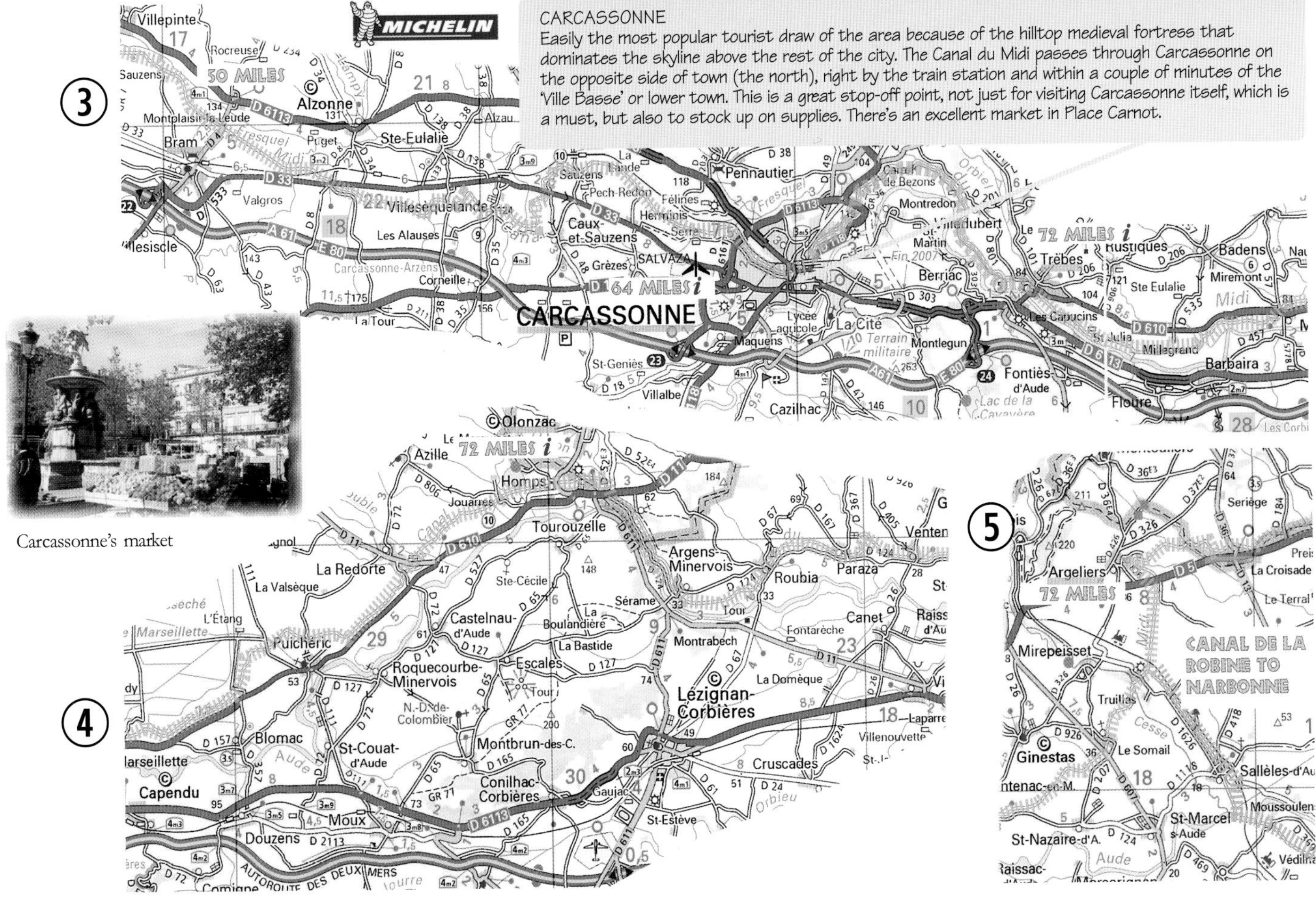

CARCASSONNE

Easily the most popular tourist draw of the area because of the hilltop medieval fortress that dominates the skyline above the rest of the city. The Canal du Midi passes through Carcassonne on the opposite side of town (the north), right by the train station and within a couple of minutes of the 'Ville Basse' or lower town. This is a great stop-off point, not just for visiting Carcassonne itself, which is a must, but also to stock up on supplies. There's an excellent market in Place Carnot.

Carcassonne's market

NARBONNE
The Canal de la Robine has been made a lovely feature as it passes through the city centre here, with mini-fountains pouring into it and flowers bedecking the banks. Narbonne's centre itself is based around the imposing cathedral which features a stretch of Roman road in front of it as a major feature of the shopping area that has many classy places to eat and drink.

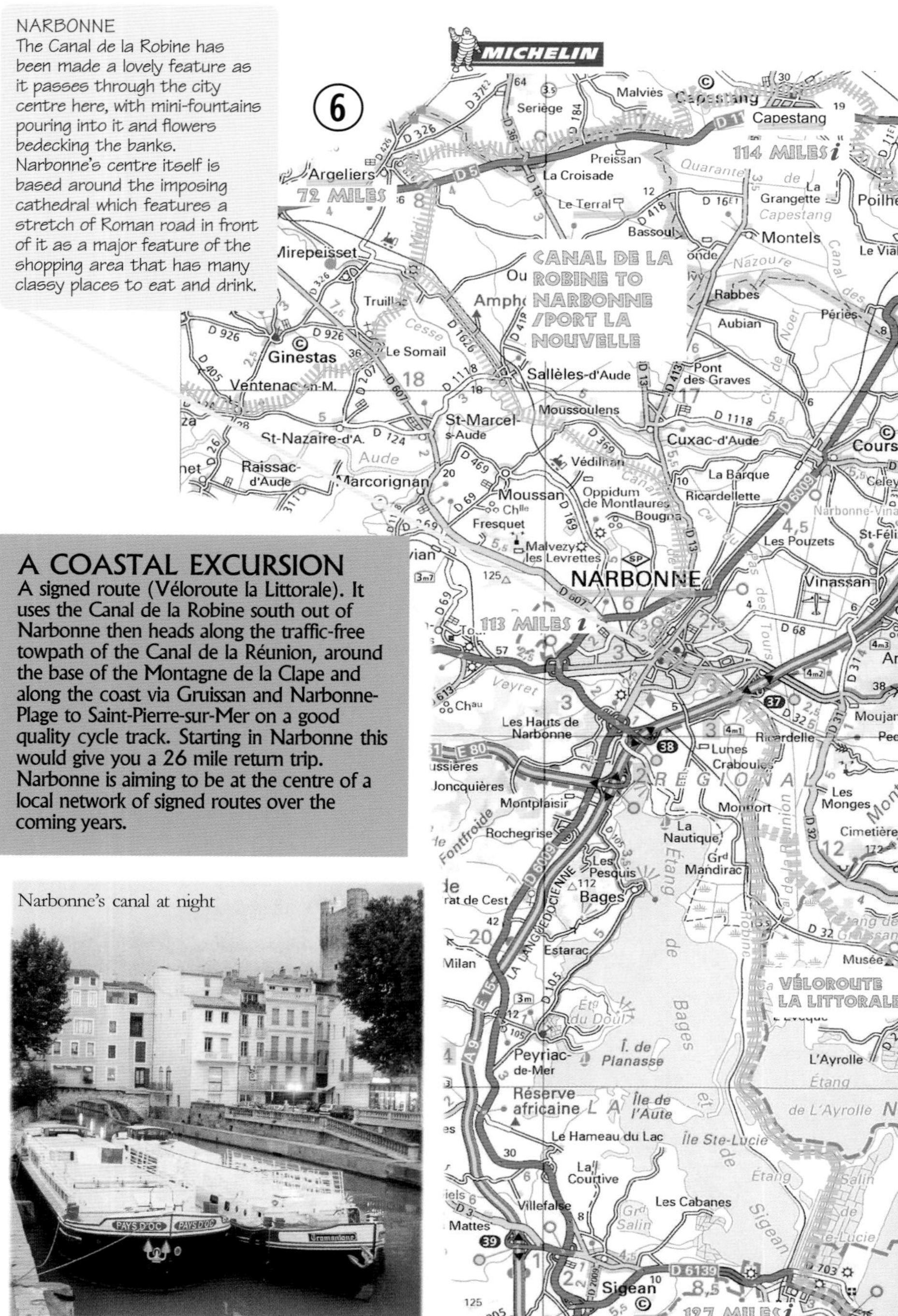

A COASTAL EXCURSION

A signed route (Véloroute la Littorale). It uses the Canal de la Robine south out of Narbonne then heads along the traffic-free towpath of the Canal de la Réunion, around the base of the Montagne de la Clape and along the coast via Gruissan and Narbonne-Plage to Saint-Pierre-sur-Mer on a good quality cycle track. Starting in Narbonne this would give you a 26 mile return trip. Narbonne is aiming to be at the centre of a local network of signed routes over the coming years.

Narbonne's canal at night

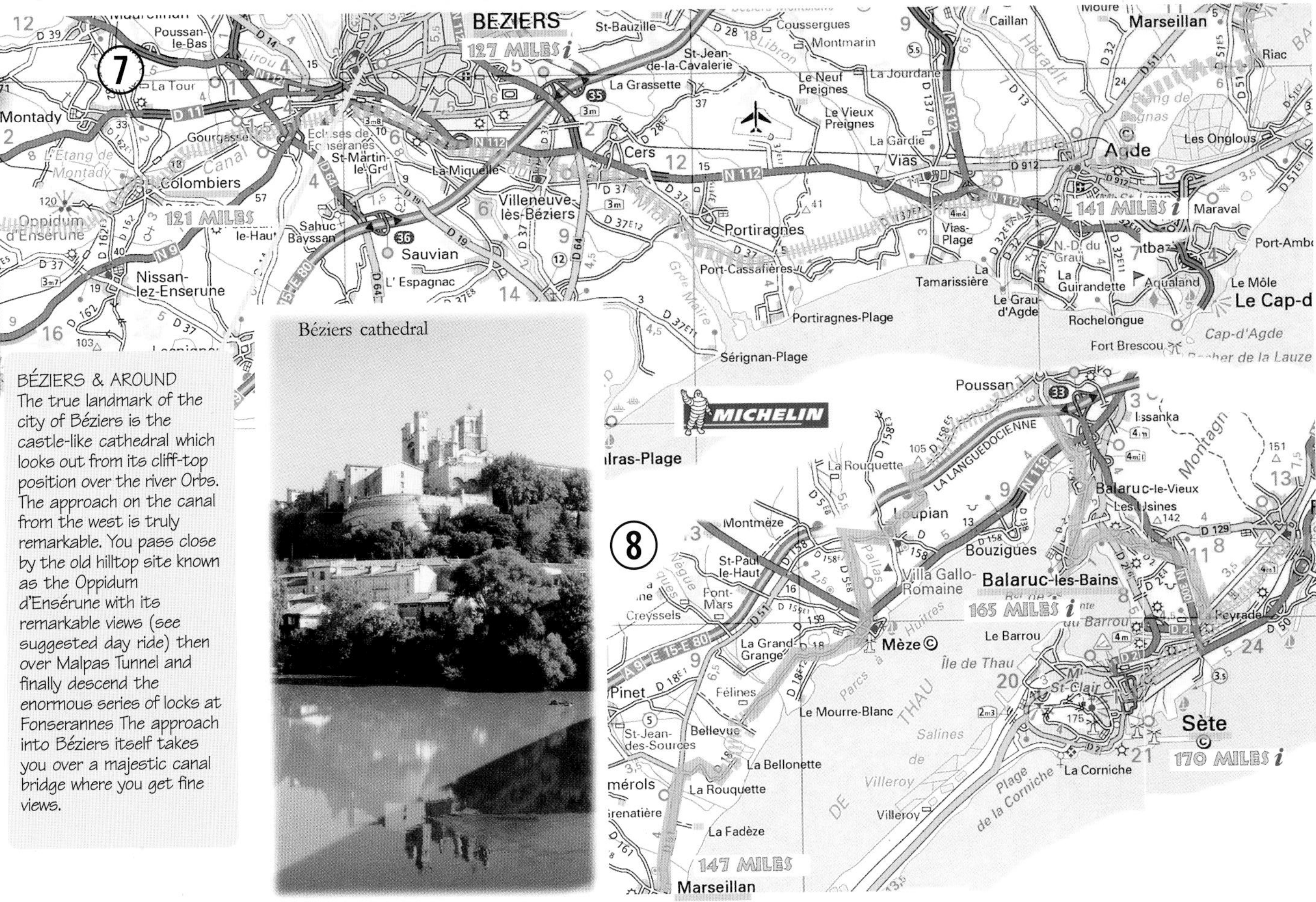

Béziers cathedral

BÉZIERS & AROUND

The true landmark of the city of Béziers is the castle-like cathedral which looks out from its cliff-top position over the river Orbs. The approach on the canal from the west is truly remarkable. You pass close by the old hilltop site known as the Oppidum d'Ensérune with its remarkable views (see suggested day ride) then over Malpas Tunnel and finally descend the enormous series of locks at Fonserannes The approach into Béziers itself takes you over a majestic canal bridge where you get fine views.

Along the Atlantic Coast

Route Info

Along the Atlantic Coast
Starting in the foothills of the Basque Pyrenees the route soon turns into a marathon route for lovers of coastal wilderness. Settlements of any size are scant for lengthy distances, although at the height of summer you shouldn't have any problem finding accommodation or food (a different picture out of holiday season). Scenery is a mixture of huge beaches, some not accessible by motor vehicle and therefore little populated, and vast stretches of sand dune backed by pine forest. You leave the Atlantic coast around Arcachon basin, known for its oyster farming and the jolly resort of Arcachon.

Grade EASY

Start / finish Ustaritz to Pointe de Grave (mouth of the Gironde estuary)

Route length 196 miles / 315km. There are various route options as marked on the map but this total is for one of the shortest routes - ie most other options add a few miles.
Total height climbed 6287ft
Total height descended 6291ft
(Reverse the figures if biking east - west)
Average climb - Ustaritz to Gironde 32 ft per mile Average climb - Gironde to Ustaritz 32 ft per mile

Route advice Mainly traffic-free with quality ranging from wide tarmac to looser surfaces and narrower tracks.
* Ondres-Plage to Biscarrosse-Plage is generally very smoothly surfaced and lies a mile or so from the coast, linking a number of small bathing resorts along the way, each with shops, campsites and hotels.
* 12 miles of road link St Paul en Born and Parentis en Born, avoiding a military no-go area.
* North of Cap-Ferret things are more complicated; for example, you have a choice of routes through the forest between Lacanau-Océan and Hourtin Plage, the one nearest the sea often being rougher concrete slabs with a better quality track just inland of it.
* North of here to Soulac, it's generally a very well-surfaced route, but there is a small hill of about 60 metres.

Train access A TGV line runs parallel but about 20 miles inland from most of the route between Arcachon and Bayonne (fairly regular stations and direct access at Arcachon and Bayonne). There's a branch line from Bordeaux up to Pointe de Grave and one comes down from Saintes to Royan, from where you can hop on a ferry to Pointe de Grave.

Nearby routes
Direct links inland: Mios-Bazas (41 miles / 66km) and Lacanau-Océan - Bordeaux (37 miles / 59km) pg47 (Bordeaux link only shown) The ferry to Royan at the northern end of the trail links to the Côte Sauvage (wild coast) greenway.

Maps, guides and websites
http://www.tourisme-gironde.fr/cdt_piste_cyclable.asp has a handy interactive map of the northern part of the route
www.tourisme-aquitaine.fr
English version of the region's tourist board site available

Signage

No unified scheme for the whole Atlantic Coast route but the Bordeaux to Lacanau-Océan track is recognised as a separate route and signed as such. Note that, at the time of writing, there was no signed route at all between Bayonne and Labenne / Labenne-Océan. The route given here is therefore an 'interim' route and you should check locally as to the existence of any new signed route immediately to the north of Bayonne.

Suggested Day Rides on the Route

Bordeaux To Arcachon Pgs 47, 46, 45
74 miles. Train return. This would prove a marathon day ride to all but the superfit but is easily spread over two days with an overnight break at Lacanau-Océan. You could also allow yourself a day at the end of the riding to explore Dune du Pyla and Arcachon.

In Bordeaux pick up the lovely riverside cycle lane at Pont de Pierre and then before heading 90 degrees left up the Crs. du Medoc and bending left onto Allées de Boutaut. As you approach the southern end of the lake you will pick up the cycle track signs to Lacanau from where you head west on a tarmac cycle track through expansive forests (the largest forest in Europe) to Lacanau. Use more good quality cycle tracks to head around the northern end of Lacanau lagoon to Lacanau-Océan. Here you follow the cycle track south, just behind a magnificently long stretch of beach - a hybrid or touring bike with reasonably wide tyres is recommended for this section as it follows some unmetalled forest tracks and narrow cycle lanes. At Cap Ferret you can take the boat across to Arcachon before visiting the vast sandy expanse of the Dune du Pylat - again the biggest in Europe! You can then use a mixture of cycle lanes and roads to follow the coast north to Arcachon.

From Bayonne Along the River Nive Pg 43
17 miles return ride. Simply follow the River Nive upstream from Bayonne where it flows into the River Adour. Most of the route actually follows a 'residents only' road on which motor traffic is so rare it's actually classed as a greenway.

Arcachon to Le Teich Nature Reserve Pg 45
There are over 75 miles of cycle lanes and paths around the basin and this 34 mile circuit explores the more interesting southern side of it. Start on the seafront, just north of Arcachon's town centre and head east, using the cycle track along the front. Sections of this are on boards over the back of the beach before you reach the port area. Follow behind the port and bend right up Rue Coste then right again to pick up cycle tracks along the main road. It's then a case of following the cycle tracks south then east to head towards Le Teich. These skirt the main RN250 road before using some lovely sections through forest. Enter the 'back' of Le Teich and head across the rail line by the station then pick up the track that follows the dyke around the edge of Le Teich reserve. It's actually part of the *Tour du Bassin d'Arcachon* walking route but bikes are allowed. Head back into Le Teich and follow your route back towards Arcachon (you can get the train back if you want to cut the journey short). Coming back into Arcachon you can return the same way you came. However, the ride over the large open area to the south of the centre, passing behind various colleges, then using streets to drop down to the Plage du Moulleau and picking up the seafront cycle track north back to your start is a lovely addition to the route. If you want to visit the incredible Dune du Pyla it's about 6 miles return trip south on the coast road from Le Molleau.

NOTE There is a dense network of cycle tracks in the area but it isn't always well-signed or obvious where they run. The best solution is to pick up local maps of the network (available at Arcachon tourist office) and to take your time to discover it.

Traffic-free cycling along the River Nive

Don't Miss

Bayonne and French Basque Country

The Basque country as a whole has a reputation as a proud, separatist area, a sentiment occasionally spilling over into terrorist acts. This activity is largely restricted to Spanish Basque country. Whilst the French Basques are equally proud of their ancient language, still widely used here, they are certainly not separatist today, though certain areas of Bayonne had this reputation in the past.

Indeed, the town of Bayonne is one of the best places to get a flavour of the real Basque culture in its French form, with the language widely on display alongside French and the characteristic Basque flag colours of red and green much in evidence on the town's paintwork. Most curiously of all there is also a distinct Gascon flavour to Bayonne, most notably in some colourfully fronted buildings and trilingual street signs.

The Sahara Comes to Europe

The incredible monster sand dune that is the Dune du Pyla lies right by the route, just south of the popular resort of Arcachon. At over 350 ft high and around 1.5 miles long it is the biggest dune in Europe - and it's moving inland, most slowly but surely. So far it has engulfed roads and villas and since 1863 has moved more than a kilometre inland. You can cycle up to the base of the dune and helpfully there is a set of moveable fibreglass steps that allow you access to the dune's 'plateau' with spectacular seaviews. Apparently you can see the Pyrenees around 60 miles to the south on a clear day.

THE ULTIMATE CHALLENGE?

New for 2008 is the *Route des Cols* - an amazing sounding but *extremely* challenging signed route, taking in a staggering 34 cols (high mountain passes) going from valley to valley through the 6 *départements* on the French side of the Pyrenees. Legendary names such as the Col du Tourmalet make this for the very fit only. There are also plans for 17 signed loops off the main route. www.routedescols.com

Dune du Pyla - Europe's biggest dune and literally one of the highpoints of your ride along the Atlantic

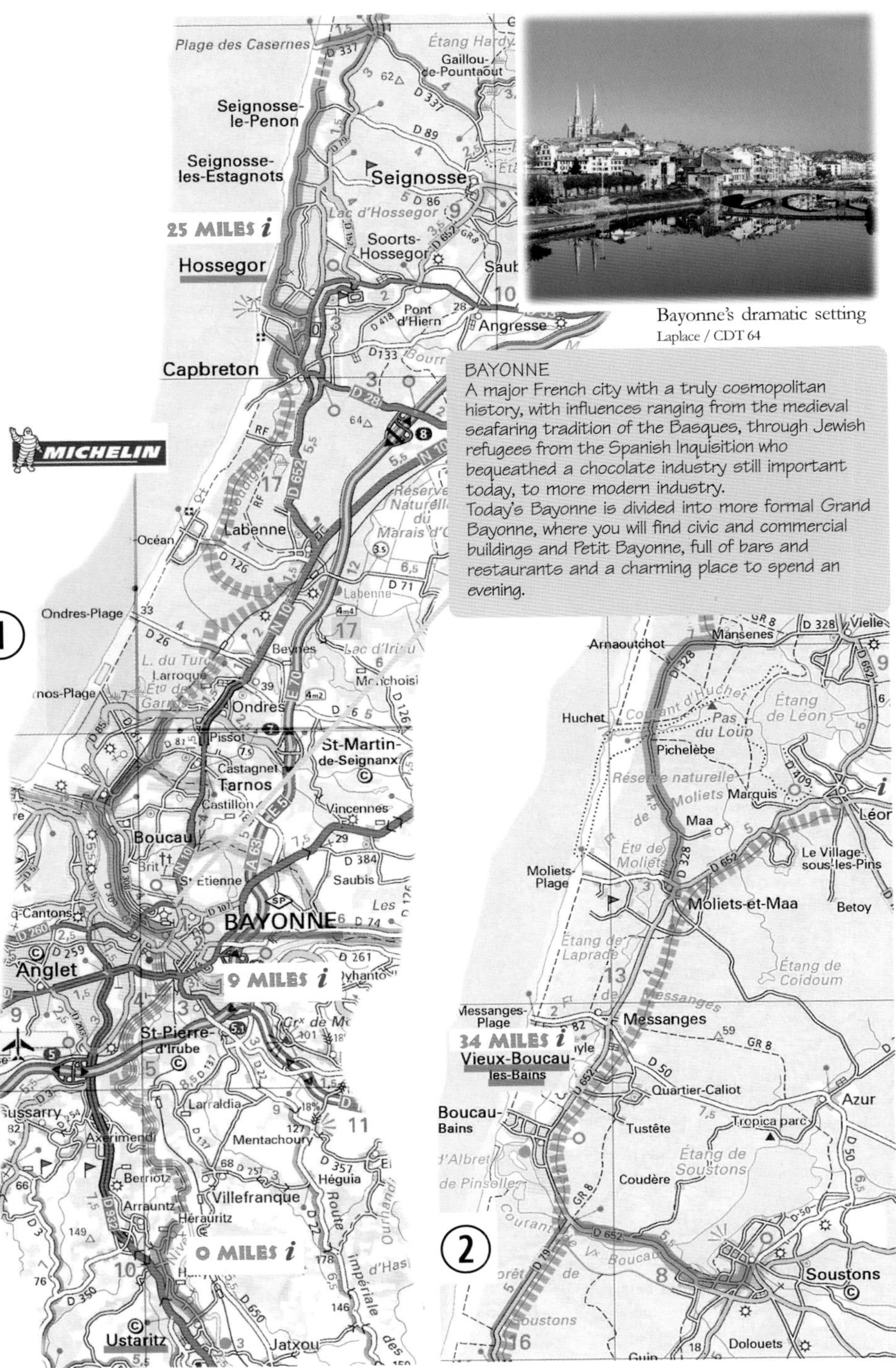

Bayonne's dramatic setting

Laplace / CDT 64

BAYONNE

A major French city with a truly cosmopolitan history, with influences ranging from the medieval seafaring tradition of the Basques, through Jewish refugees from the Spanish Inquisition who bequeathed a chocolate industry still important today, to more modern industry.

Today's Bayonne is divided into more formal Grand Bayonne, where you will find civic and commercial buildings and Petit Bayonne, full of bars and restaurants and a charming place to spend an evening.

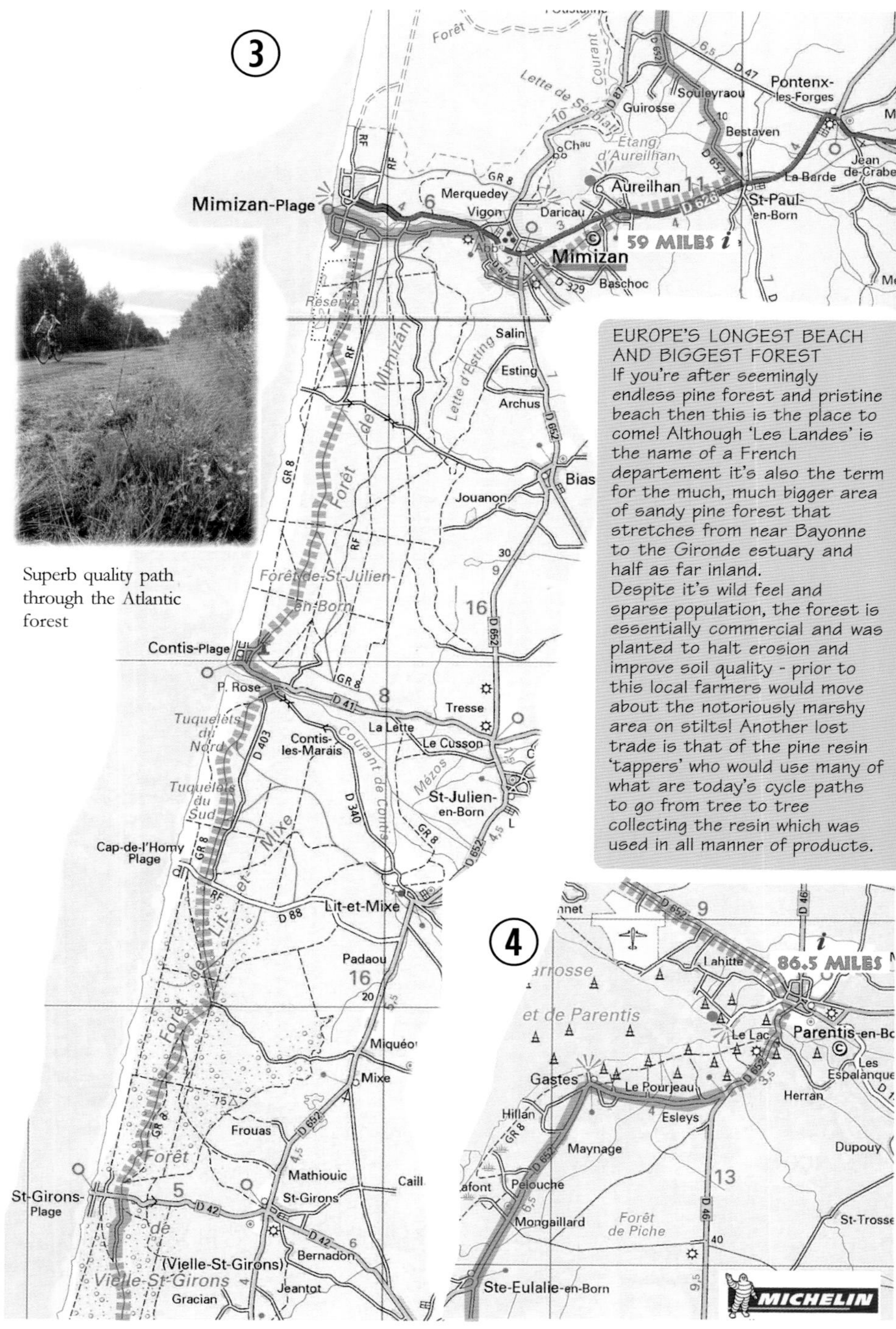

Superb quality path through the Atlantic forest

EUROPE'S LONGEST BEACH AND BIGGEST FOREST

If you're after seemingly endless pine forest and pristine beach then this is the place to come! Although 'Les Landes' is the name of a French departement it's also the term for the much, much bigger area of sandy pine forest that stretches from near Bayonne to the Gironde estuary and half as far inland.

Despite it's wild feel and sparse population, the forest is essentially commercial and was planted to halt erosion and improve soil quality - prior to this local farmers would move about the notoriously marshy area on stilts! Another lost trade is that of the pine resin 'tappers' who would use many of what are today's cycle paths to go from tree to tree collecting the resin which was used in all manner of products.

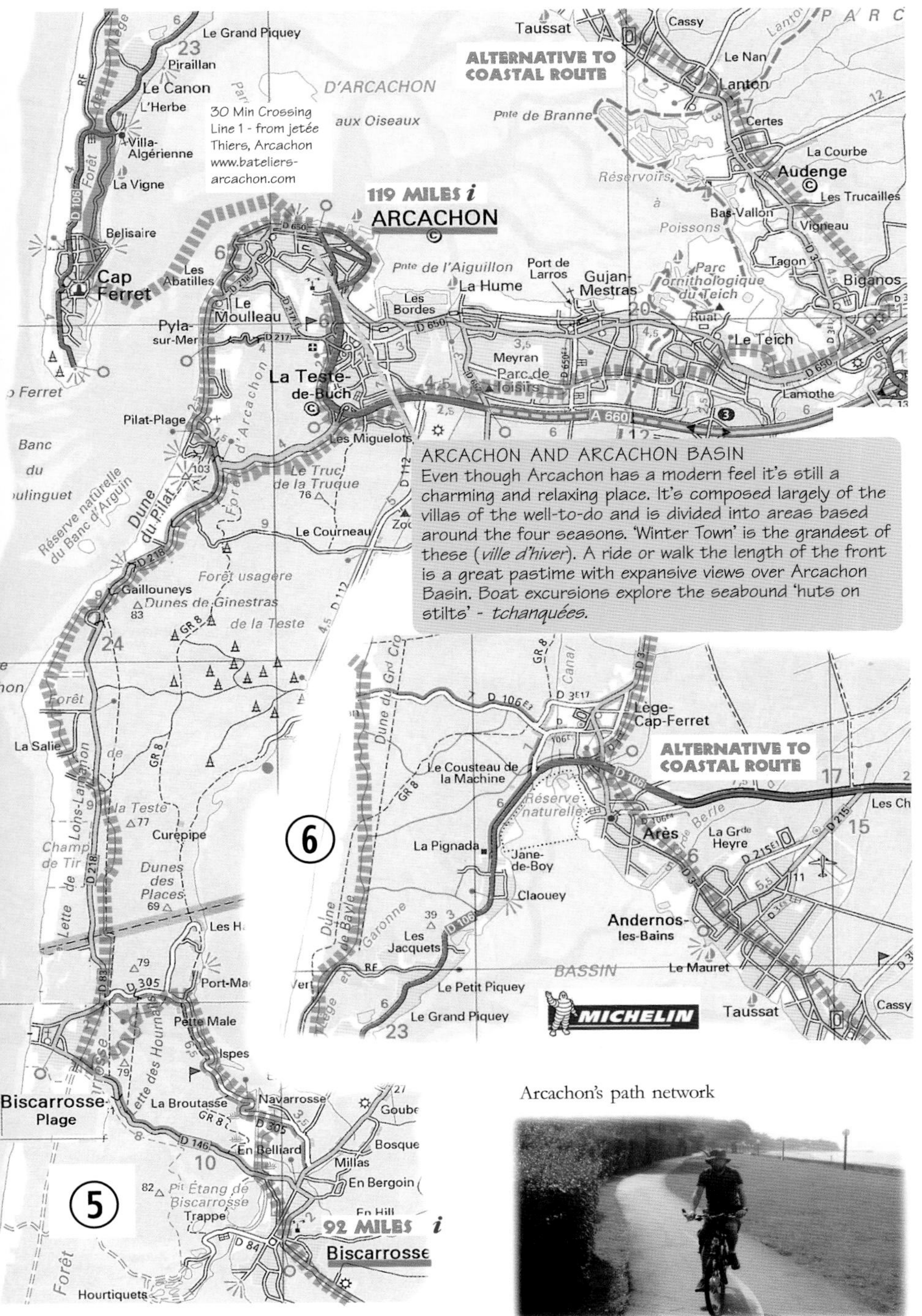

Arcachon's path network

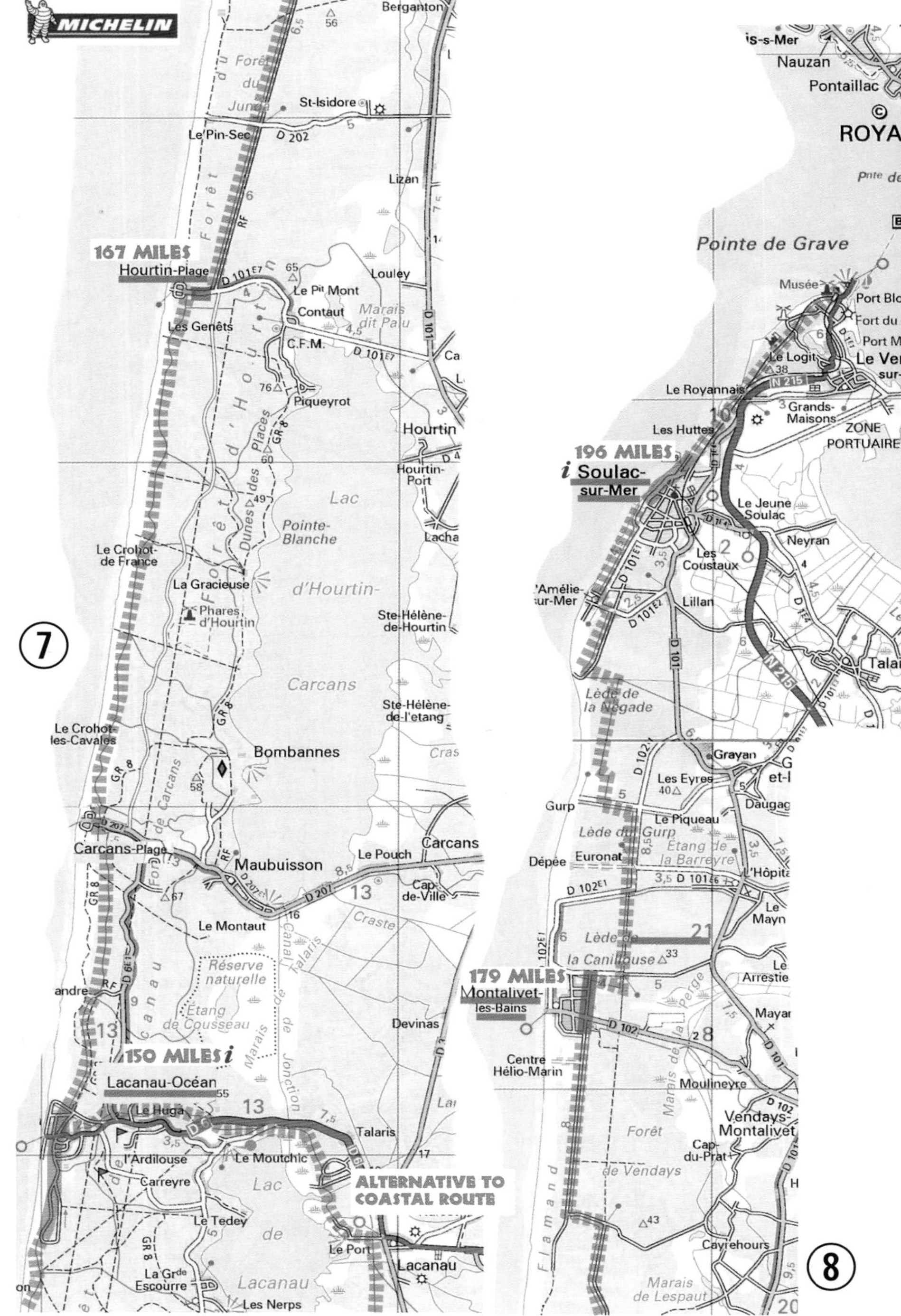
MICHELIN
167 MILES
Hourtin-Plage
Bergantor
St-Isidore
Le Pin-Sec
Lizan
Louley
Le Pit Mont
Contaut
Marais dit Palu
Les Genêts
C.F.M.
Piqueyrot
Hourtin
Hourtin-Port
Lac
Pointe-Blanche
Le Crohot-de France
La Gracieuse
Phares d'Hourtin
d'Hourtin-
Ste-Hélène-de-Hourtin
Carcans
Ste-Hélène-de-l'etang
Le Crohot-les-Cavales
Bombannes
Carcans-Plage
Maubuisson
Le Pouch
Carcans
Cap-de-Ville
Le Montaut
Réserve naturelle
Etang de Cousseau
Devinas
150 MILES
Lacanau-Océan
Le Huga
Talaris
l'Ardilouse
Le Moutchic
Carreyre
Lac
de
Lacanau
ALTERNATIVE TO COASTAL ROUTE
Le Tedey
Le Port
Lacanau
La Grde Escourre
Les Nerps
7
Nauzan
Pontaillac
ROYAN
Pointe de Grave
Musée
Port Bloc
Le Logit
Le Royannais
Grands-Maisons
Les Huttes
ZONE PORTUAIRE
196 MILES
Soulac-sur-Mer
Le Jeune Soulac
Neyran
Les Coustaux
Lillan
Talais
Lède de la Négade
Grayan
Les Eyres
Gurp
Le Piqueau
Lède du Gurp
Etang de la Barreyre
Dépée
Euronat
Lède de la Canillouse
179 MILES
Montalivet-les-Bains
Centre Hélio-Marin
Moulineyre
Vendays-Montalivet
Forêt de Vendays
Cap-du-Prat
Cayrehours
Marais de Lespaut
8

Lacanau-Océan - Bordeaux link

Bordeaux - ancient city, modern trams

BORDEAUX'S RIVERFRONT

The cycle track that runs along the west bank of the Garonne has to be one of the nicest of all French city rides. It passes in front of the grand Place de la Bourse and the Customs Museum and the 'mist fountain' only adds to the elegance of the buildings. The whole riverside is a parade of fine eighteenth century buildings looking across the broad Garonne.

If you head to the city centre from Place de la Bourse down Cours du Chapeau Rouge and Cours de L'Intendance you will see a great collection of elaborate buildings with some fine shops.

Just north of here is what claims to be the largest open pedestrian area in Europe - the Esplanade de Quinconces, with a marvellously over the top statue at its western end. It's a tribute to the Girondins, a moderate faction in the French Revolution who were ousted by a bloodier more radical faction.

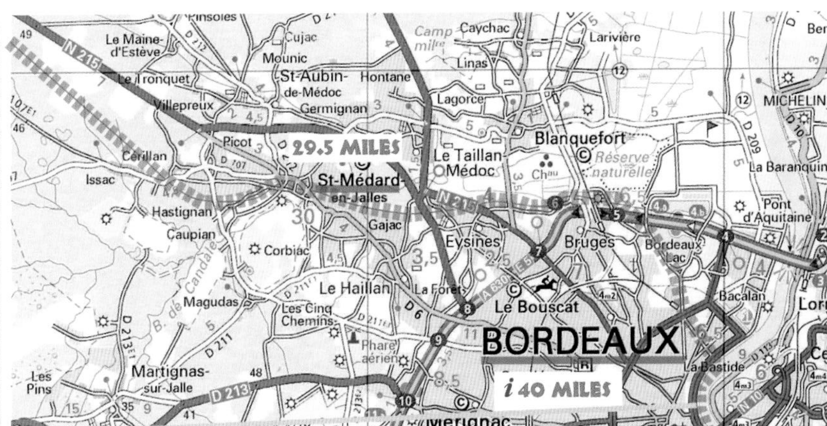

EuroVelo 6

Across France along the Loire, Saône and Doubs Valleys

Route Info

EuroVelo 6
EuroVelo 6 links many existing trails with new sections of route to come up with Europe's longest cycle trail. Although currently not signed along its entire length (huge sections are well-signed though) it follows many of France's major river valleys across the entire width of France. The French section is due to be fully completed by 2009 but the majority of the route is currently in place.
Beginning at the mouth of the Loire it follows the course of the river, swapping banks and sometimes meandering a few miles away from the river itself, leaving the Loire at the town of Digoin. Although there is no Loire towpath as such, the route frequently comes alongside the river, using many of the lovely bridges that cross it.
From Digoin you follow minor roads and towpath along the course of the Canal du Centre before picking up the River Saône at Chalon-sur-Saône. The Rhône-Rhine canal and the River Doubs are then followed for much of the rest of the route to the Swiss border at Basel (Basle).
Beyond France's borders EuroVelo 6 passes through nine more countries, covering nearly 4000km to reach the Black Sea.

Grade EASY

Start / finish St-Brevin-Les-Pins (near St Nazaire) / EV6 leaves France at the Swiss border heading to Basel (Basle)

Route length 737 miles / 1185km
Total height climbed 28,407ft
Total height descended 27,567ft
(Reverse the figures if biking east - west)
Average climb -St Brevin to Basel 38ft per mile
Average climb -Basel to St Brevin 37ft per mile

Route advice Many superbly surfaced traffic-free tarmac sections combine with tracks and minor roads. The vast majority of the route is flat or on easy gradients. Occasional sections take in some hills e.g. Paray-le-Monial to St-Léger-sur-Dheune.

Train access Lots of north/south TGV access to the western end of the route, including Nantes, Angers and Tours. For TGV access to the eastern end you can use the lines passing through Le Creusot, Dole or Besançon. Local services run east/west along much of the route. The only real gap is between Chalon-sur-Saône and Dole, where you'll have a detour north via Dijon.

Nearby routes
Poitou Charentes & Pays de La Loire - Vélocéan network pg 117
Along the Jura . Direct link - pgs 66-67
Vineyard Way / Chalon - Mâcon Greenway. Direct link - pgs 82-86
Blois. Direct link - pgs 98-100
Sologne. Direct link - pgs 101-103

Maps, guides and websites
As yet there is no comprehensive EuroVelo 6 guide - the following cover much of the route:
* *Loire by Bike* handbook. Produced annually. Detailed maps and accommodation listings between Tours and Sancerre.
* *Welcome by Bike* accommodation booklet with providers pledging to provide certain minimum standards such as secure storage, repair equipment and weather forecasts.
* *www.eurovelo6.org* Brief stage by stage descriptions of the entire route
* *www.loire-a-velo.fr* Mainly in French but useful as you can download *Loire by Bike* and *Welcome by Bike*.

Signage

Loire à Vélo St Brevin-Les-Pins to Sancerre. Currently route and signing gaps between St Brevin and Paimboeuf, Tours and Chaumont-s-Loire and Orléans and Bonny-s-Loire. Eventually the route will extend beyond Sancerre to Cuffy.

Where the route is temporary (route may change in future) the background is yellow.

Canal du Centre Handy signs showing nearby services on the canal towpath.

Doubs Valley The route between Besançon and St Vit is signed with the major settlements at either end of EuroVelo 6.

Note EV6 sections not mentioned here are not yet signed consistently

Don't Miss

Châteaux of the Last Wild River

Whilst many people will associate the Loire with the idea of Châteaux fewer will be able to tell you exactly what they mean by the term. The actual French dictionary term includes a variety of meanings, from castles designed for a military purpose to grand residences designed simply to impress - and everything in between. Later châteaux of one type may incorporate all or parts of an earlier one. In the context of the Loire though, a combination of the area's location at the heart of The Hundred Years War and the later flowering of Renaissance culture has resulted in a series of archetypal 'fairytale' palaces of turrets, battlements and towers, each highly individual. No wonder UNESCO simply made the whole area a World Heritage Site.

The route between Angers and Orléans is Châteaux country par excellence, the famous names linked by EV6 just tripping off the tongue; Chambord, Chinon, Villandry, Azay-le-Rideau to name but a few.

The fact that the Loire is still largely a wild river simply adds to the historic grandeur; it has not been dredged and opened up to large scale commercial shipping, thus allowing a huge variety of birdlife and larger mammals such as the coypu to flourish.

Note - because of strong currents and treacherous quicksand the Loire is off-limits to bathers.

Attractions of the Canal du Centre

The highlights of this little known eighteenth century canal lie at either end. At the western end a lovely canal bridge at the working town of Digoin leads to a well-surfaced section of canal towpath to the town of Paray-le-Monial, home to the beautiful Basilica of Sacré Coeur. Paray is also a major pilgrim centre.

After Paray some 77km of signed cycle route, mainly minor roads, rejoins the Canal du Centre at St-Léger-sur-Dheune. Easy well-surfaced pedalling leads past the lovely wine town of Santenay a stone's throw from the route.

After the pleaseant town of Chagny the towpath heads into the city of Chalon-sur-Saône,whose most attractive areas are by the river and around the town hall .

The Doubs Valley - Dole to Besançon

Dole is a very low key but elegant town, especially the area around the River Doubs. Between here and Besançon the Rhône-Rhine canal runs into and out of the river, the valley twisting and turning and providing some quite spectacularly grand scenery. Besançon is a very stately town sitting on a tongue of land in the river, surrounded by wooded hills. It has a decent cycle network and makes a good base for exploring this section of EV6.

The heavily wooded Doubs valley between Dole and Besançon

Tours cathedral

Suggested Day Rides on the Route

Nantes to St Florent le Viel Pgs 52-53
33 miles one way. Train return. After the bustle and city pleasures of Nantes you are soon on a traffic-free route along the north bank of the Loire before crossing onto minor roads on the south bank (new traffic-free section avoidng D751 planned for 2008). Recross the Loire to Oudon, not forgetting to take a look at the tower here. After the town of Ancenis, known for its Château and its restaurants, you use a mix of traffic-free paths and minor roads to St Florent le Viel (interesting museum in the old Sacré-Coeur chapel). Station across the bridge.

Saumur to Port Boulet via Chinon Pg54
35 miles. Train return. A fantastic ride in an area packed with the Loire's riches. The route leads out of Saumur by climbing past the hilltop Château before heading through the 'cave' dwelling villages of Parnay and Turquant. Lovely Montsoreau and Candes St Martin lead to a section north of the Vienne river to the incredible Château and village at Chinon. The loop is completed by heading north on quiet roads to the Loire, then 'inland' to Avoine and Savigny-en-Véron before recrossing the Loire to the train station at Port Boulet.

Blois, Beaugency, Château Chambord Pg56
26 miles one way. Train return. For Blois details see pg56. The sheer size of Château Chambord makes it a highlight of this route. You also dip into the 5000 hectares of wildlife rich forest that surround it (see also Around Blois pgs 98-100). After crossing the river at Muides-sur-Loire you skirt its north bank to arrive in beautiful Beaugency.

Nevers to La Charité-sur-Loire pgs 60-59
28.5 miles one way. Train return. Follow the canal link just south of Nevers centre along a beautifully surfaced towpath then pick up the Canal Lateral à la Loire towpath to cross over the River Allier on the spectacular canal bridge. A minor road leads to le Bec d'Allier from where you follow a tiny road leading to a wooden bridge back over the canal and into Cuffy. From here largely minor roads take you through some lovely countryside all the way to picturesque La Charité-sur-Loire.

Bourbon Lancy to Paray-le-Monial Pgs 60-61
35 miles one way. Train return. The pleasant village of St Bourbon Lancy is next to a high qulaity greenway that leads to Gilly-Sur-Loire. From here you are on a fast but generally quiet road, the D979, into the pleasant working town of Digoin. Here pick up another high quality section of traffic-free route along the north bank of the Canal du Centre into Paray-le-Monial, with its amazing basilica (pg61). Return by train to Gilly-S-Loire then retrace the greenway to Bourbon Lancy.

Dole to Besançon Pg63
37 miles one way. Train return. From Dole follow the canal towpath to Rochefort-sur-Nenon then follow minor roads on the south side of the Doubs valley through Eclans Nenon, Our, Etrepigny and Rans to rejoin the canal at Fraisans. From here you soon pick up a signed route all the way to Besançon, following the Doubs Valley, usually on well-surfaced traffic-free trail. The section after Torpes is particularly spectacular as is your entry into Franche-Comté's 'capital' Besançon.

East of Mulhouse Pg65
There are numerous signed rides east of Mulhouse that allow you to invent all sorts of circuits. They include an 18 mile north-south traffic-free tarmac route through the Hardt forest and links to a section of the Rhine véloroute along the German border.

Camping at Nevers

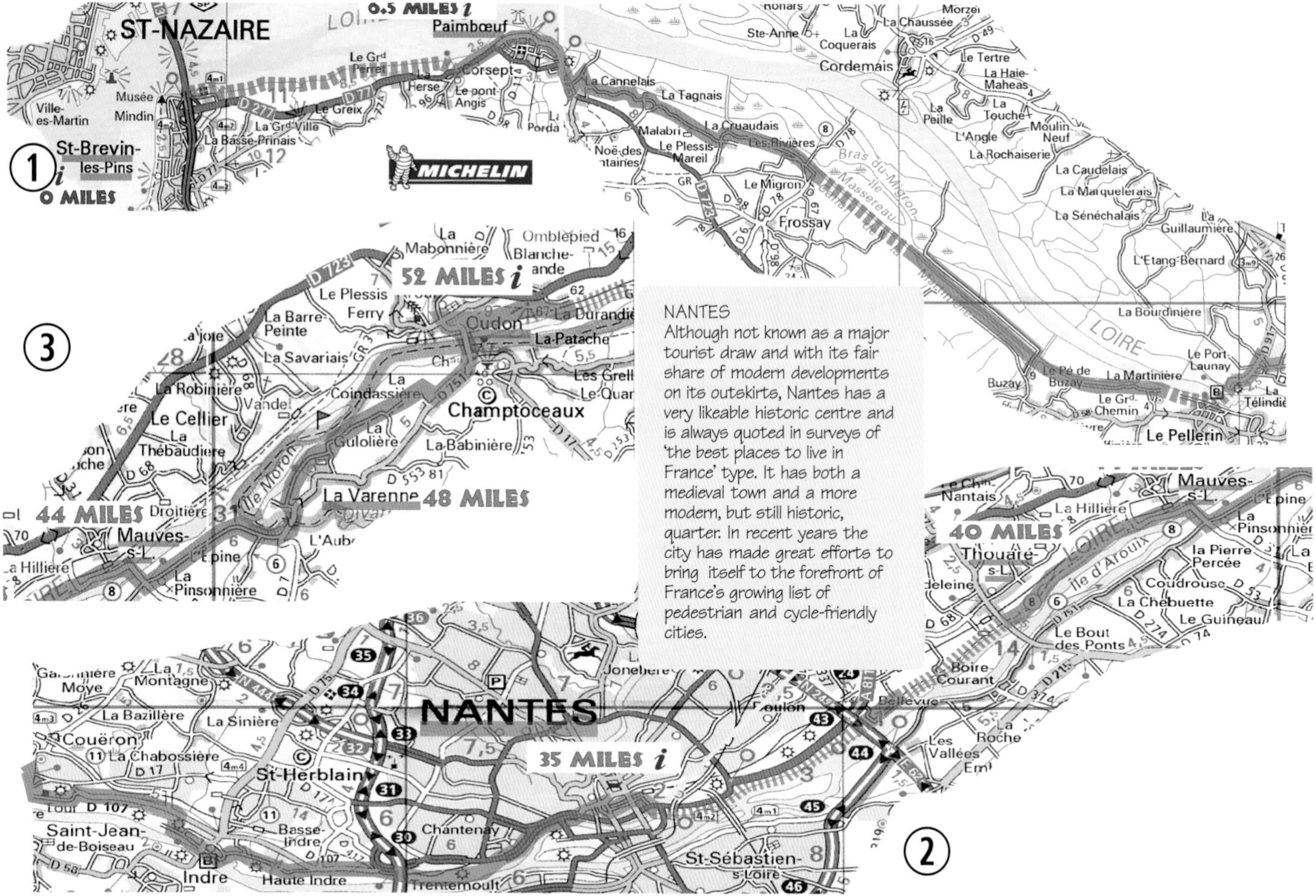

1 ST-NAZAIRE St-Brevin-les-Pins 0 MILES

6.5 MILES Paimbœuf

52 MILES Oudon

48 MILES La Varenne

44 MILES Mauves-s-L.

40 MILES Thouaré-s-L.

35 MILES NANTES

NANTES
Although not known as a major tourist draw and with its fair share of modern developments on its outskirts, Nantes has a very likeable historic centre and is always quoted in surveys of 'the best places to live in France' type. It has both a medieval town and a more modern, but still historic, quarter. In recent years the city has made great efforts to bring itself to the forefront of France's growing list of pedestrian and cycle-friendly cities.

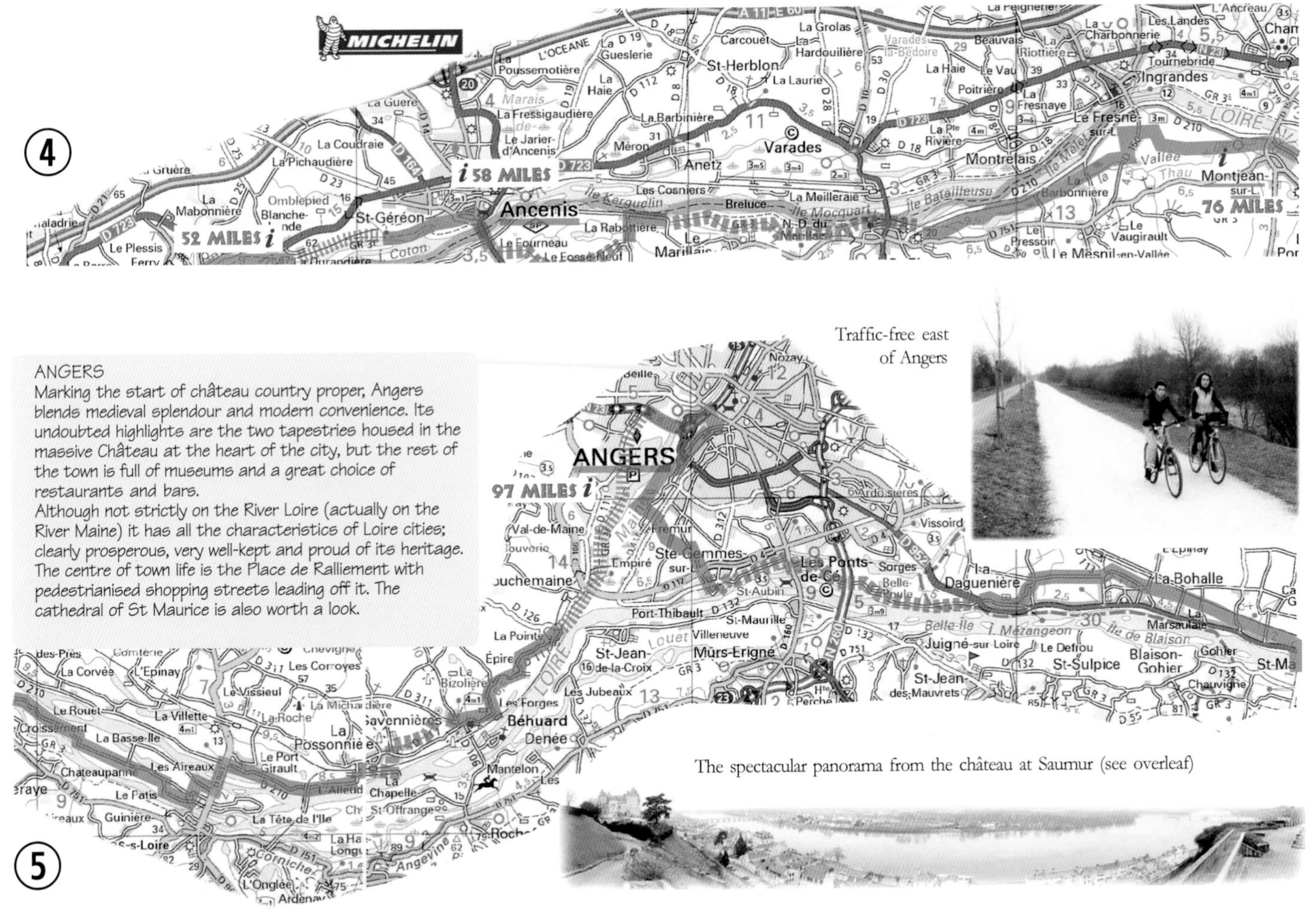

ANGERS
Marking the start of château country proper, Angers blends medieval splendour and modern convenience. Its undoubted highlights are the two tapestries housed in the massive Château at the heart of the city, but the rest of the town is full of museums and a great choice of restaurants and bars.
Although not strictly on the River Loire (actually on the River Maine) it has all the characteristics of Loire cities; clearly prosperous, very well-kept and proud of its heritage. The centre of town life is the Place de Ralliement with pedestrianised shopping streets leading off it. The cathedral of St Maurice is also worth a look.

Traffic-free east of Angers

The spectacular panorama from the château at Saumur (see overleaf)

6 Chinon Option

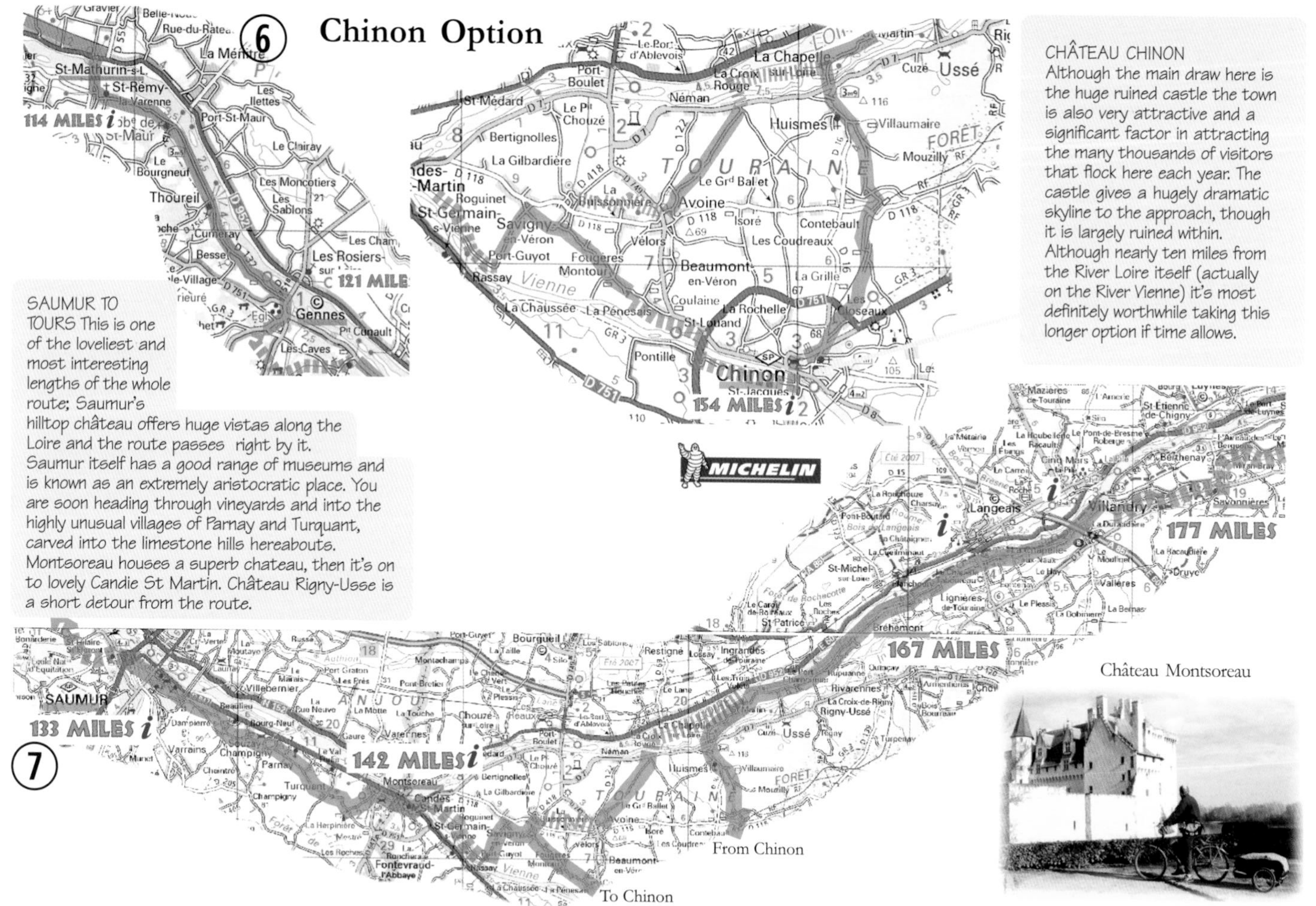

CHÂTEAU CHINON
Although the main draw here is the huge ruined castle the town is also very attractive and a significant factor in attracting the many thousands of visitors that flock here each year. The castle gives a hugely dramatic skyline to the approach, though it is largely ruined within.
Although nearly ten miles from the River Loire itself (actually on the River Vienne) it's most definitely worthwhile taking this longer option if time allows.

SAUMUR TO TOURS This is one of the loveliest and most interesting lengths of the whole route; Saumur's hilltop château offers huge vistas along the Loire and the route passes right by it.
Saumur itself has a good range of museums and is known as an extremely aristocratic place. You are soon heading through vineyards and into the highly unusual villages of Parnay and Turquant, carved into the limestone hills hereabouts.
Montsoreau houses a superb chateau, then it's on to lovely Candie St Martin. Château Rigny-Usse is a short detour from the route.

Château Montsoreau

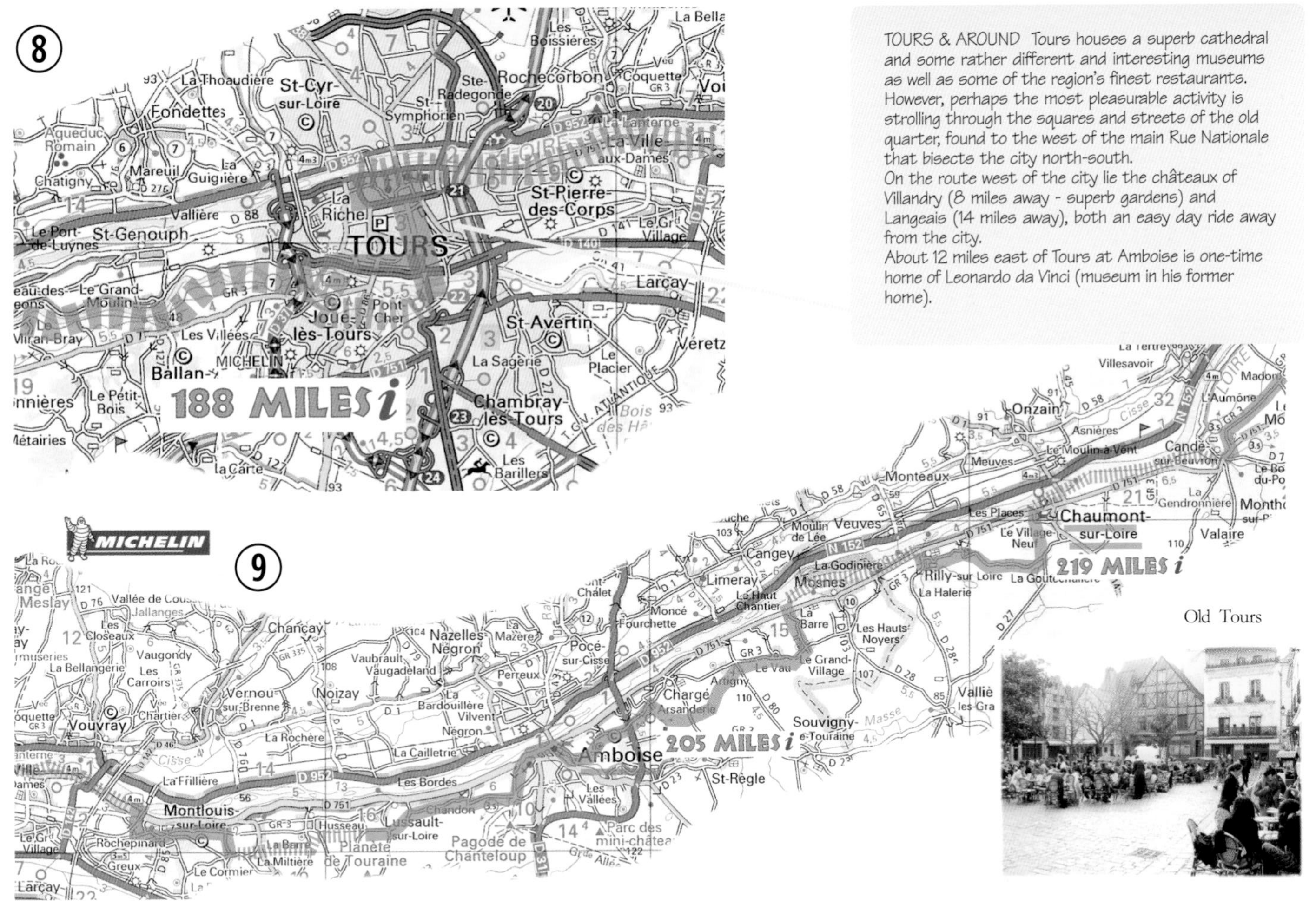

TOURS & AROUND Tours houses a superb cathedral and some rather different and interesting museums as well as some of the region's finest restaurants. However, perhaps the most pleasurable activity is strolling through the squares and streets of the old quarter, found to the west of the main Rue Nationale that bisects the city north-south.

On the route west of the city lie the châteaux of Villandry (8 miles away - superb gardens) and Langeais (14 miles away), both an easy day ride away from the city.

About 12 miles east of Tours at Amboise is one-time home of Leonardo da Vinci (museum in his former home).

Old Tours

A misty Blois seen from the south bank of the Loire. From here you can follow the river directly to Beaugency or detour via spectacular Chambord.

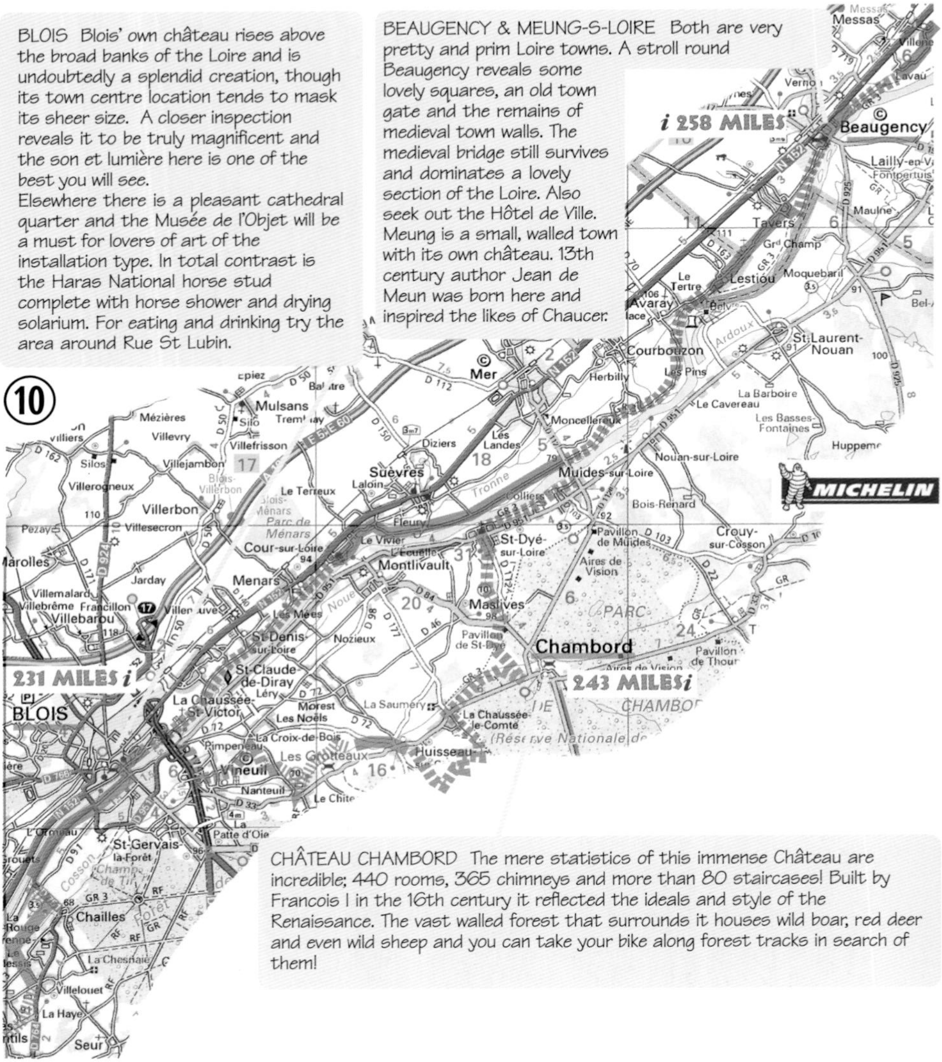

BLOIS Blois' own château rises above the broad banks of the Loire and is undoubtedly a splendid creation, though its town centre location tends to mask its sheer size. A closer inspection reveals it to be truly magnificent and the son et lumière here is one of the best you will see.
Elsewhere there is a pleasant cathedral quarter and the Musée de l'Objet will be a must for lovers of art of the installation type. In total contrast is the Haras National horse stud complete with horse shower and drying solarium. For eating and drinking try the area around Rue St Lubin.

BEAUGENCY & MEUNG-S-LOIRE Both are very pretty and prim Loire towns. A stroll round Beaugency reveals some lovely squares, an old town gate and the remains of medieval town walls. The medieval bridge still survives and dominates a lovely section of the Loire. Also seek out the Hôtel de Ville. Meung is a small, walled town with its own château. 13th century author Jean de Meun was born here and inspired the likes of Chaucer.

10

i 258 MILES

231 MILES i

243 MILES i

CHÂTEAU CHAMBORD The mere statistics of this immense Château are incredible; 440 rooms, 365 chimneys and more than 80 staircases! Built by Francois I in the 16th century it reflected the ideals and style of the Renaissance. The vast walled forest that surrounds it houses wild boar, red deer and even wild sheep and you can take your bike along forest tracks in search of them!

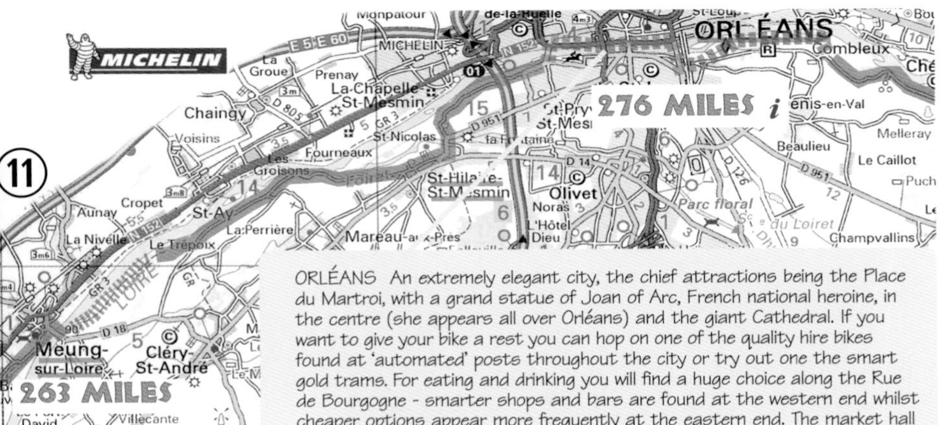

ORLÉANS An extremely elegant city, the chief attractions being the Place du Martroi, with a grand statue of Joan of Arc, French national heroine, in the centre (she appears all over Orléans) and the giant Cathedral. If you want to give your bike a rest you can hop on one of the quality hire bikes found at 'automated' posts throughout the city or try out one the smart gold trams. For eating and drinking you will find a huge choice along the Rue de Bourgogne - smarter shops and bars are found at the western end whilst cheaper options appear more frequently at the eastern end. The market hall is to the south-east of Rue de Bourgogne.

Bike hire in Orléans

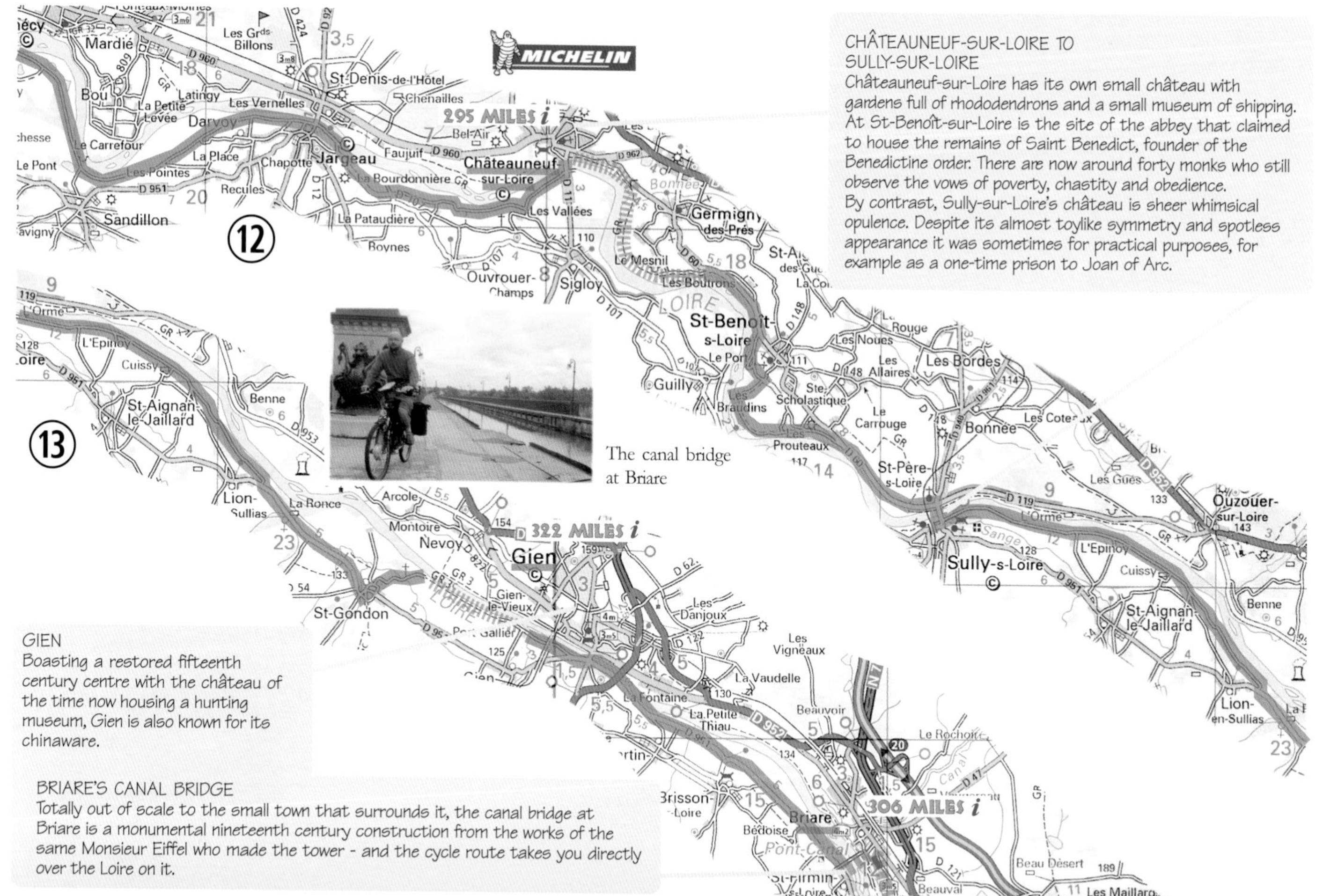

The canal bridge at Briare

CHÂTEAUNEUF-SUR-LOIRE TO SULLY-SUR-LOIRE

Châteauneuf-sur-Loire has its own small château with gardens full of rhododendrons and a small museum of shipping. At St-Benoît-sur-Loire is the site of the abbey that claimed to house the remains of Saint Benedict, founder of the Benedictine order. There are now around forty monks who still observe the vows of poverty, chastity and obedience.

By contrast, Sully-sur-Loire's château is sheer whimsical opulence. Despite its almost toylike symmetry and spotless appearance it was sometimes for practical purposes, for example as a one-time prison to Joan of Arc.

GIEN

Boasting a restored fifteenth century centre with the château of the time now housing a hunting museum, Gien is also known for its chinaware.

BRIARE'S CANAL BRIDGE

Totally out of scale to the small town that surrounds it, the canal bridge at Briare is a monumental nineteenth century construction from the works of the same Monsieur Eiffel who made the tower - and the cycle route takes you directly over the Loire on it.

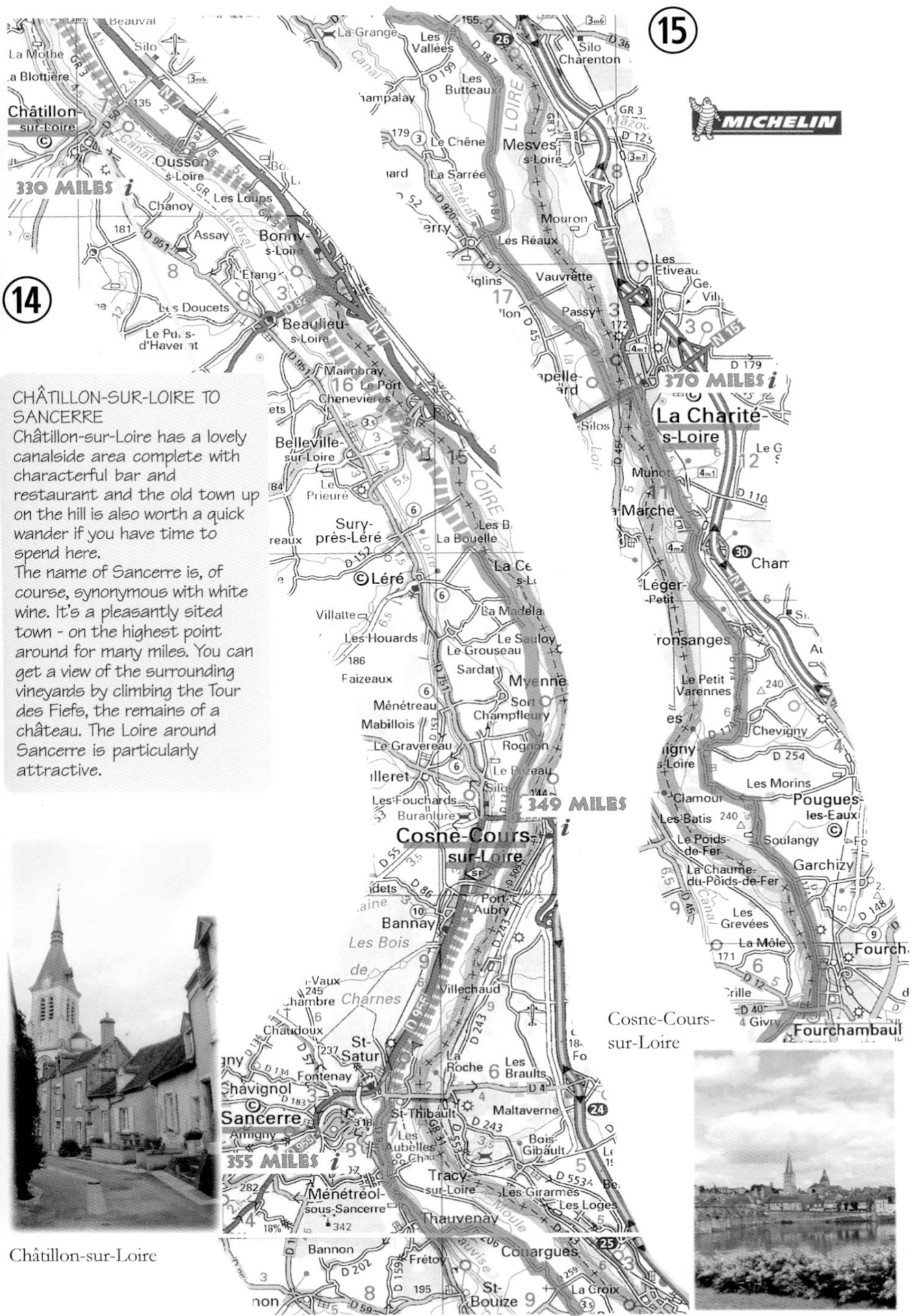

CHÂTILLON-SUR-LOIRE TO SANCERRE

Châtillon-sur-Loire has a lovely canalside area complete with characterful bar and restaurant and the old town up on the hill is also worth a quick wander if you have time to spend here.

The name of Sancerre is, of course, synonymous with white wine. It's a pleasantly sited town - on the highest point around for many miles. You can get a view of the surrounding vineyards by climbing the Tour des Fiefs, the remains of a château. The Loire around Sancerre is particularly attractive.

Châtillon-sur-Loire

Cosne-Cours-sur-Loire

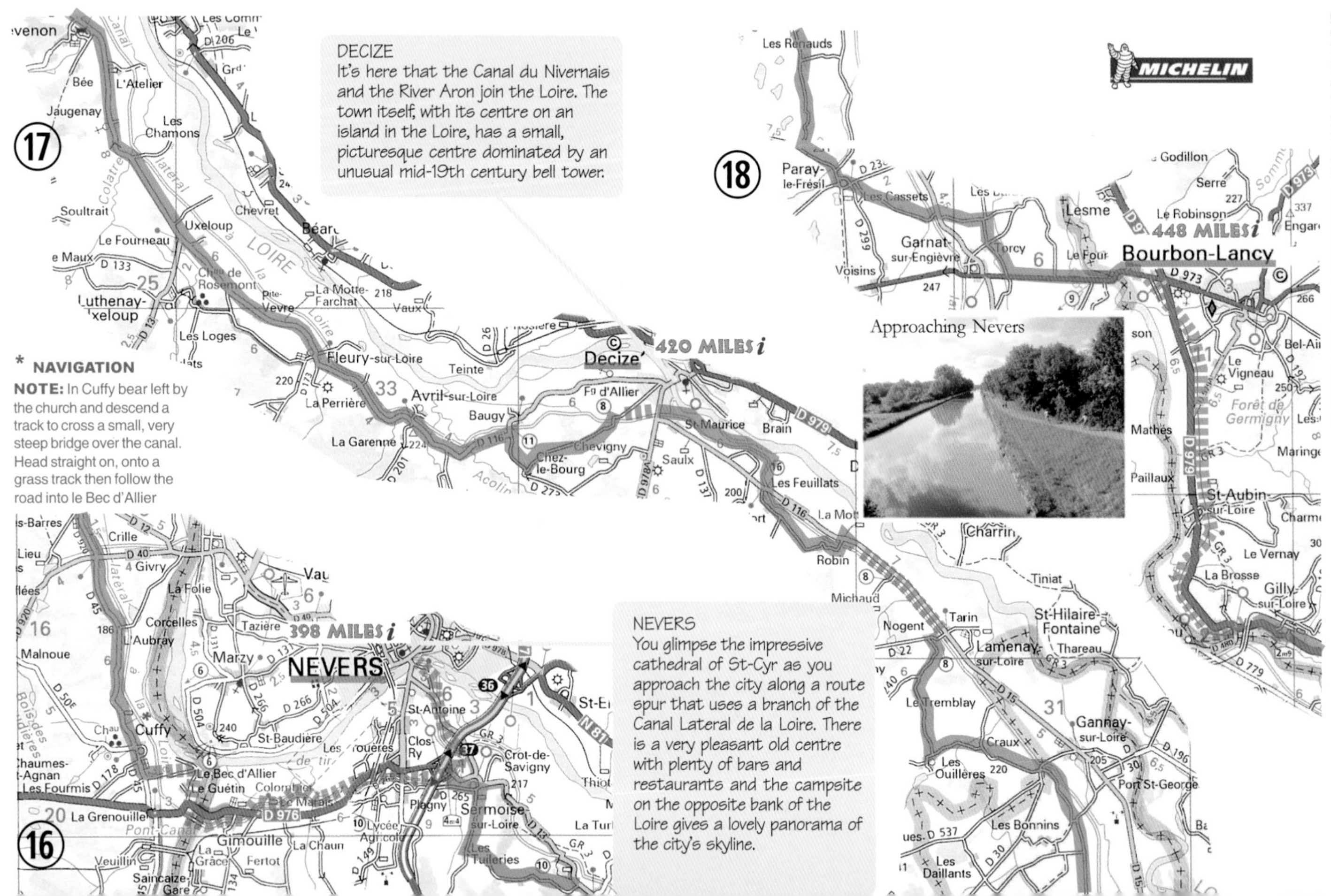

Approaching Nevers

DECIZE
It's here that the Canal du Nivernais and the River Aron join the Loire. The town itself, with its centre on an island in the Loire, has a small, picturesque centre dominated by an unusual mid-19th century bell tower.

* **NAVIGATION**

NOTE: In Cuffy bear left by the church and descend a track to cross a small, very steep bridge over the canal. Head straight on, onto a grass track then follow the road into le Bec d'Allier

NEVERS
You glimpse the impressive cathedral of St-Cyr as you approach the city along a route spur that uses a branch of the Canal Lateral de la Loire. There is a very pleasant old centre with plenty of bars and restaurants and the campsite on the opposite bank of the Loire gives a lovely panorama of the city's skyline.

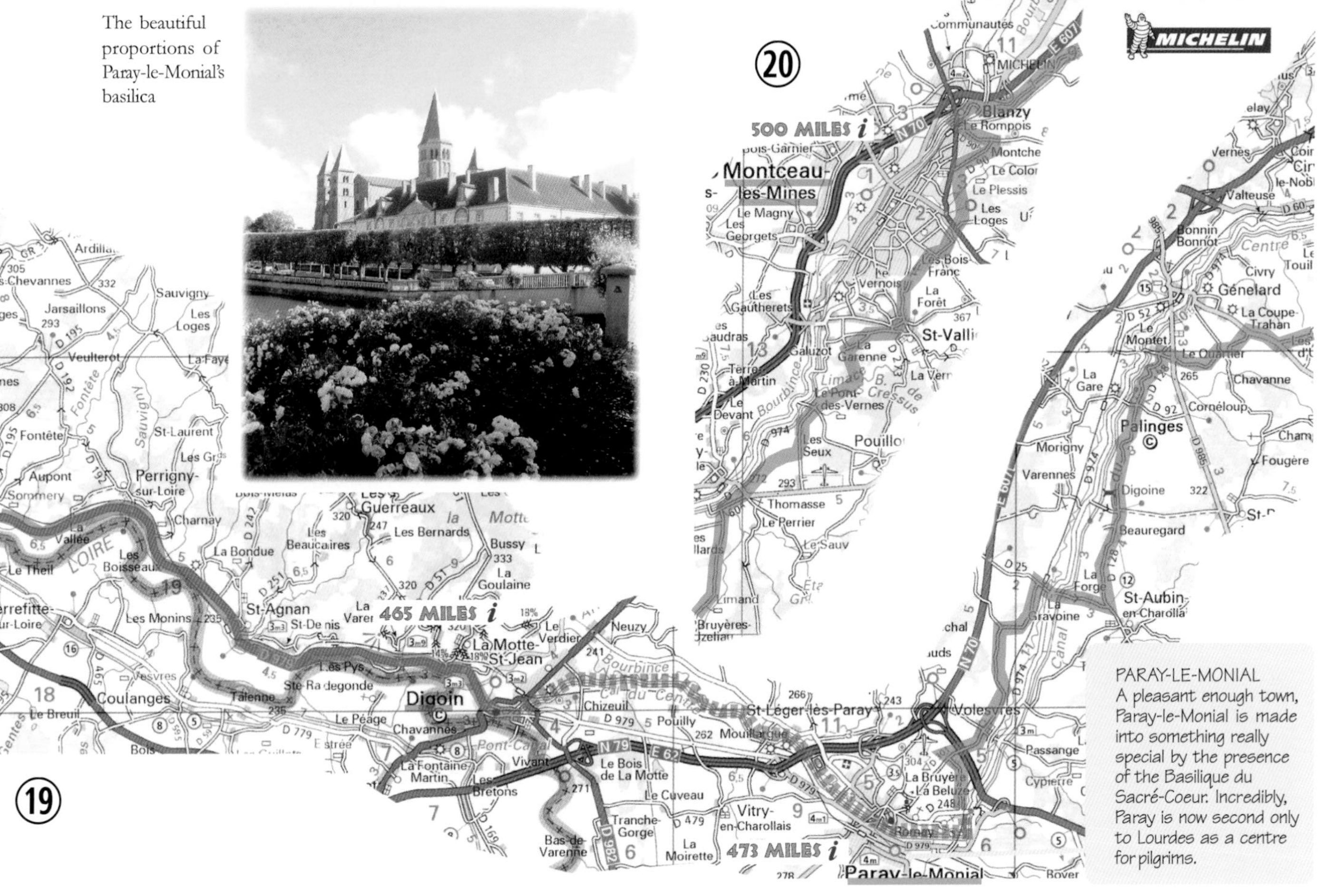

The beautiful proportions of Paray-le-Monial's basilica

PARAY-LE-MONIAL
A pleasant enough town, Paray-le-Monial is made into something really special by the presence of the Basilique du Sacré-Coeur. Incredibly, Paray is now second only to Lourdes as a centre for pilgrims.

CHALON-SUR-SAÔNE

Impressively set on the river Saône, Chalon has a fine riverside promenade / cycle lane and a pleasant old town just near the river, as well as a small selection of interesting museums. Like many less touristy places in France accommodation is still pretty plentiful but significantly cheaper than visitor hotspots - a nice place to spend a day but not too much money. It will also develop as a cycling route 'hub' for the area over the coming years, with Burgundy's Vineyard Way and the Givry to Mâcon greenway passing through or close by. There are also plans to put a route along the river Saône itself.

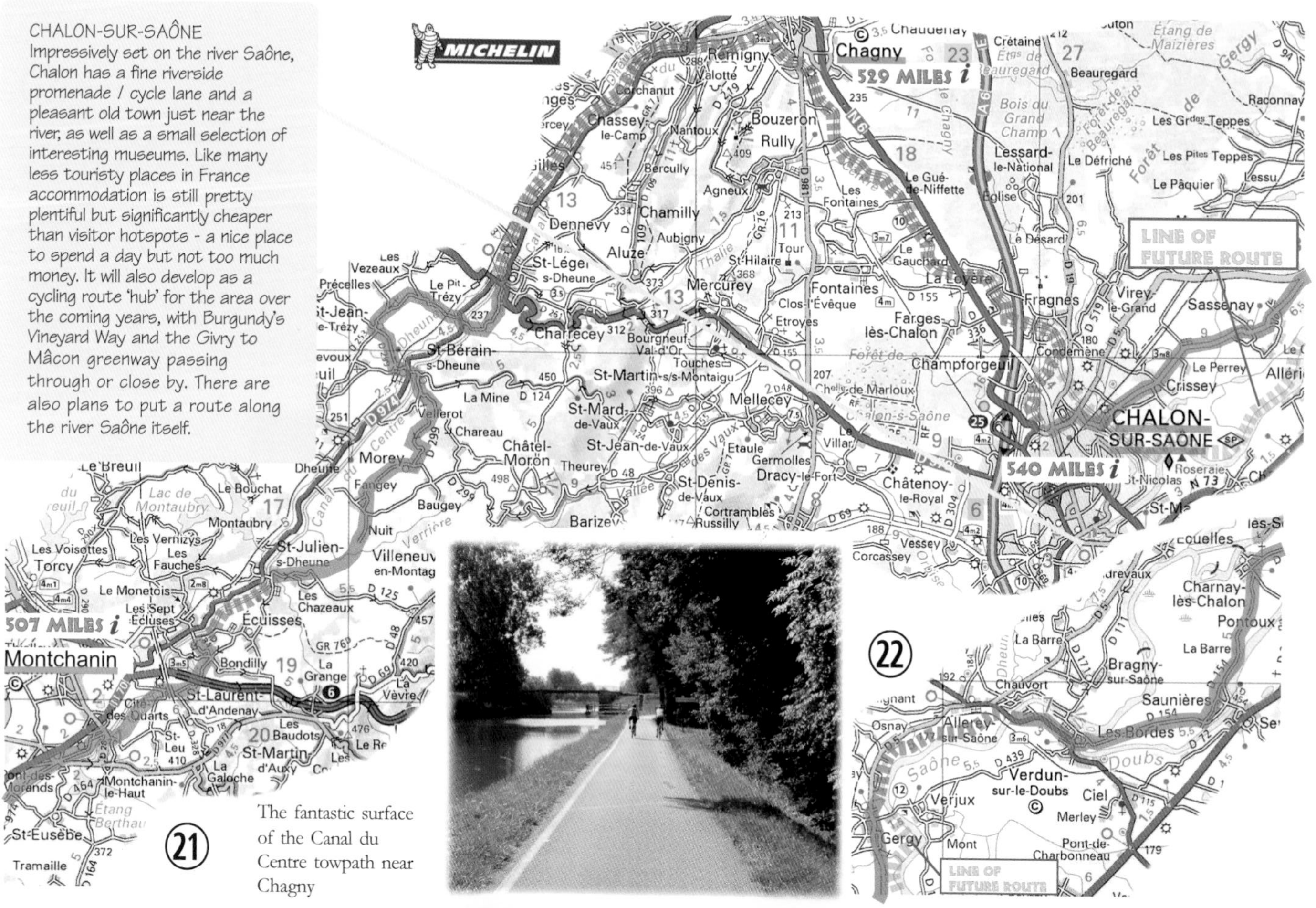

The fantastic surface of the Canal du Centre towpath near Chagny

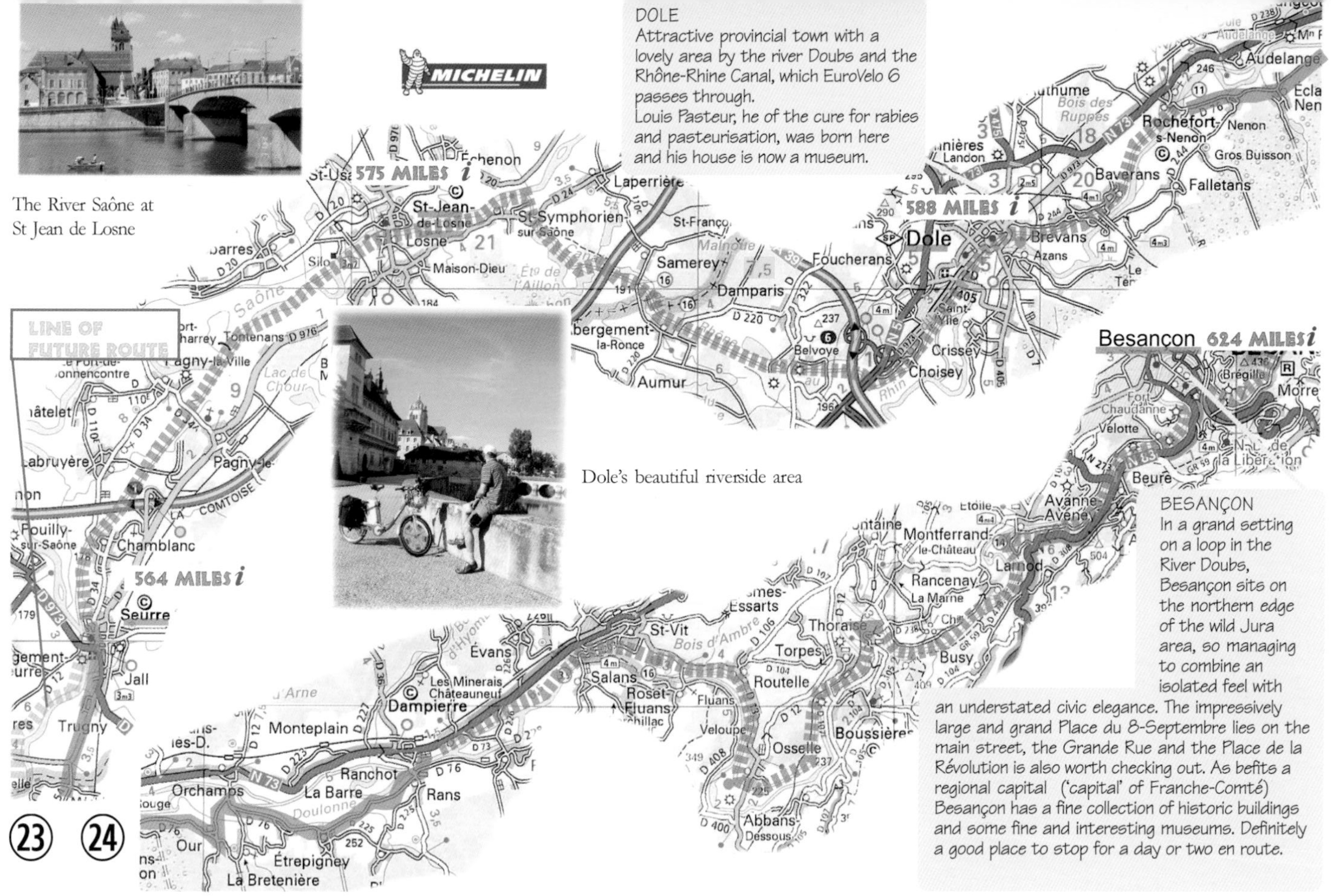

The River Saône at St Jean de Losne

Dole's beautiful riverside area

DOLE
Attractive provincial town with a lovely area by the river Doubs and the Rhône-Rhine Canal, which EuroVelo 6 passes through.
Louis Pasteur, he of the cure for rabies and pasteurisation, was born here and his house is now a museum.

BESANÇON
In a grand setting on a loop in the River Doubs, Besançon sits on the northern edge of the wild Jura area, so managing to combine an isolated feel with an understated civic elegance. The impressively large and grand Place du 8-Septembre lies on the main street, the Grande Rue and the Place de la Révolution is also worth checking out. As befits a regional capital ('capital' of Franche-Comté) Besançon has a fine collection of historic buildings and some fine and interesting museums. Definitely a good place to stop for a day or two en route.

MONTBÉLIARD
Montbéliard, has only been part of France since the late eighteenth century and so many of the older buildings here have a distinctly Germanic feel to them. Modern exhibitions are housed in the fifteenth century castle of the Dukes of Würtemberg. In nearby Sochaux there's the Peugeot Museum and the cars are still made in the southern suburb of Audincourt. It is also at the northern end of the Jura traverse.

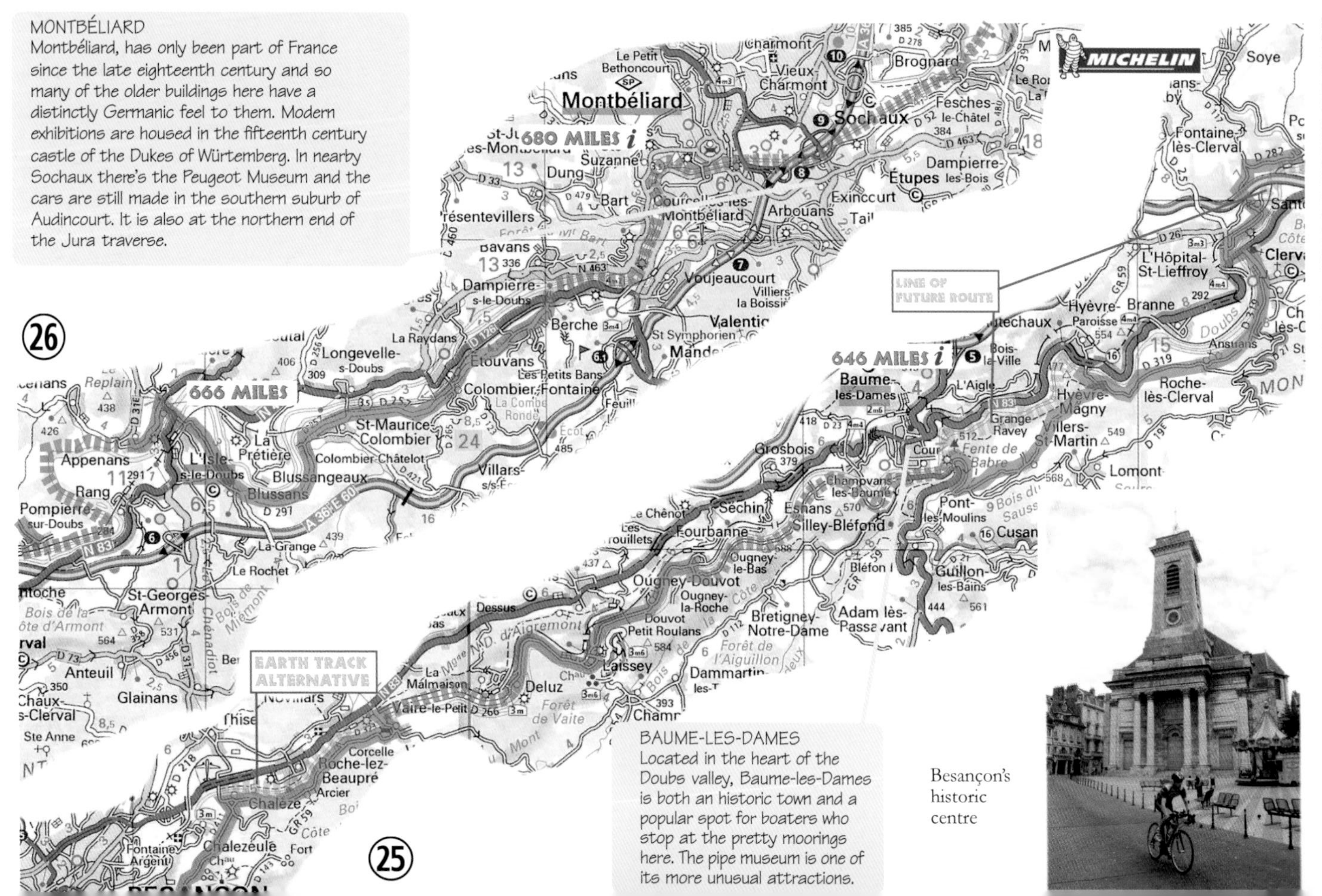

BAUME-LES-DAMES
Located in the heart of the Doubs valley, Baume-les-Dames is both an historic town and a popular spot for boaters who stop at the pretty moorings here. The pipe museum is one of its more unusual attractions.

Besançon's historic centre

EUROVELO 6 CONTINUES

Heading east, EuroVelo 6 continues out of France and into Switzerland at the border city of Basel (Bâle in French), which also shares a border with Germany. Indeed it is at a junction of several major European cycle routes; the Rhine route and the Three Countries Cycle Route (a route through France, Switzerland and Germany).

EV6 follows the Rhine, actually the Swiss-German border, before picking up the Danube through southern Germany, heading for Regensburg and Passau. Its mammoth course then leads through Austria, Slovakia, Hungary, Croatia, Serbia and Romania before finishing on Bulgaria's Black Sea coast!

MULHOUSE

Historically Swiss, Mulhouse voted to become part of France in the late eighteenth century, but still has many strong ties to Switzerland.

It is fairly and squarely an industrial city and consequently less attractive on the face of it than many other French cities, but the variety of this industry has bequeathed a number of interesting museums. The fabric museum displays the city's rich textile tradition whilst the outskirts of the city house the vast Automoile City with over 600 cars, dating from the late 19th century and the national railway museum which includes rolling stock from Napoléon III's era.

It's also a good place to try Alsatian cookery.

Along the Jura

Route Info

Along the Jura
The idea of travelling along the extended ridges of the Jura is clearly not limited to touring cyclists; there are also mountain biking, walking and cross-country ski routes!
As this route is in its infancy and only signed in the Ain *département* at the time of writing, it's dealt with briefly. However, despite the lack of comprehensive signing if you fancy some touring in Alpine scenery of pine-clad ridges, green upland pastures and chalet-style architecture - without the killer cols of the Alps proper - then this could be the route for you. If so, you'll need more detailed info as listed in the Maps, guides and websites section.

Grade DIFFICULT Many climbs, even though you are travelling along the length of the elongated Jura mountains.

Start / finish Montbéliard / Culoz

Route length 214 miles / 344km. This assumes using only one of the optional routes, the spectacular Corniche du Goumois (other options add more).
Total height climbed 32,128ft
Total height descended 32,387ft
(Reverse the figures if biking south - north)
Av. climb - Montbéliard to Culoz 150 ft per mile
Av. climb - Culoz to Montbéliard 151 ft per mile

Route advice Mainly on quiet minor roads.

Train access Montbéliard, Portarlier, Bellegarde and Culoz are serviced by TGV trains and Morteau and Morez locally.

Nearby routes
At Montbéliard join Eurovelo 6 - pg48
Ain à Vélo - pgs 87-97
Alps Easy Riding - pgs 74-80

Maps, guides and websites
Montagnes de Jura à Vélo High quality French guidebook worth buying for the detailed maps. Lists details of bike shops, though no accommodation. From local tourist offices.

Signage

GTJ is the handily short form for any of the several types of crossings of the Jura (see above) and stands for *Grande Traversée de Jura* - the Great Jura Crossing in other words. Although the Ain was the only local area to have put comprehensive signing in place at the time of writing, the route is relatively easily followed with the French-language guide maps as it is mainly on minor roads.

Don't Miss

Germany Comes to France

The route's starting point, Montbéliard, has only been part of France since the late eighteenth century and so many of the older buildings here have a distinctly Germanic feel to them. Modern exhibitions are housed in the fifteenth century castle of the Dukes of Würtemberg. In nearby Sochaux there's the Peugeot Museum and the cars are still made in the southern suburb of Audincourt.

Along the Corniche

This variant on the main route is certainly a tough option but offers some of the most astounding views on the route. The river Doubs snakes away beneath you from the road that hugs the side of the valley. You also get the chance to visit the village of Goumois, partly in France and partly in Switzerland.

Near the Corniche de Goumois
Association GTJ

SMUGGLERS' LADDERS

If you continue on the easterly route option (not passing through the village of Damprichard) you'll get the chance to make a short there and back detour on the road to the electricity plant at Refrain. Here are the 'ladders of death' (*echelles de la mort*), which those with a head for heights can climb for a great view over the Doubs valley. They were once a handy smugglers' route across the Franco-Swiss border.

LAKES AND PEAKS

Just south of Pontraltier (museum of futuristic car design called *ESPERA-Sbarro*) is the lovely Saint Point lake with a greenway running around much of its shore.

The harder southern route option here gives you the chance to visit the 1463m / 4800ft summit of Le Mont d'Or. Although this involves a 4 mile climb it's worth it on a clear day for the views of the Swiss and French Alps.

Alternatively have a rest and try the other Mont d'Or - the name of the local cheese.

VILLERS-LE-LAC & MORTEAU

From the village of Villers-le-Lac you can visit the *Saut de Doubs* waterfall some 4 miles upstream of the village. This is 'clock country' you are now in so you could pay a visit to the clock museum here too.

At the more sizeable Morteau you can see the even more impressive Clock Museum of the Haut Doubs (*Musée de l'Horlogerie de Haut-Doubs*).

Morteau is also known for its high quality smoked sausages.

LAJOUX AND BELLEGARDE

The final 60 miles or so are largely downhill as you descend off the Jura and to the Rhône.

Just before Lajoux you will pass the Jura's highest lake, Lamoura, also one of its smallest.

You then head down the Valserine Valley with the nature reserve of the High Jura occupying much of the immense ridge on the south side of the valley - home to such rare wildlife as the peregrine falcon and the lynx.

You climb out of Bellegarde onto the lovely Retord plateau and the very final leg of the route gives you the option to sample one of the hardest cols in all of France, so only for experienced and fit climbers. Known as *Le Grand Colombier*, it takes you to a height of 1531m or over 5,000ft with a 360 degree panorama over countryside including the Alps and Lakes Léman, Bourget and Annecy.

Classic Jura countryside
Association GTJ

The Vaucluse

Route Info

The Vaucluse
Fine cycling in a land of lavender fields and vineyards Provence's heart.

Grade MEDIUM to DIFFICULT

Route length
Route lengths vary between 2.5 miles / 4 km and 49 miles / 78 km

Route advice
Valréas, in L'Enclave des Papes, is at the centre of a fairly level plateau. However, there some stiff hills to the south-east, en route. Other routes in the Haute Vaucluse cover a range, from easy plateau riding to the challenging *Dentelles,* just to the west of towering Mont Ventoux - extremely challenging country. However, the Montagne de Lure is also very challenging. Les Ocres à Vélo country is typified by rolling hills.

Train access
The line from Marseille to the Alps has a station at Manosque which is the nearest to Forcalquier and the eastern side of the area. To the west of Avignon lines skirt the riding area, the most useful station probably being Orange. A line heads north up the Durance valley, skirting the Montagne de Lure circuit.

Nearby routes
Les Ocres à Vélo and the Forcalquier ride are off the northern length of the long distance Luberon route, described in *Long Distance Rides*.

Maps, guides and websites
Leaflets with detailed mapping to all routes available locally or through sources given in information boxes. For specific route websites see area boxes accompanying the map.

HAUT VAUCLUSE
A group of nine circular signed routes in the area west of Mont Ventoux and around Orange are all described on www.hautvaucluse.com (includes information in English) along with L'Enclave des Papes. Each has a downloadable bilingual map leaflet (printed ones available locally) and there are details of participants in a "Cyclists Welcome" scheme. Distances range from 5.5 to 28 miles / 9 to 45 km. Some of the rides also feature on www.provenceguide-velo.com

LES OCRES À VÉLO
This 50 kilometre signed in both directions circular route could form a good day ride off the long distance Luberon route. Starting in Apt, a nice old market town known for its crystallised fruit, pottery and Saturday market. Places along the route include Rustrel and Roussillon, old ochre mining villages and an unusual landscape including brightly coloured former ochre quarries. For info and downloadable leaflet (bilingual) see www.ot-apt.fr (has English version).

Mont Ventoux's light stone cap as seen in the February sun

L'ENCLAVE DES PAPES
This little bit of Provence that seems to have drifted northwards reportedly originated from the liking of a 14th century Avignon pope for the local wine - he just bought the estate. These days the vineyards, the woodland and the lavender fields provide the backdrop for this 33.5 kilometre circular ride. Valréas, the main town, is ancient with imposing castle tower, a town hall in a former château and a history of printing. Grillon, Richerenches and Visan are well worth a stop. See www.provenceguide-velo.com/velo-hautvaucluse.asp (excellent English version). Route leaflet available locally.

MONT VENTOUX
Mont Ventoux (1912 metres high) and its western foothills, the Dentelles de Montmirail, offer many cycle routes. Some, but certainly not all, will benefit from a mountain bike and some are unsigned, although an increasing number are being signed. The mountain dominates a huge area of countryside and can be seen from afar. Its white limestone means it can look snow-covered at some very unlikely times of year. There is a pack available locally of 18 small mapsheets of rides (3 of them need a mountain bike) in the area or see http://perso.wanadoo.fr/cyclo-provence-alpes (which tells you to phone 04.90.70.57.22) if you want one beforehand.

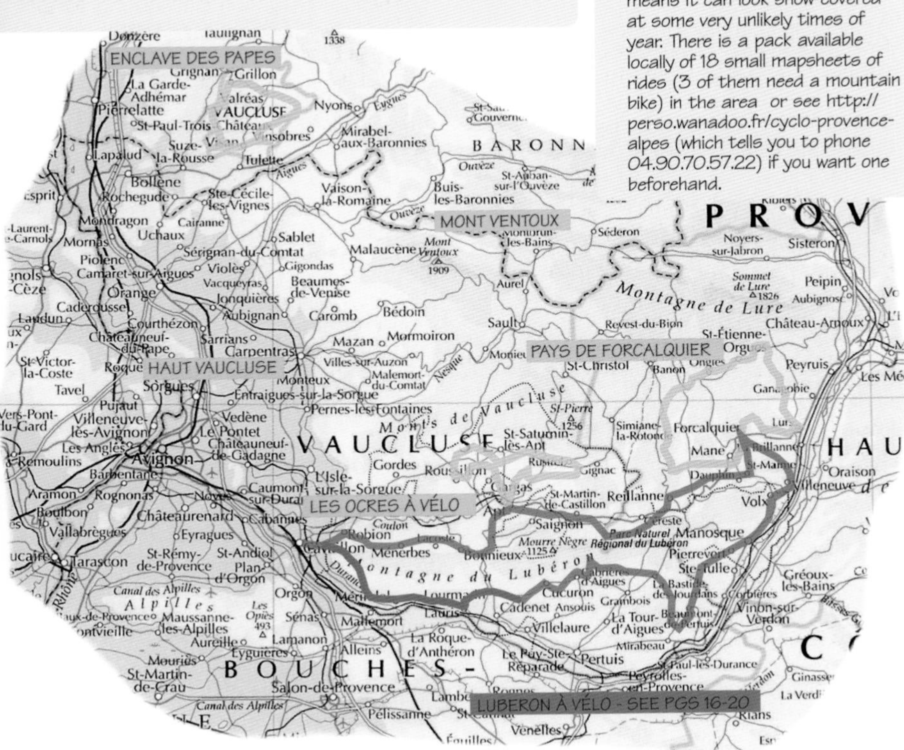

AUBENAS
Le Pays de Forcalquier en vélo.
Chambres d'Hôtes

Routes in the Vaucluse are well-signed

LE PAYS DE FORCALQUIER ET MONTAGNE DE LURE EN VÉLO
Another nice ride off the long-distance Luberon route, this 78 kilometres passes through ancient hilltop Lurs, St. Etienne les Orgues at the foot of the 1800+ metre Montagne de Lure with its magnificent views and many other villages, often set amidst colourful lavender fields. Forcalquier is described on page 20 of "Around the Luberon". Information may be available on or via www.veloloisirluberon.com

Around the Côte d'Azur

Route Info

Around the Côte D'Azur
Planned as a 63 mile / 102 km traffic-free route between Toulon and St. Raphael, the western part between Toulon and Le Lavandou is largely complete, offering 33 miles / 53km of easy, well-signed cycle route much of it on a former railway. Further inland in the Var *département* are 20 signed routes, covering more difficult terrain.

Grade EASY Toulon to Le Lavandou
Grade MEDIUM to **DIFFICULT** Var circular routes

Start / finish
Toulon / Le Lavandou (traffic-free section). Plenty of small towns along the route and a rail link between Hyères and Toulon make it easy to split the route into short sections or couple it up to some of the Var rides.

Route length 33miles/53km

Route advice
Good, wide tarmac path with few significant climbs and the one or two road sections are short. Whilst the path doesn't actually run along the coast for the most part, it's sometimes near enough for a short detour to put sand between your toes. Quite a lot of the route has no tree shade. Signage is good and there are information boards from time to time. A good variation on the coastal route is to head around the spit of land known as the Presqu' Île de Giens, which boasts extensive stretches of cycle lane, opening up the possibility of a ferry to Porquerolles. Here you can try out the earth tracks of this virtually traffic-free and barely developed island.
The signed circular routes have their own rating system, from easy to difficult but all will be significantly more difficult than the traffic-free coastal trail, as you will have several mountain chains to contend with. All are road routes, the majority on minor roads. They range from 34 miles / 55km to 62 miles / 99km and present a great challenge through some spectacular scenery for keen road riders.

SIDE TRIP - MONT FARON'S ADRENALINE RUSH

Just above the port city of Toulon's city centre a cable car will take you and your bike to near the summit of Mont Faron. Once there you can explore the memorial museum to the Allied landings in Provence or take a trip round the small nearby zoo. You have a choice of short but hair-raising descents on barrier-free mountain roads back down to Toulon (eastern and western options) or even more vertiginous mountain bike tracks down the side of the mountain.

Train access Plenty of trains between Hyères and Toulon. It's a TGV line so not all trains will carry bikes.

Nearby routes
The Luberon route (pg 16) and the associated rides around the Vaucluse (pg 68-69) are next door to the Var, to the north-west of the area.

Maps, guides and websites
* *Plan Vélo* - a reasonably detailed free map of the area between Toulon and Hyères showing this cyclepath and others along with advisory routes. From local Tourist Offices.
* *Parcours Cyclable du Littoral* Handy little free leaflet with overview plan of the whole Toulon to St - Raphael route and explanations of signs used on the route. From local Tourist Offices.
* *www.var.fr* Basic route information.
* *http://voiescyclables.free.fr/cotedazur.html*

All of the more difficult signed circular routes are detailed in a handy free booklet (French language only), *22 Circuits de promenades et randonnées pour cyclotouristes* that is worth having for the maps alone. Available at local tourist offices.

Signage

The coastal traffic-free route is well-signed and is in anycase obvious. It appears the circular Var routes were signed sometime ago and so some signs may be missing or wrong so be sure to take the free booklet detailing them.

THE VERDON GORGE
Twenty miles long and hundreds of metres deep, this enormous gorge, Europe's largest, is a dramatic sight. It's popular for rock-climbing, rafting and canoeing and bungee jumping from the amazing Pont de l'Artuby, but for simple open-mouthed gawping, It's the tops. The Corniche Sublime is the D71 road running along the southern bank of the gorge and the northern side of ride 5.

COTIGNAC
Backed by a cliff full of troglodyte dwellings, Cotignac is one of the prettiest villages in the rocky Haut Var area. It has a very picturesque Place de la Mairie, but if it is food and drink you are after head for the Cours Gambetta.

MONS
A truly unspoilt mountain village in a gorgeous setting with only minor evidence of tourism. Although well inland, at 800 metres plus altitude it offers views of the Mediterranean and even Corsica on a good day.

THE CALANQUES
Calanques are the secluded coves, many harbiuring fine beaches, found all along the Côte D'Azur and ideally explored by bike and foot,
The southern section of Route 19 runs parallel to one of the finest sections of coastline so take your time, get a detailed map and you'll find heading just a short distance off the route will reward you with fine, golden-white sand and turquoise sea. In particular many dead-end roads and tracks lead to some fine stretches of coastline around the St Tropez peninsula.

FRÉJUS
The best of both worlds - Fréjus has huge, long beaches and busy marinas a mile or so from the town centre. Holiday entertainment is plentiful but a Roman and medieval history leaves Fréjus with the remains of a Roman amphitheatre and aqueduct and an eleventh century cathedral and other medieval church buildings. The Buddhist pagoda you pass on the ride return into Fréjus was built by Vietnamese soldiers fighting in France in WW1. There's a chapel designed by Jean Cocteau and perhaps more family style entertainment at the zoo. October sees the annual 'Roc d'Azur' 5 day mountain bike event attracting thousands of competitors and spectators.

Toulon

Toulon is well-known as a French naval base but has other maritime traffic also. A boat trip across to St. Mandrier is a good way of seeing this huge natural harbour and for spectacular views of it all, there's a cable car up Mont Faron behind the city - take your bike on the cable car and have a whizz back down! There's also a small zoo (mainly big cats) and a WWII museum up there.

Hyères

With its streets lined with palm trees and its nice markets and wide variety of shops, Hyères is well worth a visit. Some of the villas from the town's heyday are quite splendid and the place has an atmosphere all its own.

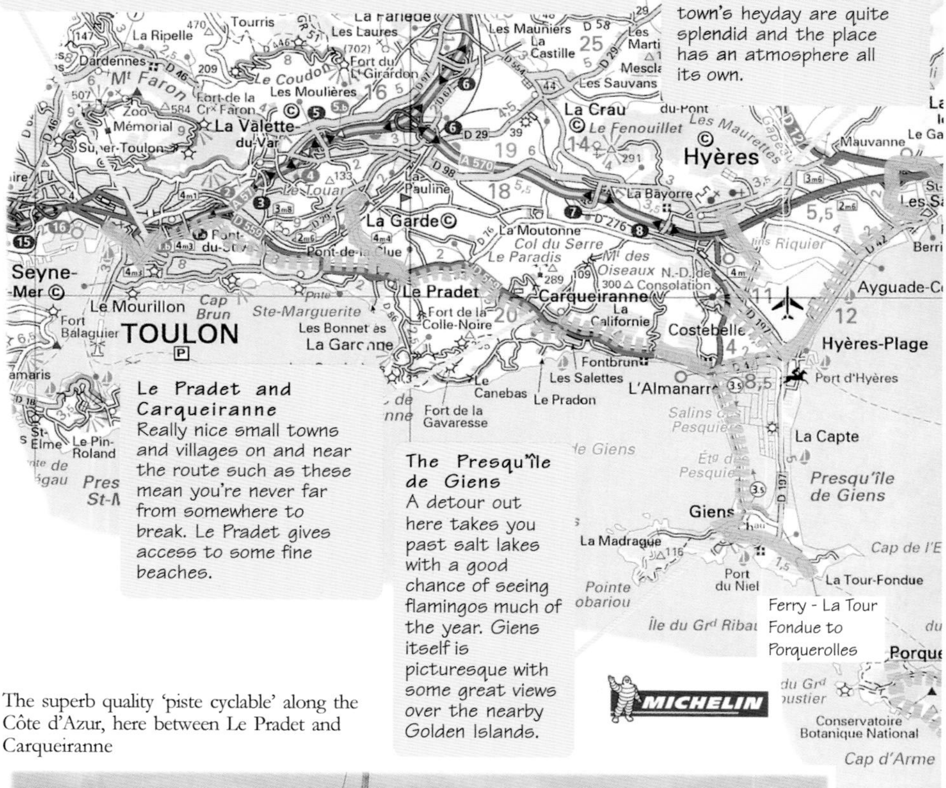

Le Pradet and Carqueiranne

Really nice small towns and villages on and near the route such as these mean you're never far from somewhere to break. Le Pradet gives access to some fine beaches.

The Presqu'île de Giens

A detour out here takes you past salt lakes with a good chance of seeing flamingos much of the year. Giens itself is picturesque with some great views over the nearby Golden Islands.

Ferry - La Tour Fondue to Porquerolles

The superb quality 'piste cyclable' along the Côte d'Azur, here between Le Pradet and Carqueiranne

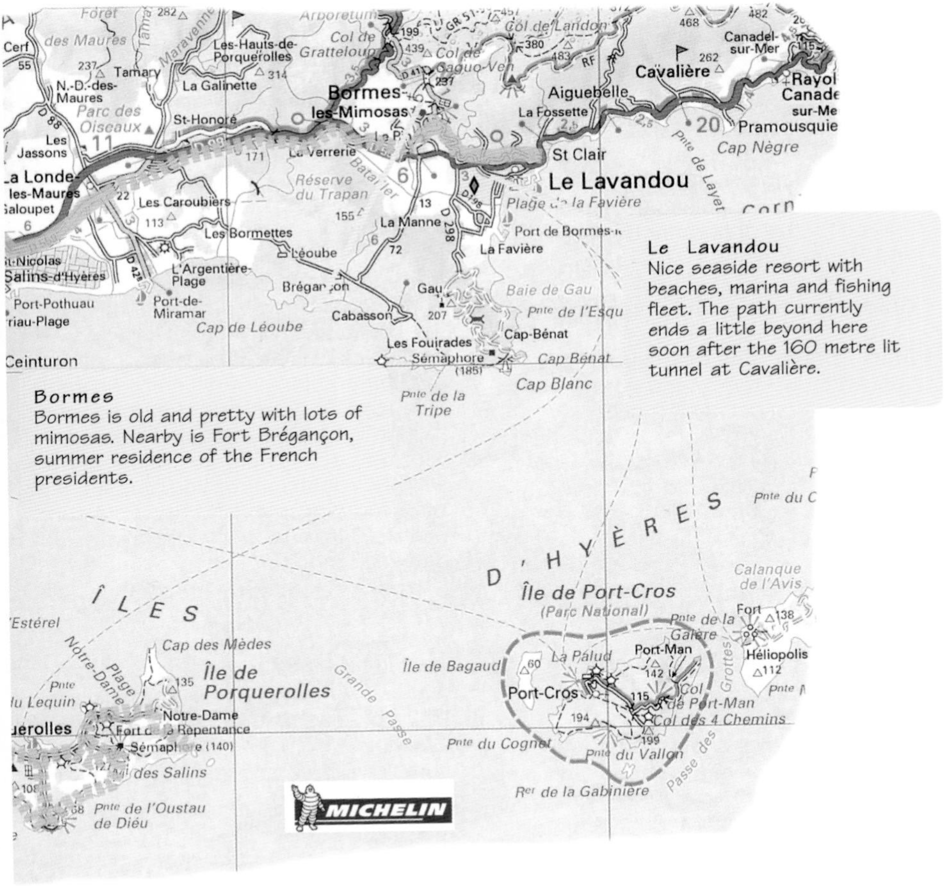

Le Lavandou
Nice seaside resort with beaches, marina and fishing fleet. The path currently ends a little beyond here soon after the 160 metre lit tunnel at Cavalière.

Bormes
Bormes is old and pretty with lots of mimosas. Nearby is Fort Brégançon, summer residence of the French presidents.

Earth track riding on the virtually traffic-free island of Porquerolles; here the route takes you around small coves at the western end of the island

Alps Easy Riding

Route Info

Routes in the Savoy
A network of routes ranging from gentle railpaths to dizzying alpine rides in the outstandingly scenic area offered by the departments of Savoie and Haute Savoie.

Grade See below for section grades

Start / finish The main suggested ride starts in Annecy and heads to Moutiers. You could stay in Chambéry, Aix-les-Bains or Albertville for easy-riding day excursions. The following maps also show other suggested centres for riding in the Alps, though these are usually for fitter riders only (Grenoble and Bourg St. Maurice being the exceptions with some riding possibilities on relatively gentler gradients).

Route advice
Lake Annecy Circular Tour The eastern side of the lake route uses a mixture of minor and busier roads (**Grade MEDIUM**), though the traffic is only moderate out of tourist season. The traffic-free path along the western side of the lake (**Grade EASY**) is simply a beautiful ride.
Annecy to Aix-Les-Bains **Grade MEDIUM**
Generally quiet minor roads along part of signed route 51
Aix-Les-Bains to Myans **Grade EASY**
Generally easy going traffic-free riding on tarmac.
Myans to Albertville **Grade MEDIUM**
Generally quiet minor roads along part of signed route 44
Albertville to Moutiers **Grade EASY**
Generally quiet minor roads along part of signed route 44
Signed routes in Savoie and Haute Savoie are 8 miles / 13km to 79 miles / 127 km. Some very, very serious climbs.

Train access
Bicycle-carrying TGVs serve the area and local trains usually carry bicycles.

Nearby routes
Along the Jura - pages 66-67
Ain by Bike - pgs 87-97

Maps, guides and websites
For a good overview of these routes and information to help in choosing, the bilingual booklet *Vélo tourisme* gives basic route details, maps, profiles and level of difficulty. (Doesn't give surface types or on/off road ratio though). It's available locally along with a map showing the whole area with the routes on, or you can see it at *www.tourism.savoiehautesavoie.com* (English version available) along with other cycling information.
Chambéry has a good printed cycle route map available locally or see *www.chambery-metropole.fr*
A leaflet on the Promenade Cyclable du Lac d'Annecy is available locally.
Grenoble has its own city cycle map available locally and downloadable from *www.grenoble-isere-tourisme.com*

The *départements* of Savoie and Haute Savoie contain a dense network of signed routes, though many routes have steep climbs and you'll need a route map of the area as the signing isn't always perfect.

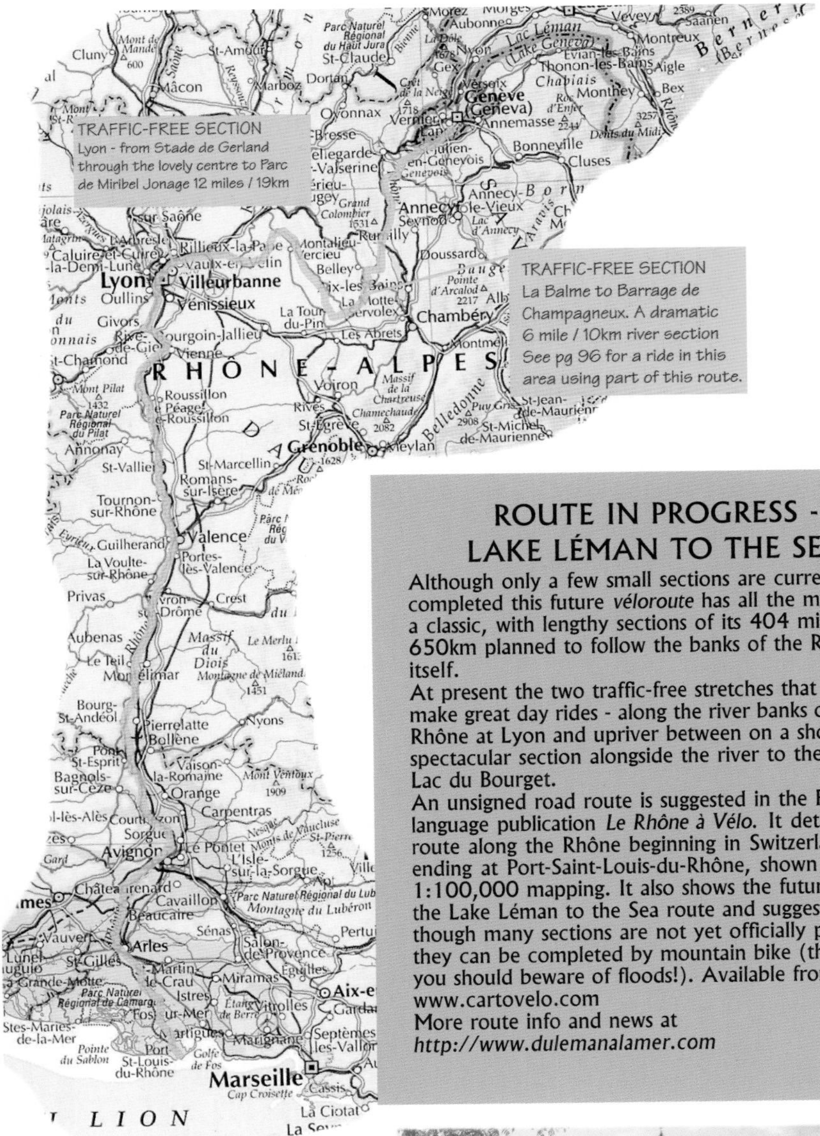

TRAFFIC-FREE SECTION
Lyon - from Stade de Gerland through the lovely centre to Parc de Miribel Jonage 12 miles / 19km

TRAFFIC-FREE SECTION
La Balme to Barrage de Champagneux. A dramatic 6 mile / 10km river section See pg 96 for a ride in this area using part of this route.

ROUTE IN PROGRESS - LAKE LÉMAN TO THE SEA

Although only a few small sections are currently completed this future *véloroute* has all the makings of a classic, with lengthy sections of its 404 miles / 650km planned to follow the banks of the Rhône itself.

At present the two traffic-free stretches that are open make great day rides - along the river banks of the Rhône at Lyon and upriver between on a short but spectacular section alongside the river to the west of Lac du Bourget.

An unsigned road route is suggested in the French language publication *Le Rhône à Vélo*. It details a route along the Rhône beginning in Switzerland and ending at Port-Saint-Louis-du-Rhône, shown on IGN 1:100,000 mapping. It also shows the future line of the Lake Léman to the Sea route and suggests that, though many sections are not yet officially permitted they can be completed by mountain bike (though you should beware of floods!). Available from www.cartovelo.com

More route info and news at *http://www.dulemanalamer.com*

The superb traffic-free ride through the heart of Lyon

AIX-LES-BAINS
An elegant spa resort, reflected in the town's architecture. Its reputation reached its highpoint in the mid-nineteenth century, when Queen Victoria visited several times.
The main square in town, Place Maurice-Mollard mixes elborate spa architecture with Roman remains such as the Arc de Campanus. South of here is the maze of streets that make up the old town.
The suggested cycle route takes you down the side of Lake Bourget - at the time of writing the cycle track along the south-eastern edge of the lake was being implemented / upgraded and should be a fine traffic-free ride by the time you ride it.
Fitter riders based in Aix for a few days will revel in the signed rides around the Massif du Bauges to the east of Aix, especially those around and across the beautiful Alpine plateau around Mont Revard.

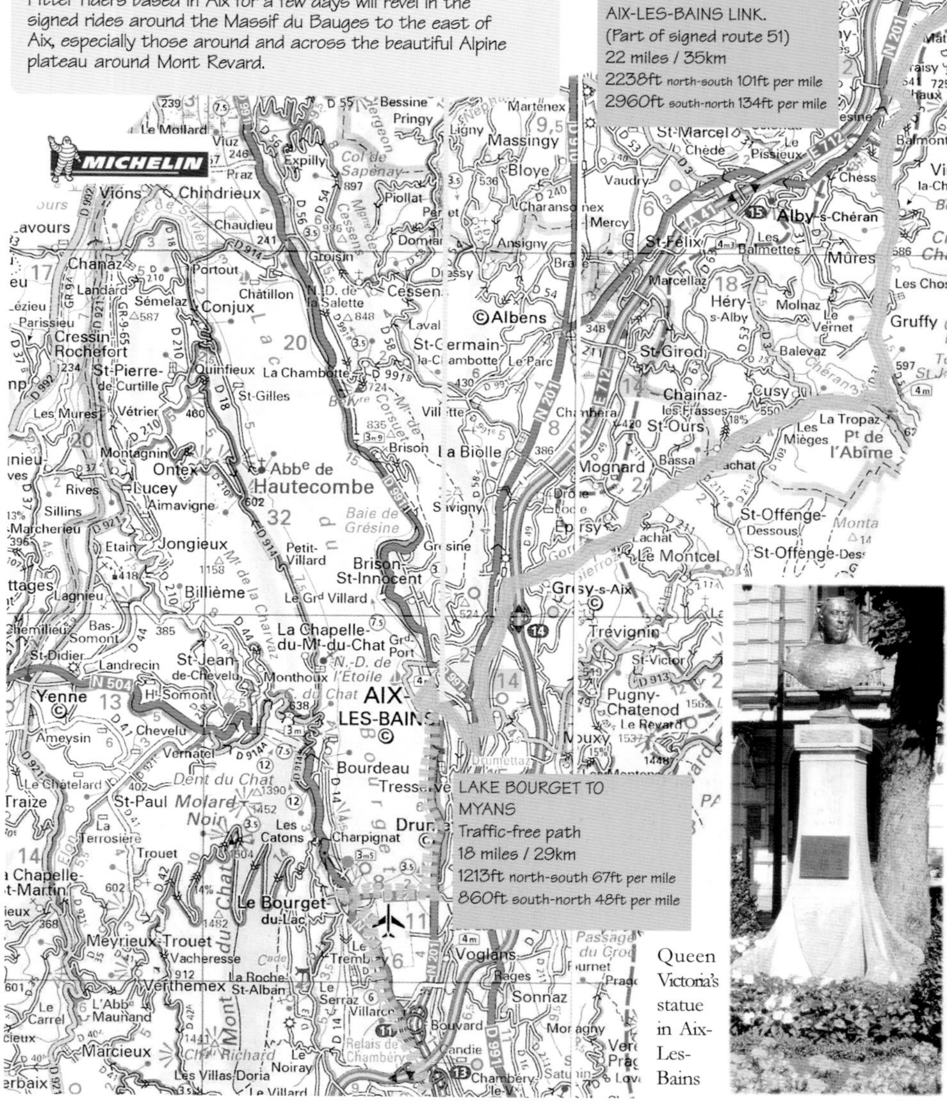

Queen Victoria's statue in Aix-Les-Bains

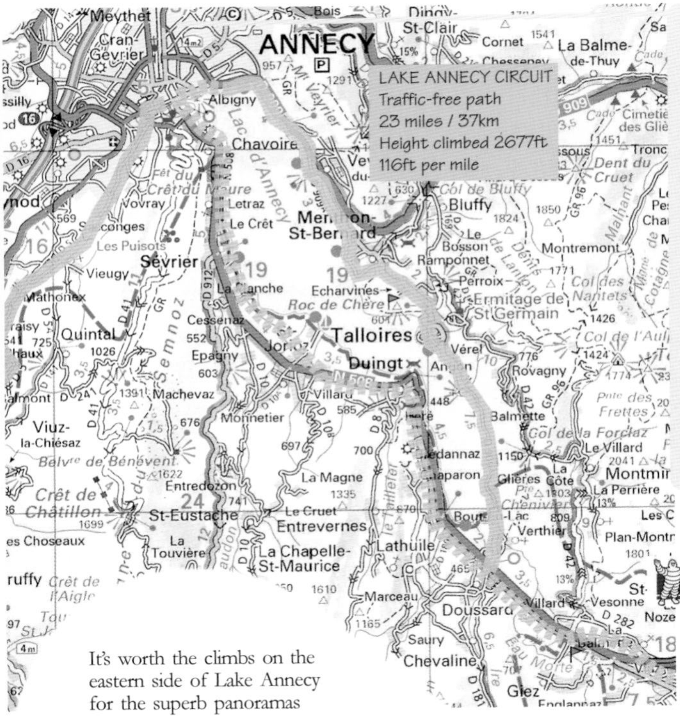

LAKE ANNECY CIRCUIT
Traffic-free path
23 miles / 37km
Height climbed 2677ft
116ft per mile

It's worth the climbs on the eastern side of Lake Annecy for the superb panoramas

ANNECY

Annecy's charms are considerable. The waterways running through the town are attractive as are the colonnaded streets in the centre. The setting is magnificent. From the grassed area at the water's edge, you can look down Lake Annecy, surrounded by alpine mountains, or take a boat trip from the canalside port. Various museums and ecclesiastical buildings are of interest, but the general atmosphere and setting are what captivate. It does get very, very busy at times though.

CHAMBÉRY

Very nice wide pedestrianised streets with lovely old pastel-coloured and shuttered buildings - a great place to relax with a drink and watch the world go by. Onetime capital of Savoy, Chambéry has the rather large castle of the Dukes of Savoy and although it's now an administrative building, guided tours are possible in the summer. The Boulevard du Théâtre, naturally enough, has an attractive theatre and at its opposite end is the nineteenth century Elephants Fountain, with the fronts of four elephants surrounding its base. If you're not headed there in any case, consider a trip to the Lac du Bourget about 10km north of Chambéry - it's France's largest and deepest natural lake and has the spa town of Aix-les-Bains near its shores (trains from Chambéry).

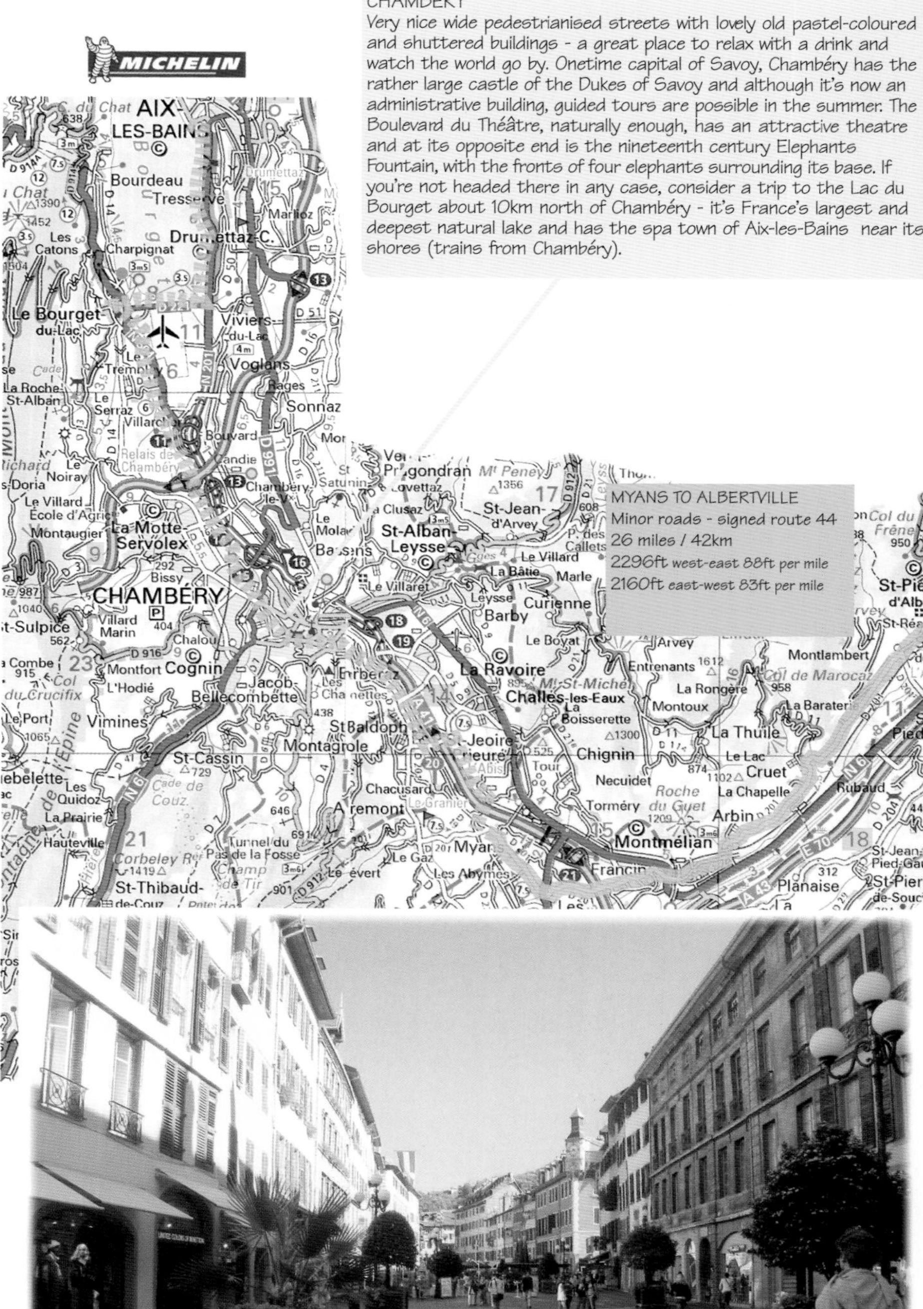

MYANS TO ALBERTVILLE
Minor roads - signed route 44
26 miles / 42km
2296ft west-east 88ft per mile
2160ft east-west 83ft per mile

Chambéry's elegant pedestrian area

ALBERTVILLE

Some great sporting facilities in and around Albertville are a legacy of the 1992 winter Olympics held there. The place de l'Europe was created for the games and looks from the more modern and developed Albertville over to the old town of Conflans across the river.

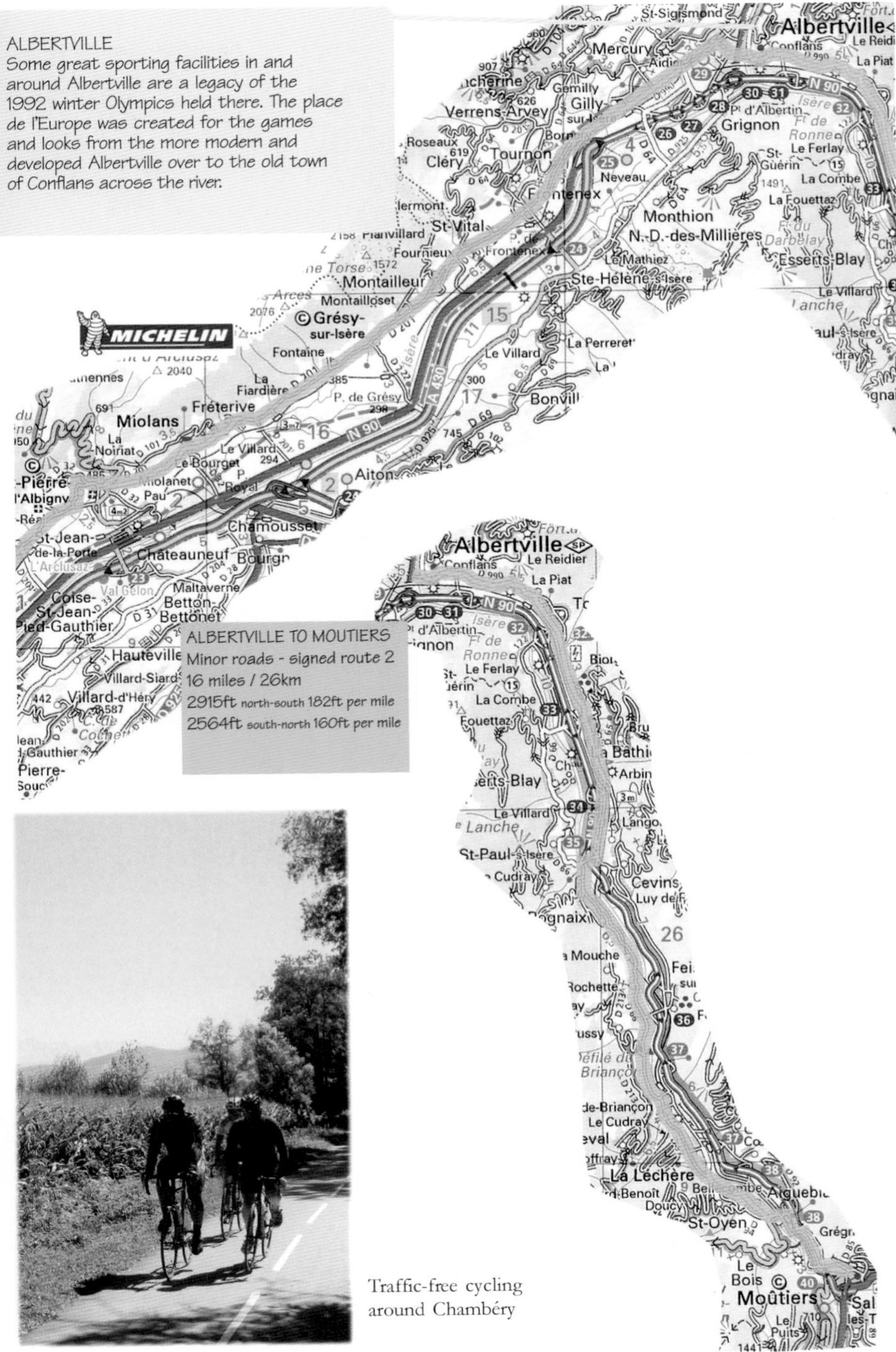

ALBERTVILLE TO MOUTIERS

Minor roads - signed route 2
16 miles / 26km
2915ft north-south 182ft per mile
2564ft south-north 160ft per mile

Traffic-free cycling around Chambéry

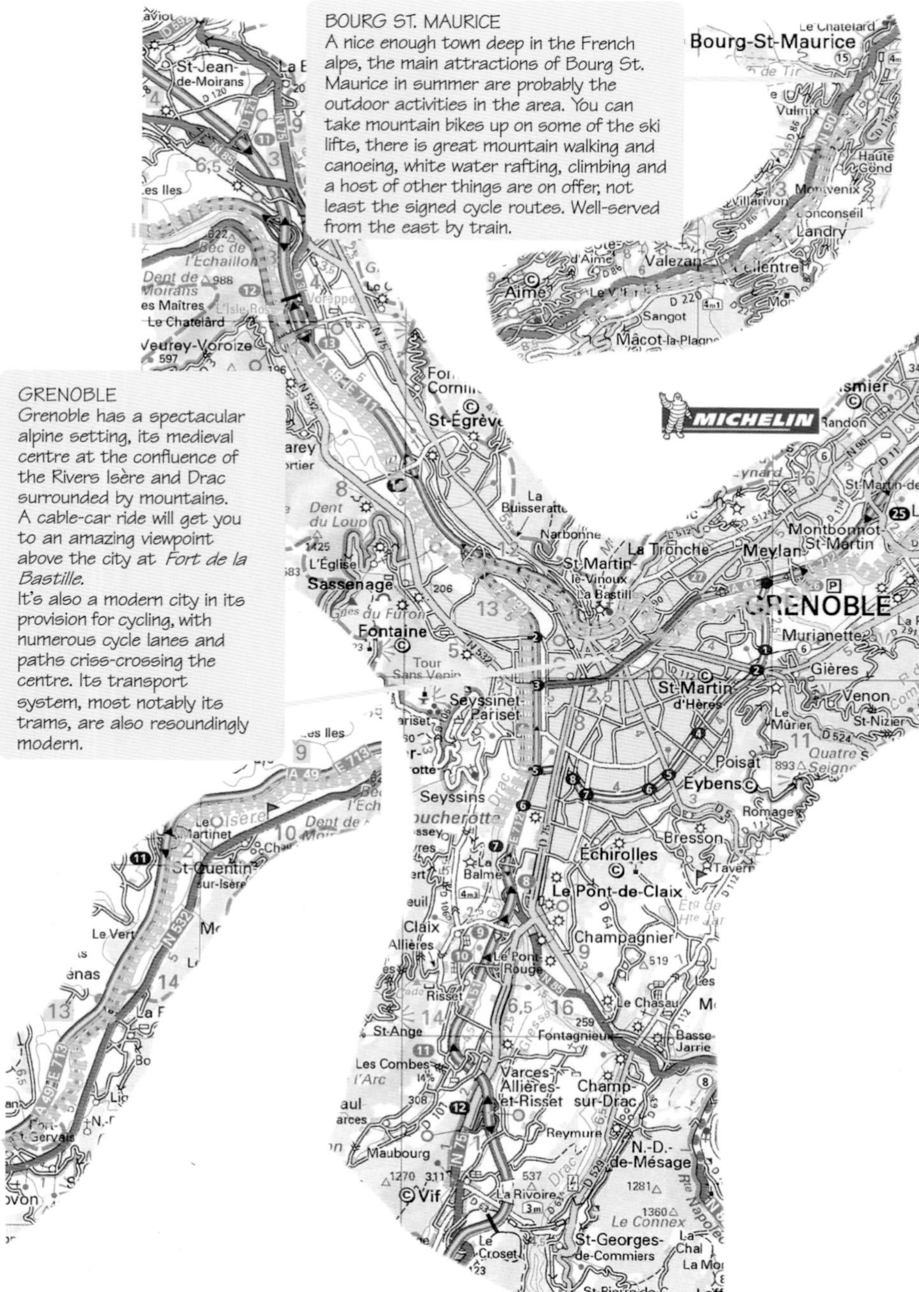

BOURG ST. MAURICE

A nice enough town deep in the French alps, the main attractions of Bourg St. Maurice in summer are probably the outdoor activities in the area. You can take mountain bikes up on some of the ski lifts, there is great mountain walking and canoeing, white water rafting, climbing and a host of other things are on offer, not least the signed cycle routes. Well-served from the east by train.

GRENOBLE

Grenoble has a spectacular alpine setting, its medieval centre at the confluence of the Rivers Isère and Drac surrounded by mountains. A cable-car ride will get you to an amazing viewpoint above the city at *Fort de la Bastille*.

It's also a modern city in its provision for cycling, with numerous cycle lanes and paths criss-crossing the centre. Its transport system, most notably its trams, are also resoundingly modern.

Route 51 - the Annecy to Aix-les-Bains route

Givry to Mâcon greenway near St. Gengoux-Le-National (see following chapter)

The Vineyard Way & The Chalon - Mâcon Greenway

Route Info

The Vineyard Way and the Chalon-sur-Saône - Mâcon Greenway
A lovely ride on a mix of minor roads and tracks and a greenway, this is a well-established route along the Côte d'Or and on to Mâcon. Towns and villages are picturesque and well-groomed and it seems, in the Côte d'Or at least, as though every place bears a legendary name in the world of wine, from the Hôtel Dieu in Beaune to the smallest village.

Grade EASY

Start / finish Beaune and Mâcon

Route length 72 miles / 115 km

Route advice
The Vineyard Way from Beaune to Santenay is a lovely ride on a mix of unfenced minor roads and tracks, sometimes tarmac, sometimes stone and gravel. The intention is to carry on extending the route at either end to connect Dijon and Digoin. The Vineyard Way is followed by a good towpath ride from Santenay along the Canal du Centre Greenway into Chalon-sur-Saône. The Chalon - Mâcon Greenway is a luxurious ride on an uninterrupted tarmacked traffic-free path from the Chalon to Charnay-lès- Mâcon. Various facilities along the way including drinking water. There's a tunnel south of Cluny over a mile long which is quite cold (overhead alternative route available). See the booklet downloadable at *www.bourgogne-du-sud.com* for lots of signed circular rides off the Chalon - Mâcon Greenway and the Canal du Centre path.

The Beaune to Santenay route can be extended to St.-Léger-sur-Dheune and a couple of loops off mean it doesn't need to be a there and back ride - this is part of the EuroVelo 6 route (see below).

Train access
Bicycle-carrying TGVs serve an area including Dijon, Beaune, Chalon-sur-Saône and Mâcon. Many local trains carry bikes.

Nearby routes
EuroVélo 6 passes through Chalon, goes north east along the Saône valley to Dole and then heads off towards Switzerland. See pgs 48-65
Ain by Bike. Pgs 87-97

Maps, guides and websites
www.bourgogne-du-sud.com for downloadable/orderable leaflet (bilingual) with map and info on the Chalon - Mâcon Greenway and the Canal du Centre
www.burgundy-tourism.com In English. Downloadable/orderable brochure covering cycling in Burgundy including the whole of this route.
www.ot-beaune.fr (English version available) for downloadable leaflet on the Beaune - Santenay Voie des Vignes and other useful information.
www.burgundy-by-bike.com Wonderful - compendious information for these routes and others covering route details, access, attractions along the way, food and drink, accommodation, cycle hire and repair, baggage transfer, guides and tourist offices. If it isn't here, you probably don't need it.

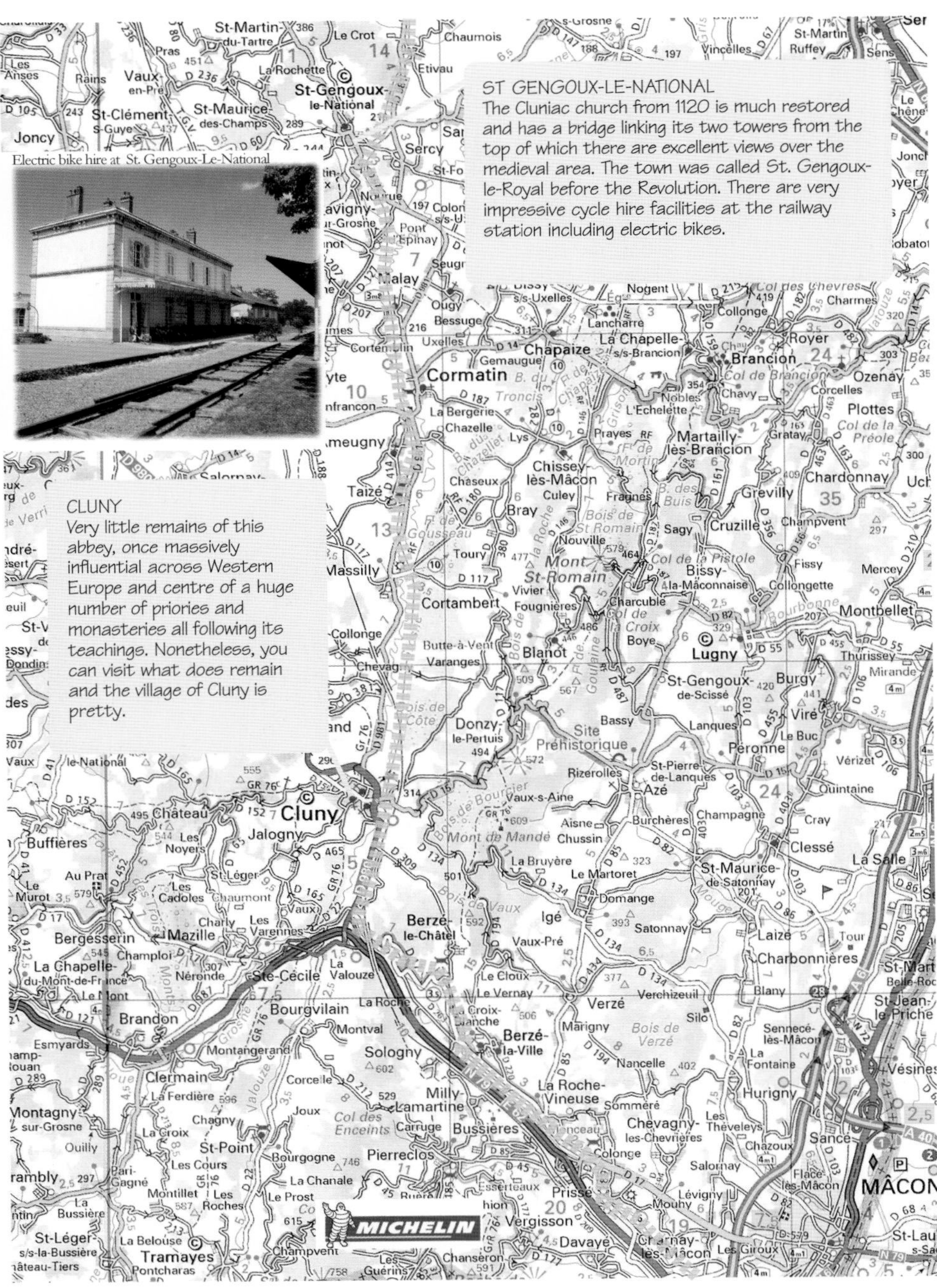

Electric bike hire at St. Gengoux-Le-National

ST GENGOUX-LE-NATIONAL

The Cluniac church from 1120 is much restored and has a bridge linking its two towers from the top of which there are excellent views over the medieval area. The town was called St. Gengoux-le-Royal before the Revolution. There are very impressive cycle hire facilities at the railway station including electric bikes.

CLUNY

Very little remains of this abbey, once massively influential across Western Europe and centre of a huge number of priories and monasteries all following its teachings. Nonetheless, you can visit what does remain and the village of Cluny is pretty.

CHAGNY
A handy stopover on the Canal du Centre with useful facilities by the canal. Interesting town architecture includes a 13th century castle tower, a 19th century Italian style theatre, an 18th century pharmacy and an old firewatch tower. Sunday and Thursday morning markets. Restaurants, cafes and fine local wine not in short supply.

SANTENAY
On the Canal du Centre, the village of Santenay has thermal waters, a casino, historic churches and a lovely castle set amidst vineyards. There's a restored nineteenth century windmill, open for visits, and panoramic views from nearby Mont Sène.

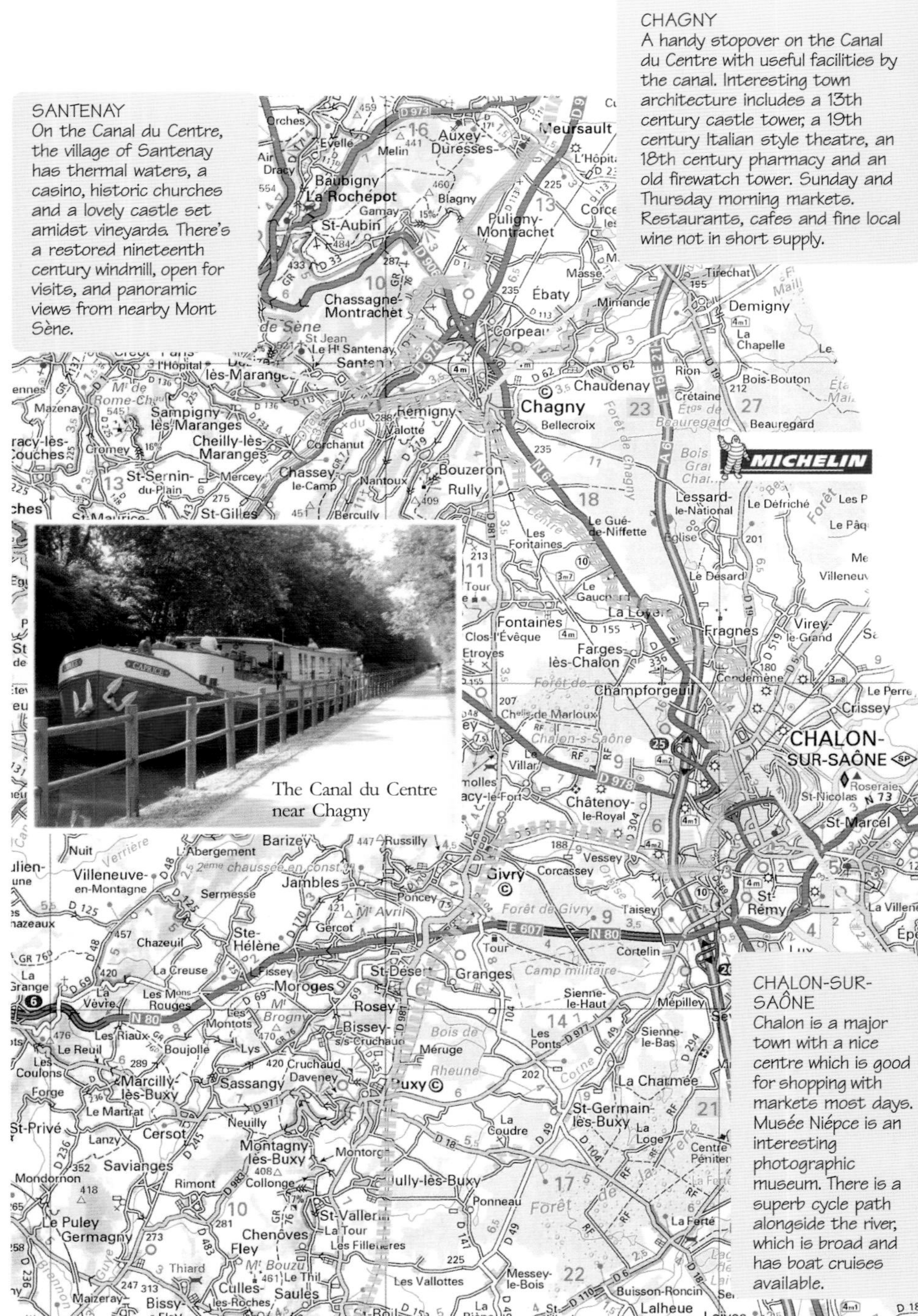

The Canal du Centre near Chagny

CHALON-SUR-SAÔNE
Chalon is a major town with a nice centre which is good for shopping with markets most days. Musée Niépce is an interesting photographic museum. There is a superb cycle path alongside the river, which is broad and has boat cruises available.

DIJON
Dijon - where the mustard comes from - is a lovely old city of ancient buildings with colourful roof tiles. It centres around the Ducal Palace and the place de la Libération and is an excellent place for shopping. Other attractions include museums and art galleries and some nice parks and gardens.

FIXIN
The colonnaded semi-circular village washhouse of 1827 is as grand a washhouse as you're likely to see. The lava-covered village oven is interesting and one of the two village churches is the oldest Romanesque building in the area. There's a museum dedicated to Napoleon Bonaparte in the Parc Noisot and it's one of the villages which can put wine into the highly respected Côte de Nuits Villages. It also has its own village appellation.

GEVREY-CHAMBERTIN
Pleasant village with a large, ancient and impressive castle. Combe Lavaux nature reserve nearby in a deep valley.

CHÂTEAU DU CLOS DE VOUGEOT
Set in the middle of its vineyards this Renaissance château producing one of the famous wines of the area offers visits to see the process and the huge and ancient wine presses they still have.

DIJON TO BEAUNE
Note: This is a suggested 'temporary' route and is unsigned but an extension of the Vineyard Way north of Beaune is planned.
From the Chenôve area of Dijon pick up the path signed 'Chemin des Grands Crus' then pick up the D122 to Vougeot. Here once again you can pick up the 'Chemin des Grands Crus' into Nuits-St-Georges where you pick up the N74 before turning left into Corgoloin. You then follow a minor road via Ladoix-Serrigny and Chorey into Beaune.
From here the Vineyard Way to Santenay is signed.

The Chemin des Grands Crus is used for part of the temporary suggested route between Dijon and Beaune

BEAUNE
Main town of the Côte d'Or wine region, Beaune is a busy but attractive old town. The Hôtel Dieu, a fifteenth century hospital well worth visiting is run by the Hospices de Beaune, famous for their charity wine auction every year.

Notre Dame Cathedral provides a superb backdrop to pavement cafes in Dijon

HEADING FOR THE HILLS? THINK ELECTRIC

A relatively new but rapidly developing way of cycling involves electric bikes. Only ten years ago they were generally very heavy and cumbersome machines, often with industrial-sized lead acid batteries. The best of today's models are barely distinguishable from 'normal' non-assisted cycles, sporting 'nano' motors in the hubs and lightweight lithium-ion batteries, often concealed in the frame or the rear pannier. Range per charge can be as much as 30 miles / 50km. They are broadly divided into two types; pedelecs give assistance whilst you pedal, usually matching the effort you put into the pedals with electric power, whilst e-bikes use a traditonal moped style throttle grip. Some bikes come with a switch that allows you to choose between the two modes. Most models, as they are limited to around 15mph / 24kph require no documentation to go on public roads and are treated just as non-motorised cycles.

As both Burgundy and the Jura (including much of the Ain *département)* are made up of rolling hills an electric bike would be the ideal way to tackle a trip in the area. If you're not ready to take the plunge and buy there are an increasing number of hire outlets where rates are reasonable and may often be discounted against the value of a final purchase, should you so choose. Outlets that I have tried and would personally recommend are:

Two Wheels Electric (Les 2 Roues Electriques) , By Lake Kir, Dijon 03 80 65 77 61 www.L2RE.com Manager Patrick Mortier speaks a little English and is very helpful. He can be contacted direct on 06 32 35 22 16.

H2 Rent, 39, avenue Félix Viallet, Grenoble (near the station) 04 76 17 21 15 www.h2rent.com In the Isere *département*, about 40 miles / 65 km south of the Ain.

Ain by Bike

Route Info

Ain by bike
The Ain stretches from the Saône to the Jura offering the cyclist a choice of rides through everything from pastureland and lakeland to valleys and mountains.

Grade EASY to DIFFICULT

Route length 12 miles / 19km to 73 miles / 116km

Route advice
These 27 circular rides and 5 circular family ones are on little country roads for the most part, some challenging, mainly in the east, and some leisurely, mainly in the west.

Train access A number of the rides can be got to by train. Rail access to the area is good generally with Bourg-en-Bresse being served by lines in from Mâcon, Lyon and Ambérieu and two lines in from the north. There's even the odd direct bicycle-carrying TGV from Paris.

Nearby routes
EuroVélo 6 (pp 48 - 65), Along the Jura (pp 66 - 67), Alps Easy Riding (pp 74 - 81) and The Wine Route and The Givry - Mâcon Greenway (pp 82 - 86). Also when it comes, the Lake Geneva to the sea route will be nearby (pg 75).

Maps, guides and websites
L'Ain à Vélo Set of 27 map leaflets giving info on each route including a map, a difficulty grading, distance and time estimate, basic directions, route profile and facilities (including cycle repair) along the way with recommendations for good places to break. 7 euros from Comité Départemental du Tourisme du l'Ain. 34, rue Général Delestraint, BP78, 01002 Bourg-en-Bresse Cedex or telephone 00 33 4 74 32 31 30 or see *www.ain-tourisme.com* (Contact for postage cost before ordering.)

VILLARS-LES-DOMBES

A town at the heart of a huge area of lakes, one of the premier fishing areas of France and rich in birdlife. Nearby, at the Parc des Oiseaux, you can see a staggering variety of species from all over the world, many of them endangered. Other attractions in the area include a farm shop reflecting the locality - carp sausages, smoked carp, carp and other fish in many forms along with cheeses, poultry and all manner of good things.

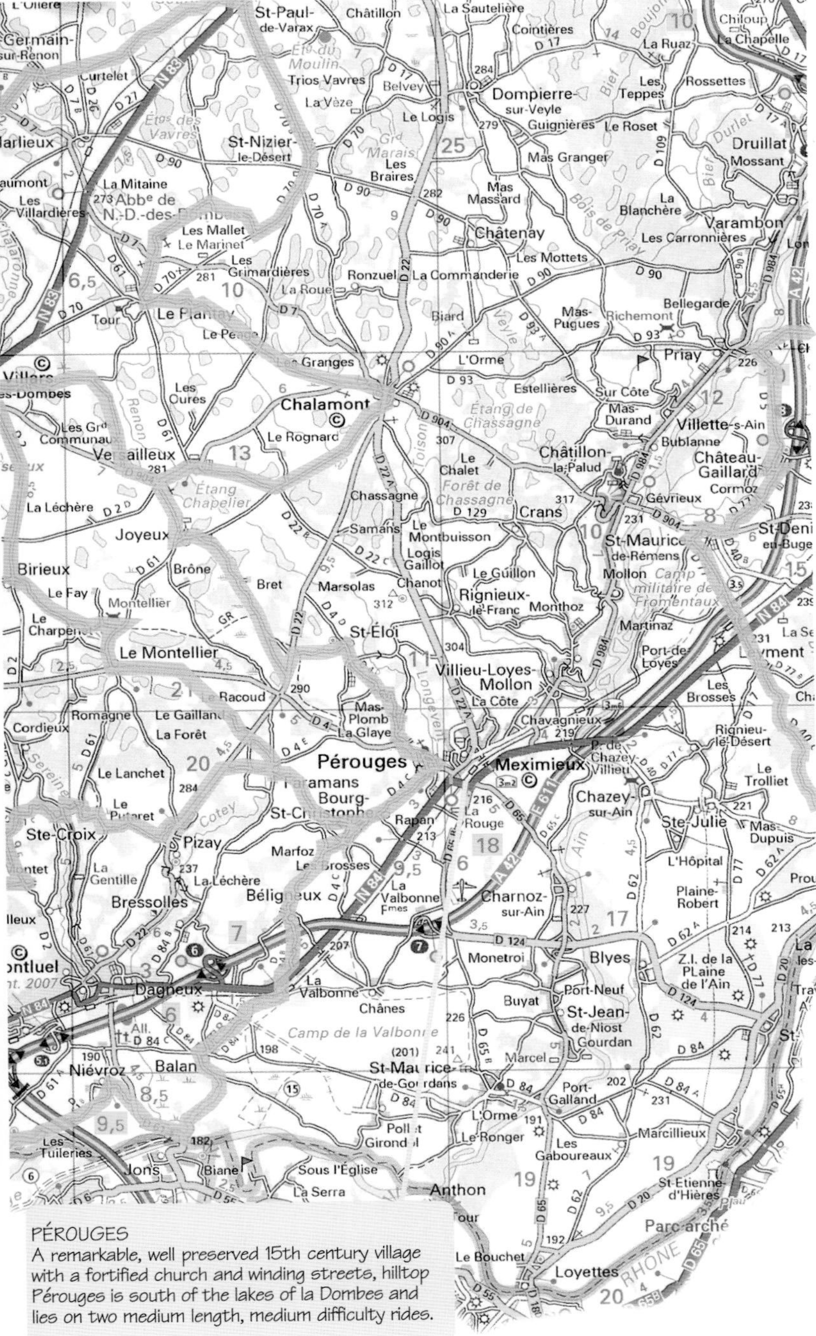

PÉROUGES

A remarkable, well preserved 15th century village with a fortified church and winding streets, hilltop Pérouges is south of the lakes of la Dombes and lies on two medium length, medium difficulty rides.

THE JURA - A GEOLOGICAL WONDER

The eastern part of the Ain *département* makes up part of the geographical area known as the Jura (see also *Along the Jura* pgs 66-67). Whilst there's plenty of steep gradients here (especially in the east) the Jura is a relatively gentle approach for cycle tourists heading north from the Ain to Switzerland.

Its unusual geology - fold after fold of limestone rock - means cycling can be either tortuous or pretty easy, depending whether you go with the 'grain' of the land (valleys usually running south-west to north-east) or across it. The age of these particular rocks has given us the wider term Jurassic, for the period in which they were formed.

It's a little frequented area, but truly lovely, full of huge forests, alpine meadows and small scale suprises such as the very rich local yellow wine, *vin jaune*. Little-known and all the better for it, the Jura is beautiful, wild cycling country.

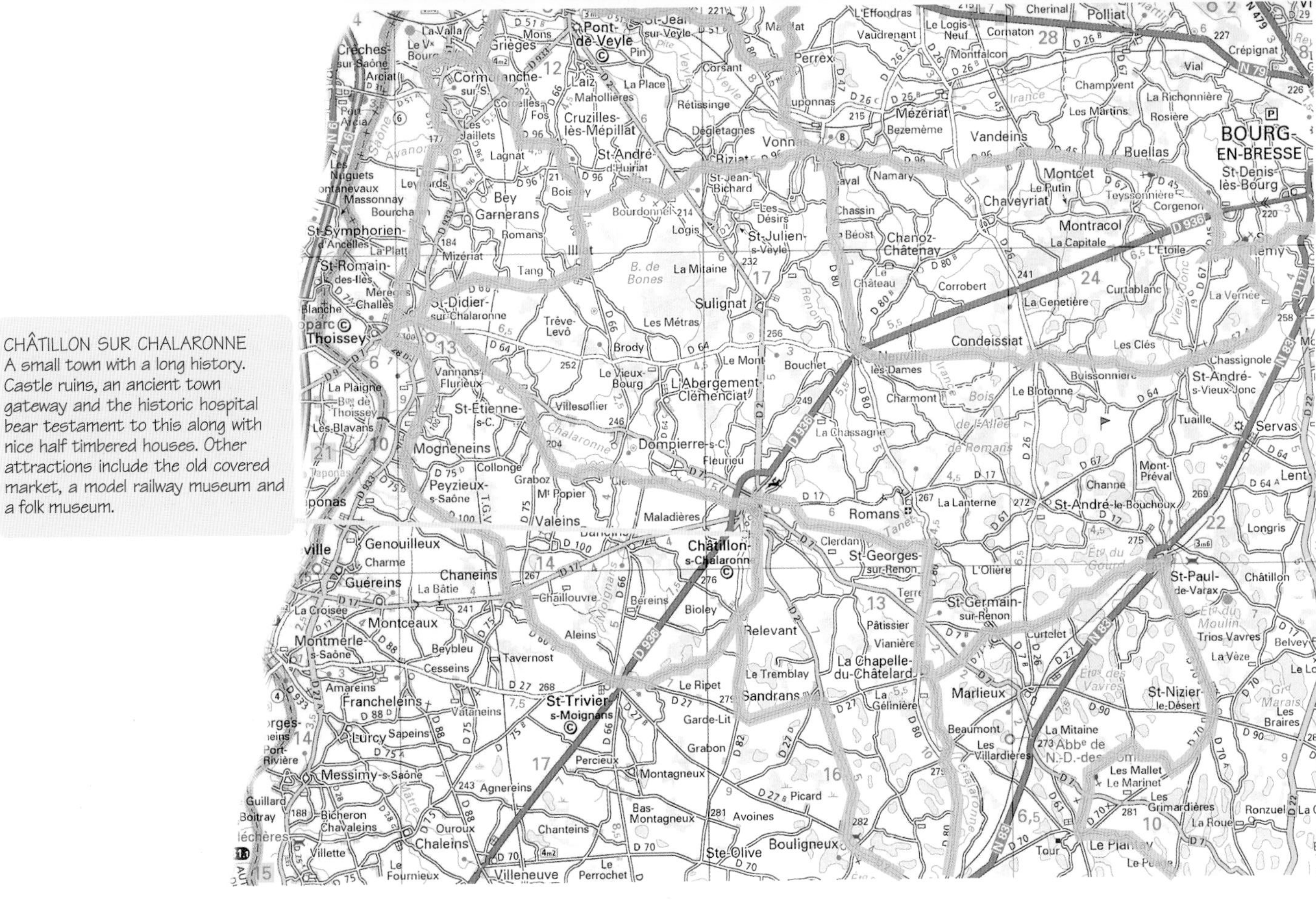

CHÂTILLON SUR CHALARONNE
A small town with a long history. Castle ruins, an ancient town gateway and the historic hospital bear testament to this along with nice half timbered houses. Other attractions include the old covered market, a model railway museum and a folk museum.

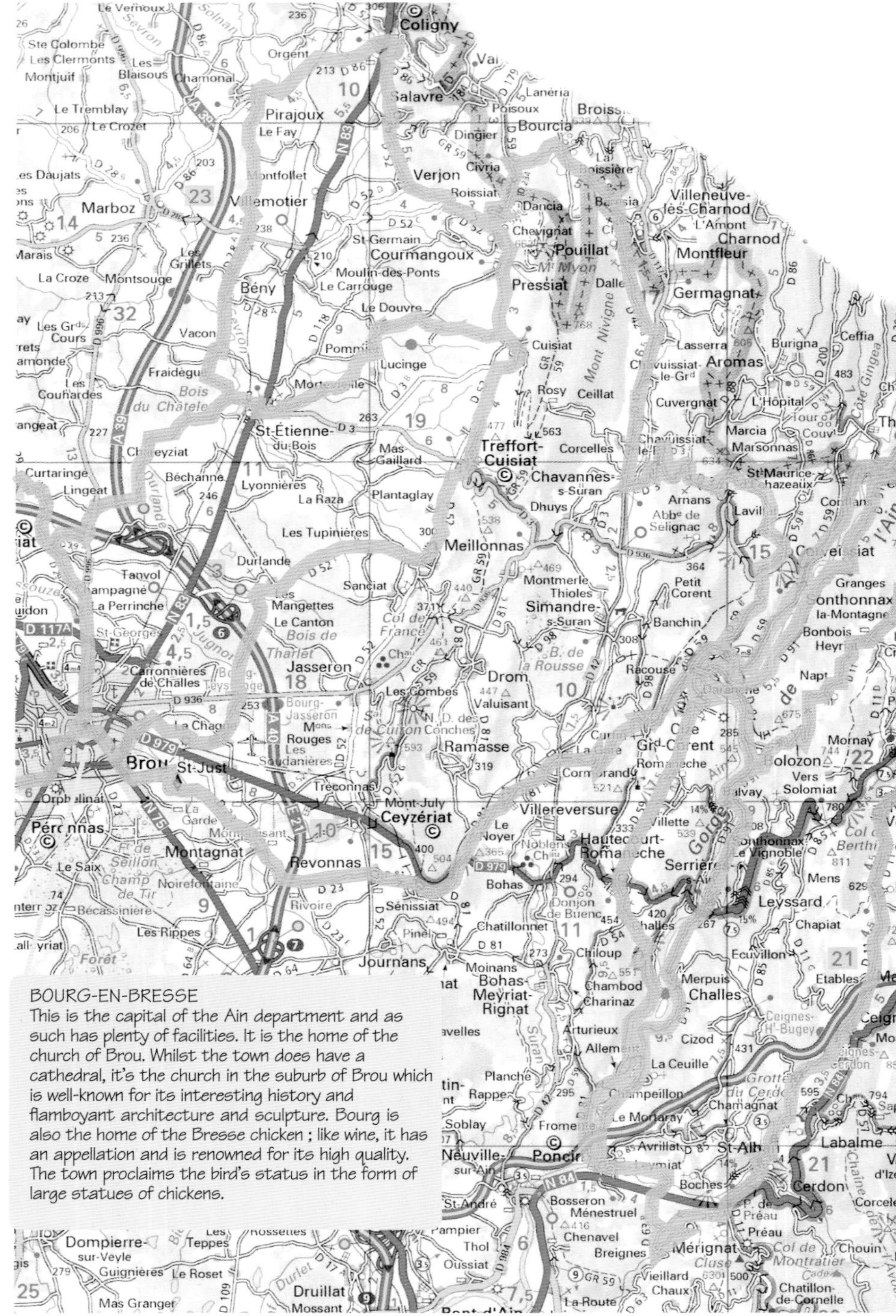

BOURG-EN-BRESSE

This is the capital of the Ain department and as such has plenty of facilities. It is the home of the church of Brou. Whilst the town does have a cathedral, it's the church in the suburb of Brou which is well-known for its interesting history and flamboyant architecture and sculpture. Bourg is also the home of the Bresse chicken ; like wine, it has an appellation and is renowned for its high quality. The town proclaims the bird's status in the form of large statues of chickens.

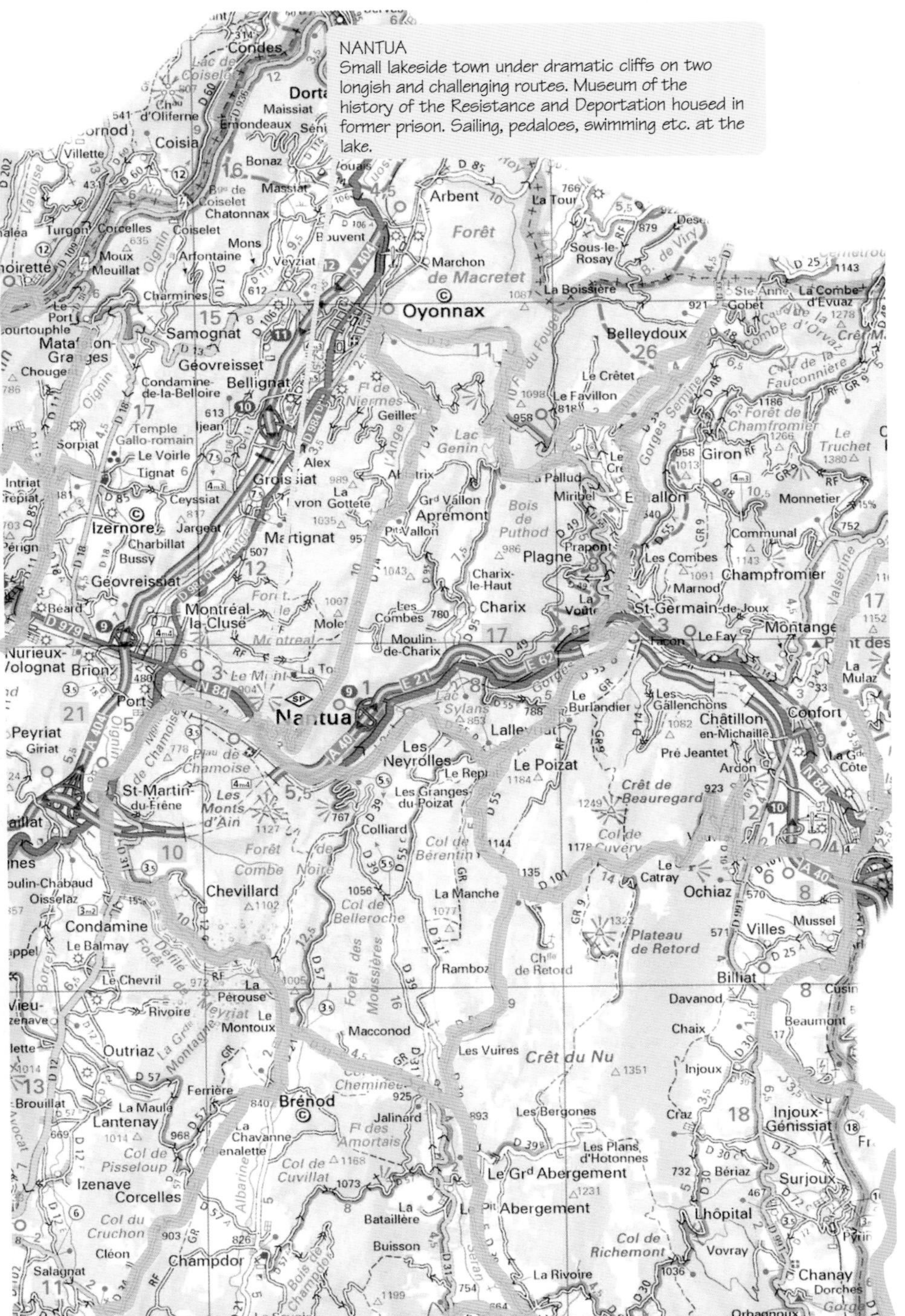

NANTUA

Small lakeside town under dramatic cliffs on two longish and challenging routes. Museum of the history of the Resistance and Deportation housed in former prison. Sailing, pedaloes, swimming etc. at the lake.

Neuville-sur-Ain
Poncin
Cerdon
Vieu-d'Izenave
Rivoire
Le Montoux
Maccon
Turgon
St-André
Bosseron
Ménestruel
Chenavel
Breignes
Mérignat
Préau
Corcelette
Outriaz
Pampier
Thol
Oussiat
Col de Montratier
Chouin
Brouillat
La Maule
Ferrière
Brénod
Vieillard
Chaux
Chatillon-de-Cornelle
Lantenay
La Chavanne
Chenalette
La Route
Jujurieux
Pont-d'Ain
Corlier
Col de Pisseloup
Izenave
Corcelles
Col de Cuvillat
Poncieux
La Courbattière
Le Blanchon
Hauterive
St-Jean-le-Vieux
Cossieux
Boyeux-St-Jérôme
Col du Cruchon
Varey
Aérium
Riez
Cléon
Champdor
Oiselon
St-Jérôme
Col du Cendrier
Salagnat
Ambronay
L'Abergement-de-Varey
Montgriffon
Aranc
Genoud
Merland
Salaport
St-Gras
Rougemont
La Savoie
Col de la Berche
Hauteville-Lompnes
Coutelieu
Douvres
Nivollet-Montgriffon
Résinand
Mt Luisandre
Brédevent
Granges-de-Luisandre
Lupieu
La Bertinière
Marbre
Nantuy
Chute
Les Allymes
Lacoux
Ambérieu-en-Bugey
Morgelaz
Gratoux
Oncieu
Vorages
Evosges
Grd Charabotte
Cormaranche-en-Bugey
Chaley
Longecombe
Vareilles
Angrières
St-Rambert-en-Bugey
Chau St-Germain
L'Albarine
Argis
Le Chaney
Dergit Ste-Anne
Vaux-St-Sulpice
Forêt de Cormaranche
Bettant
Le Chauchay
Javornoz
Serrières
Averliez
Malix
Cérarge
Ambutrix
Blanaz
Dergit-Michaud
Col de la Lebe
Vaux-en-Bugey
Tour
Vaux-Fevroux
Montferrand
Mont-de-l'Ange
Torcieu
Plomb
Tenay
Lavant
Forêt de Rouge
Cleyzieu
Indrieux
St-Sulpice-le-Vieux
Les Catagnolles
Ste-Blaizine
Forêt de Gervais
Lagnieu
Dorvan
Arandas
Hostias
Abbé
Le Vachat
Villeneuve
Le Genevray
Thézillieu
Conand
Posafol
St-Sorlin-en-Bugey
Souclin
Fay
Chairvieux
Petite
La Bourbellière
Vertrieu
Chariot
Chartreuse de Portes
Ponthieu
Col de Ballon
Brénaz
Serverin
Soudon
Les Hôpitaux
Grd Tare
Prémillieu
Salette
Sault-Brénaz
Ft de Serverin
Bouis
Calvaire de Portes
L. des Hôpitaux
Armix
Suptilieu
Villebois
Fays
La Burbanche
Egieu
Nivollet
Porcieu-Amblagnieu
Bois de Cuny
Ordonnaz
Cheignieu-la-Balme
Chamboud
Bénonces
Rossillon
Pernaz
Bois de la Morgne
Onglas
Prévezieu
Montagne de la Raie
Montalieu-Vercieu
B. de Souhait
Seillonnaz
Contrevoz
Serrières-de-Briord
Les Granges
La Serraz
Lompnas
Ste-Anne
Montbreyieu
Bouvesse-Quirieu
Montagnieu
Chosaz
Bois du Molard Dedon
Innimond
Chau de Beauretour
Briord
Crept
Marchamp
Cerin
Vercraz
Meyrieu
Brivaz
St Germain les-Paroisses
Apprengin
Buison
Tour St André
Flévieu
Millieu
Lac d'Ambléon
Dornieu
Mgne de Tentanet
Lhuis
Ambléon
Colomieu
Malville
Pusignieu
Mérieu
RHONE
St-Martin
Ansolin
Le Trieu
Grapéou
Le Poulet
Rix

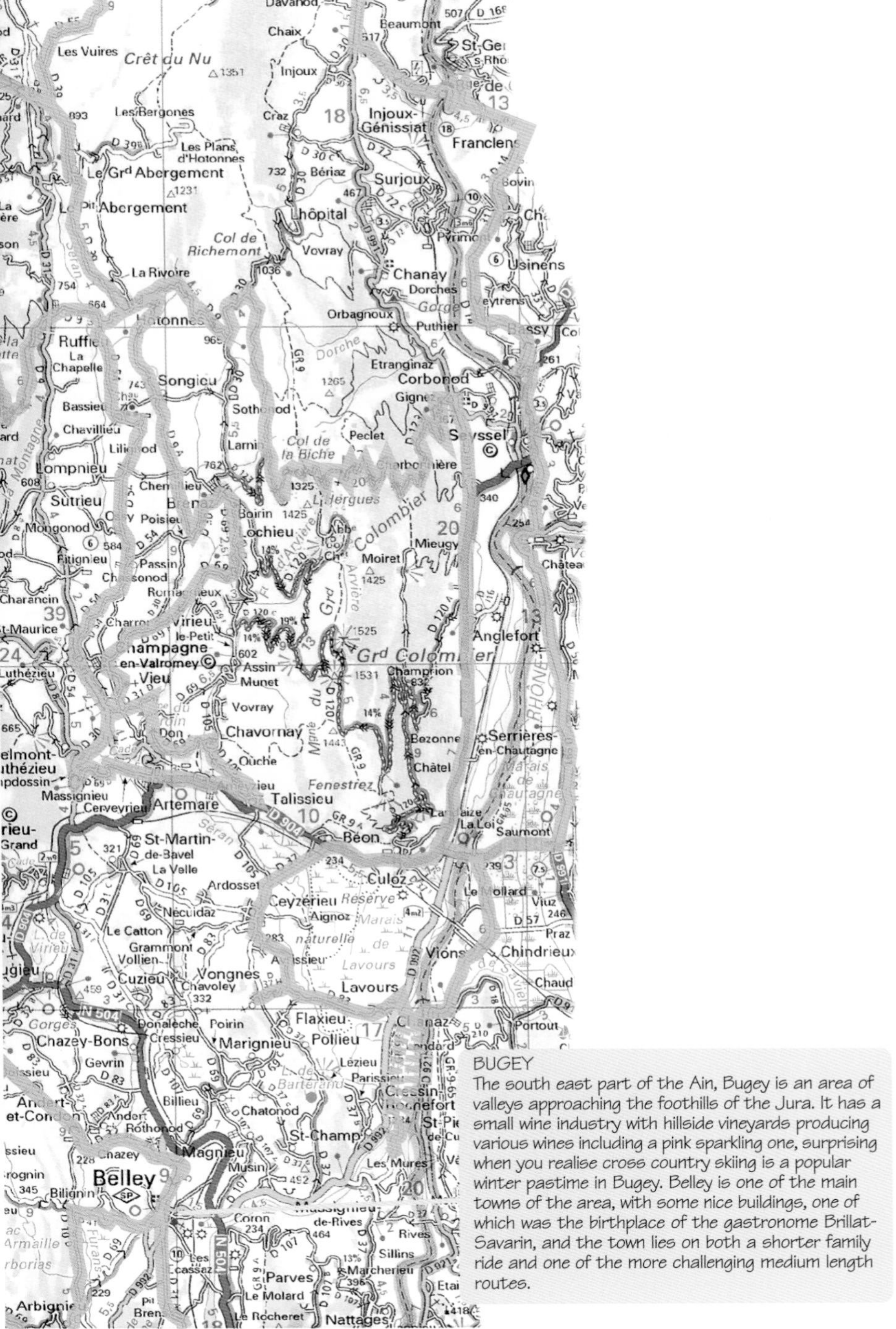

BUGEY

The south east part of the Ain, Bugey is an area of valleys approaching the foothills of the Jura. It has a small wine industry with hillside vineyards producing various wines including a pink sparkling one, surprising when you realise cross country skiing is a popular winter pastime in Bugey. Belley is one of the main towns of the area, with some nice buildings, one of which was the birthplace of the gastronome Brillat-Savarin, and the town lies on both a shorter family ride and one of the more challenging medium length routes.

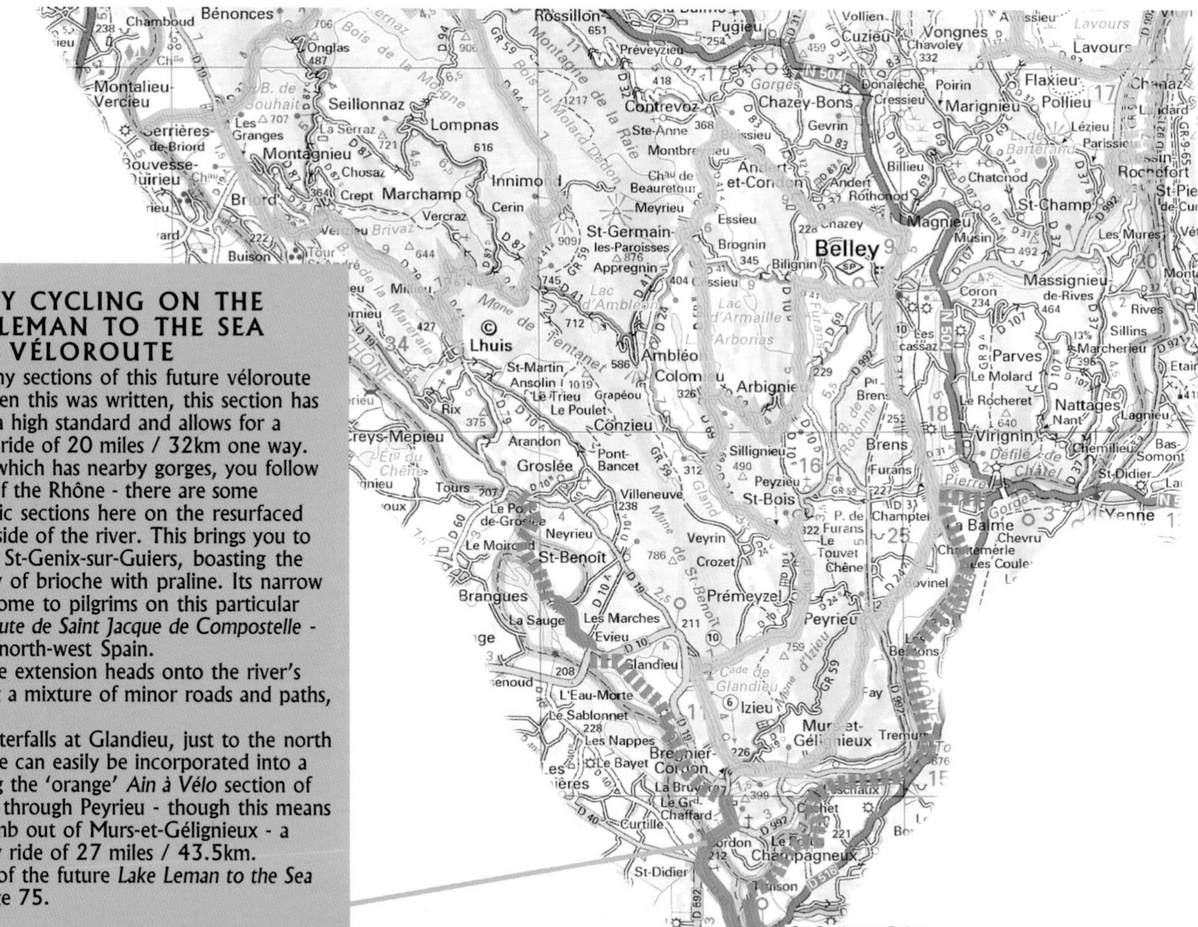

FAMILY CYCLING ON THE LAKE LEMAN TO THE SEA VÉLOROUTE

Although only tiny sections of this future véloroute were in place when this was written, this section has been finished to a high standard and allows for a lovely Rhôneside ride of 20 miles / 32km one way. From La Balme, which has nearby gorges, you follow the eastern side of the Rhône - there are some absolutely fantastic sections here on the resurfaced dike tops by the side of the river. This brings you to ancient, fortified St-Genix-sur-Guiers, boasting the culinary speciality of brioche with praline. Its narrow streets are also home to pilgrims on this particular branch of the *Route de Saint Jacque de Compostelle* - finally ending in north-west Spain.

A suggested route extension heads onto the river's north bank, using a mixture of minor roads and paths, to Groslée.

However, the waterfalls at Glandieu, just to the north of the Rhône here can easily be incorporated into a circular ride using the 'orange' *Ain à Vélo* section of route that passes through Peyrieu - though this means a steep initial climb out of Murs-et-Gélignieux - a medium difficulty ride of 27 miles / 43.5km.

For an overview of the future *Lake Leman to the Sea* véloroute see page 75.

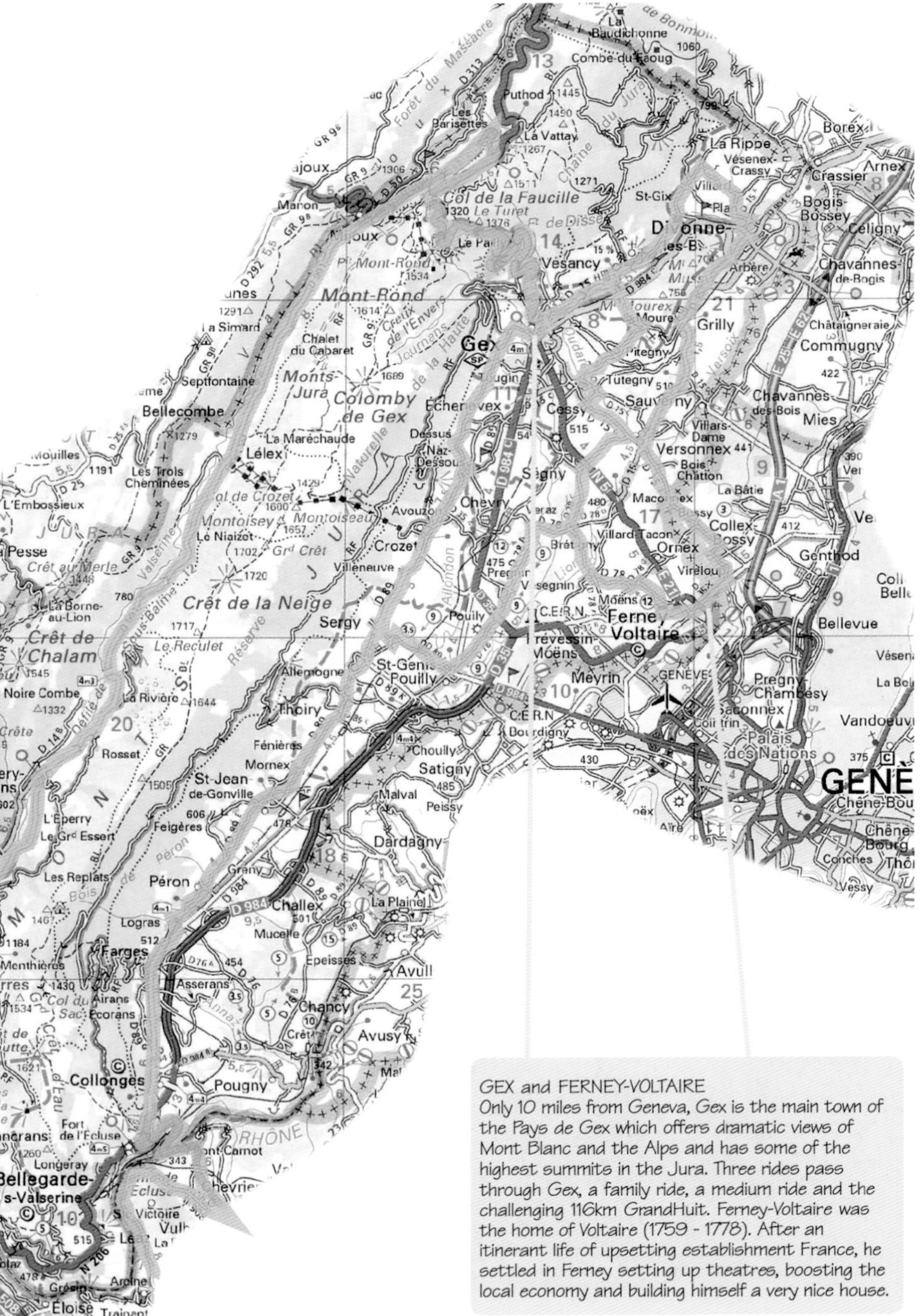

GEX and FERNEY-VOLTAIRE

Only 10 miles from Geneva, Gex is the main town of the Pays de Gex which offers dramatic views of Mont Blanc and the Alps and has some of the highest summits in the Jura. Three rides pass through Gex, a family ride, a medium ride and the challenging 116km GrandHuit. Ferney-Voltaire was the home of Voltaire (1759 - 1778). After an itinerant life of upsetting establishment France, he settled in Ferney setting up theatres, boosting the local economy and building himself a very nice house.

Around Blois

Route Info

Around Blois
Network of eleven signed rides around some of the best-known Loire château country taking in smaller châteaux as well as big name ones. Blois is a great base in a lovely riverside setting with its own magnificent château.

Grade EASY

Length 5.6 miles / 9 kilometres to 27 miles / 44 kilometres

Route advice
Country roads, tracks and cyclepaths on a variety of surfaces with little challenging in the way of gradients. From elegant château parkland to rolling vineyards to memorable riverscapes and forest rides, it's great cycling country in a UNESCO World Heritage site. Popular area for organised cycling holidays - an internet search will produce a good number of attractive-looking packages.

Train access Frequent bicycle-carrying Corail trains from Paris to Blois.

Nearby routes
EuroVelo 6 passes along the Loire here. See pg 56.
The Sologne - pgs 101-103

Maps, guides and websites
www.chateauxavelo.com (English version available) Includes individual route maps, attractions, accommodation and bike hire. It's probably the individual route maps which are the most useful thing - paper copies can be ordered through the website.

Château de Chambord - an easy ride from Blois randonnéecyclotouristiqueph.loirevalleytravel (2)

BLOIS
Beautifully set above the Loire, Blois is a good base for visiting the many châteaux nearby and has its own royal château in the town, famous for its magnificent staircase. Son et Lumière throughout the summer. The Musée de l'Objet is a gallery of contemporary and modern art containing some work by very well-known people.

CHAUMONT
The Château of Chaumont-sur-Loire is a fifteenth century fortified château. It has been owned by various people including Catherine de Medici but is now a museum owned by the state and open to the public. There are collections of furniture, tapestries and carriages and the nearby gardens, some with very up-to-date design and planting, are open spring to autumn. It's a little off the designated route but as one of the major Loire châteaux it's worth the detour.

Easy cycling at Blois - randonnéecyclotouristiqueph.loirevalleytravel (8)

CHÂTEAU DE FOURGÈRES-SUR-BIÈVRE
Small, ancient and fortified, but with an aviary and gardens where you can sit by the little River Bièvre as it runs through the castle grounds.

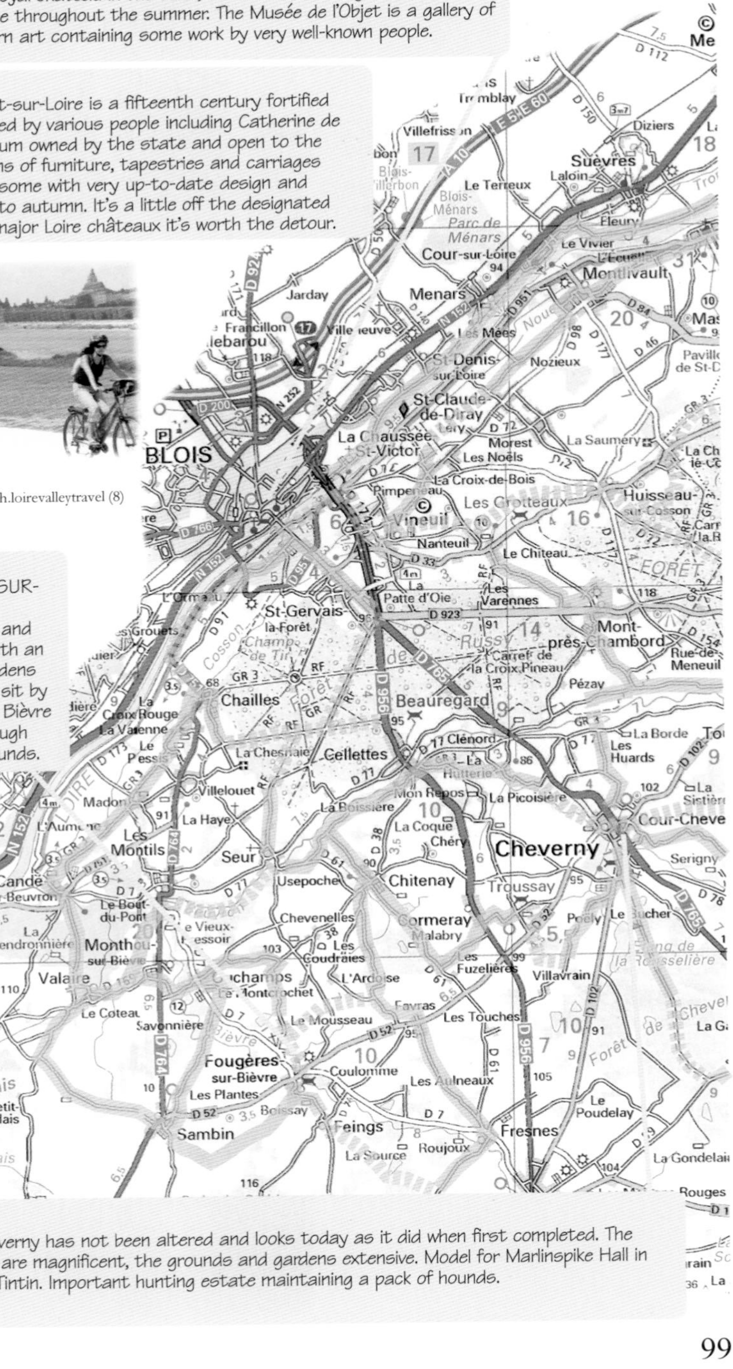

MICHELIN

CHEVERNY
Built in the 1600s, Cheverny has not been altered and looks today as it did when first completed. The interior and furnishings are magnificent, the grounds and gardens extensive. Model for Marlinspike Hall in Hergé's Adventures of Tintin. Important hunting estate maintaining a pack of hounds.

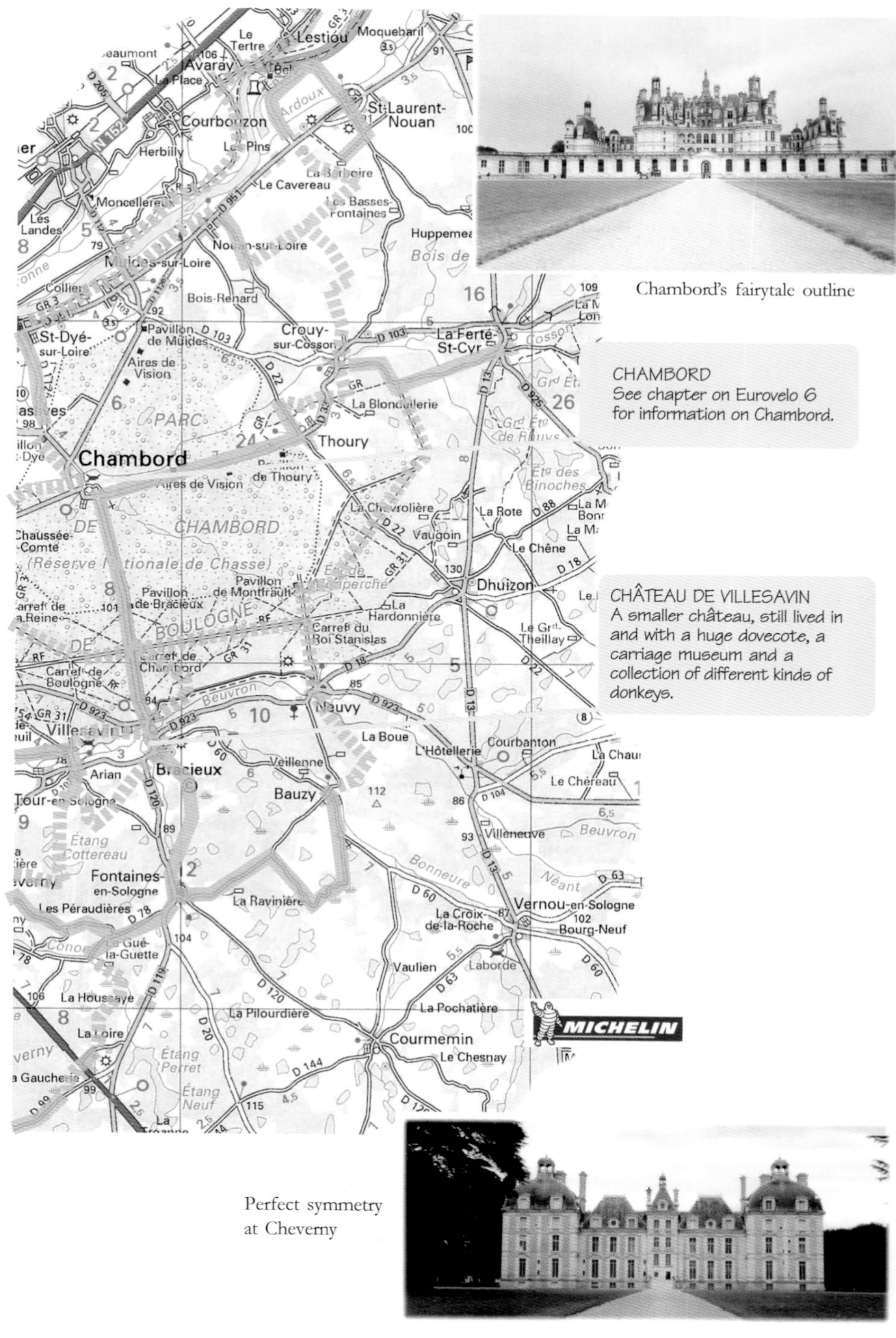

Chambord's fairytale outline

CHAMBORD
See chapter on Eurovelo 6 for information on Chambord.

CHÂTEAU DE VILLESAVIN
A smaller château, still lived in and with a huge dovecote, a carriage museum and a collection of different kinds of donkeys.

Perfect symmetry at Cheverny

The Sologne

Route Info

The Sologne
A traditional area of wooded marsh and wetland makes for an unusual landscape with a wide variety of wildlife. Largely flat, it's ideal summer cycling country when nature is at its most splendid here.

GRADE EASY

Start / finish
The four circular rides to the south of Orléans start at Cléry-St-Andre (two), Meung-sur-Loire and Sandillon.
To the south-east of these, the Canal de la Sauldre runs between Blancafort and Lamotte-Beuvron.

Route length The circular routes range from 8 to 26 miles (13 to 42 km)
The Canal de la Sauldre is around 28 miles / 45km long

Route advice The four signed routes south of Orléans are all on road and directionally signed.

The towpath of the Canal de la Sauldre is a mixture of wider, purpose-built crushed stone and single-track earth, the latter meaning an all-terrain bike is preferable. It's signed as a GR route (the GR de Sologne).

Train access There is a train line with numerous stops just to the north of The Sologne, running along the Loire Valley.

Nearby routes Long-distance véloroute Loire By Bike (part of the EuroVelo 6 route) lies just to the north of the Sologne (pgs 48-65)
Blois - pgs 98-100

Maps, guides and websites
À Vélo dans le Loiret - a handy booklet on the eight signed cycle routes in the Loiret *département.* Includes the four signed circular routes south of the Loire, as well as four more to the north in the Orléans forest.

Orléans is a great base for exploring the nearby Sologne

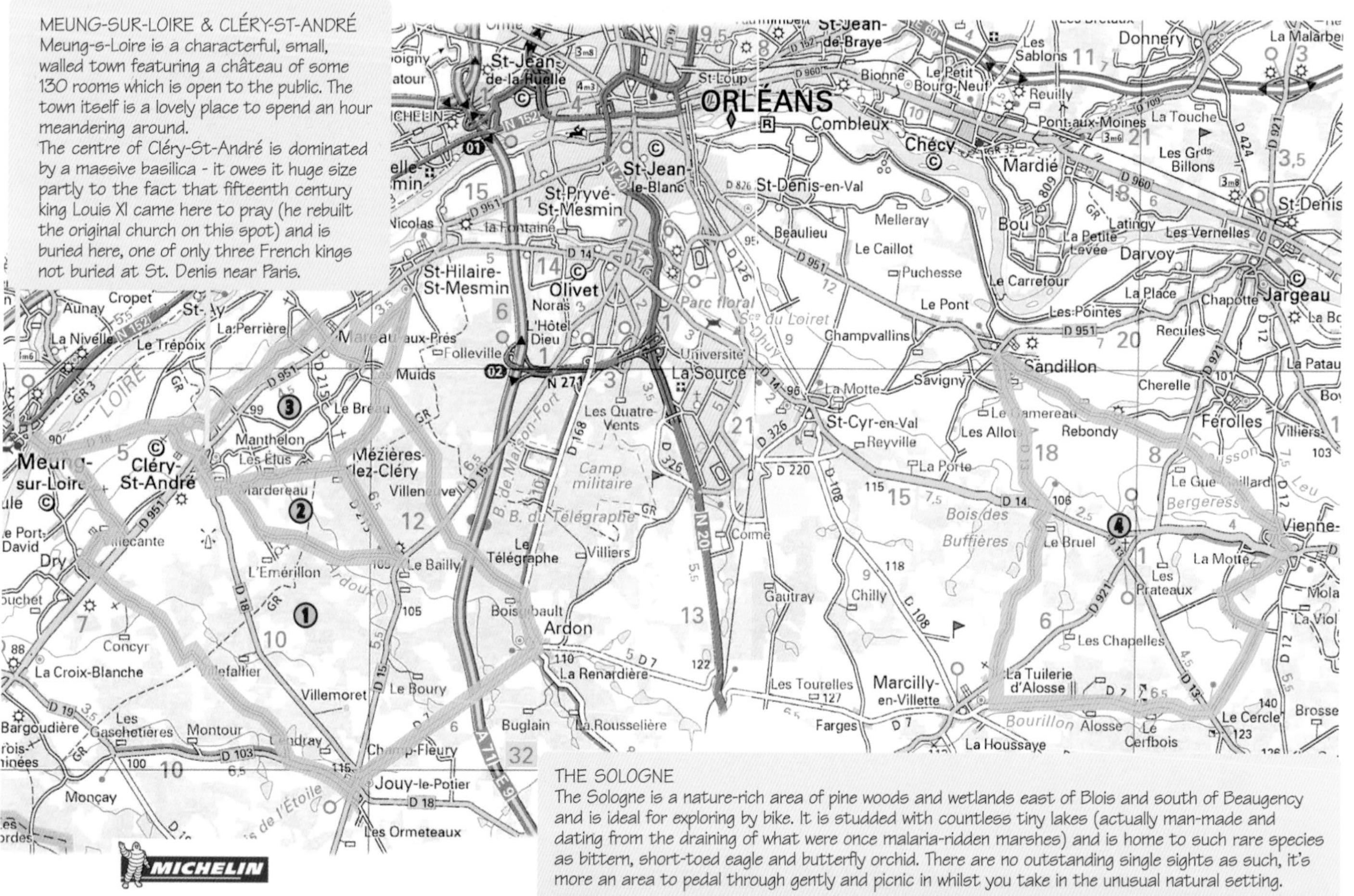

MEUNG-SUR-LOIRE & CLÉRY-ST-ANDRÉ

Meung-s-Loire is a characterful, small, walled town featuring a château of some 130 rooms which is open to the public. The town itself is a lovely place to spend an hour meandering around.

The centre of Cléry-St-André is dominated by a massive basilica - it owes it huge size partly to the fact that fifteenth century king Louis XI came here to pray (he rebuilt the original church on this spot) and is buried here, one of only three French kings not buried at St. Denis near Paris.

THE SOLOGNE

The Sologne is a nature-rich area of pine woods and wetlands east of Blois and south of Beaugency and is ideal for exploring by bike. It is studded with countless tiny lakes (actually man-made and dating from the draining of what were once malaria-ridden marshes) and is home to such rare species as bittern, short-toed eagle and butterfly orchid. There are no outstanding single sights as such, it's more an area to pedal through gently and picnic in whilst you take in the unusual natural setting.

CANAL DE LA SAULDRE

A rustic canal, known for the large number of locks and the huge manual labour required to build it, that no longer carries boat traffic - only bikes, walkers and fishermen frequent it now. Due to the historic misfortunes of the traditionally unproductive Sologne area, the canal never really had a chance to prove its profitability and was finally 'declassified' as a navigable waterway in 1926, barely more than half a century after it opened. The original idea was to improve the area's poor soil by shipping calcium-based material along the canal, but its role was quickly superseded by the arrival of the railways in the area.

Today it is a lovely backwater, leading you gently through the green world of the Sologne and a series of villages, many with their own quirky architecture. At the canal's western end Lamotte-Beuvron houses the *Hôtel Tatin*, home of the original sumptuous apple desert *Tarte Tatin*, still served there all day long.

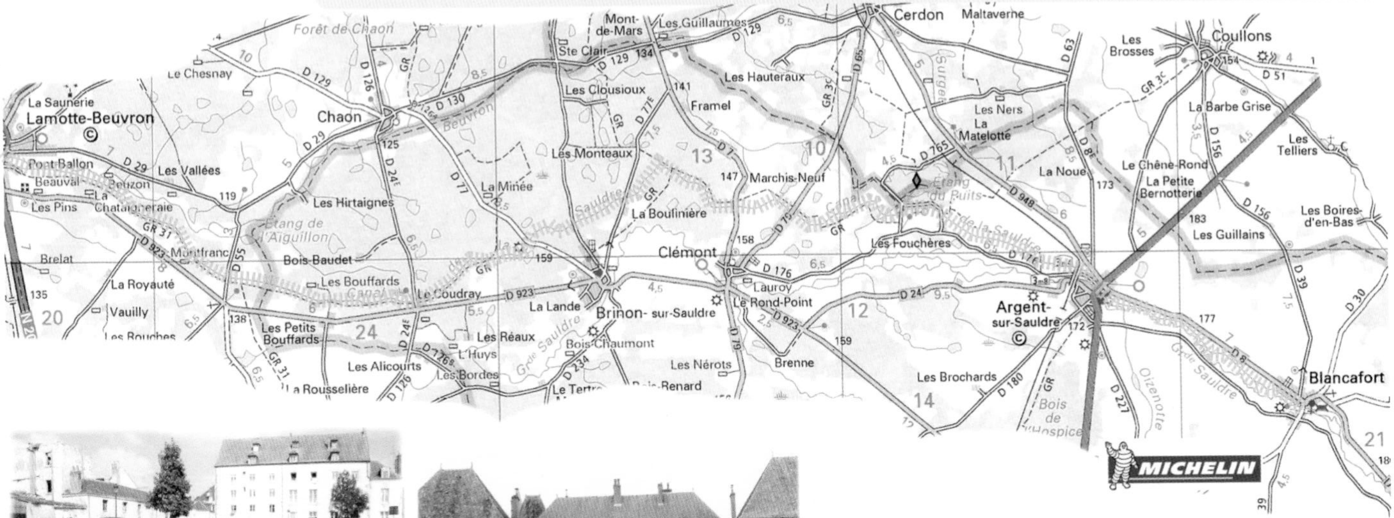

Meung-sur-Loire is a delightfully small-scale base from which to explore the rides opposite, complete with its own château

Cycling Paradise - The Marais Poitevin

Route Info

The Marais Poitevin
The Marais Poitevin - the Marshes of Poitou - contain a bewildering variety of signed routes. As you can guess from the name, the predominantly flat landscape is very easy cycling country. The heart of the area, in tourist terms at least, is the portion of the marshes to the west of the city of Niort, mainly in the *département* of Deux-Sèvres. Here you find 'typical' features of the area; beautiful tiny green canals (the smaller ones more like drainage ditches but still highly picturesque), inland ports like Arçais and Coulon and the myriad of small sluices and dams that allow water regulation - many also have small 'bypasses' for the use of the small wooden rowing boats still widely used in the area. Indeed, now that the commercial heyday of this 'green Venice' is past it is becoming something of a real-world Centreparcs-type tourist attraction with walking, cycling and various water-based activities to choose from. Niort and Coulon are both good bases, with a traffic-free route extending almost into the heart of Niort. Further east, the area around Lucon, is a very different landscape of wheat and sunflower fields with towns on small mounds that were once islands.

Grade Easy

Route advice
The routes themselves are well-signed and on a mixture of generally quiet public roads (*goudronné* or asphalted) and virtually traffic-free 'white roads' made of hardpacked calciferous material and known as *chemins blancs.* There are also 'sand tracks' which you'll see indicated on official maps as *sable* and which are more suitable for mountain bikes. Signage is good and there are information boards from time to time.

Route length The route network here is so dense you can make up your circuits of virtually any distance you like.

Train access TGV trains stop at Niort on the line between La Rochelle and Paris.

Nearby routes
Coastal Routes in Poitou-Charentes (pg 109), Charente (pg 118) and Le Loire à Vélo (pg 48)

Maps, guides and websites
Le Marais Poitevin à Bicyclette is a series of six maps showing the many signed routes in the area. 1euro each or all six for 3euros.
IGN Map 1:25,000 - Marais Poitevin des Deux-Sèvres, a detailed map of walking and cycling routes in the heart of the Marais area. Both available locally or from www.cartovelo.com, who also have a book, "Randonnées en Charente-Maritime et Marais Poitevin".
www.tourisme-deux-sevres.com to order "Le Marais Poitevin à Bicyclette - Vélo Découverte", a bilingual guide to the cyclists welcome scheme for the area.
www.poitou-charentes-vacances.com (English version available) for downloadable / orderable leaflet "Poitou-Charentes. Go Country Cycling" on biking here and in Poitou-Charentes generally.
www.bicyclette-verte.com Firm in Arcais offering bike hire, rescue and repair, route information, organised holidays and more.

Signage

The numerous routes use a variety of signing - some have pictorial direction indicators whilst others are coded by a combination of colour and number. The appropriate signs are shown in the map pack *Le Marais Poitevin à Bicyclette*

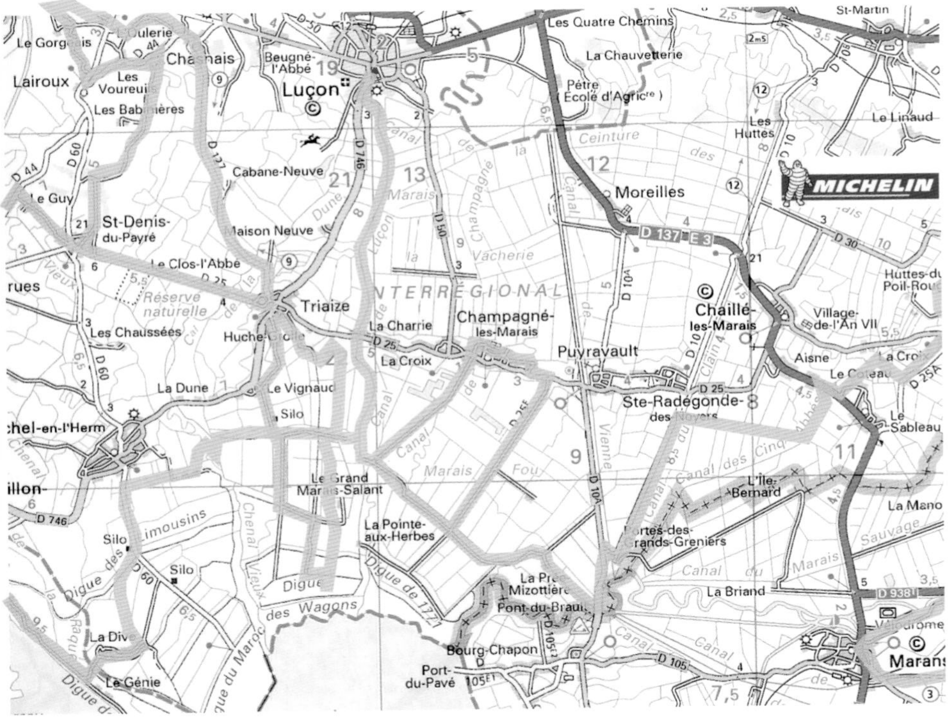

Coulon's waterside dwellings

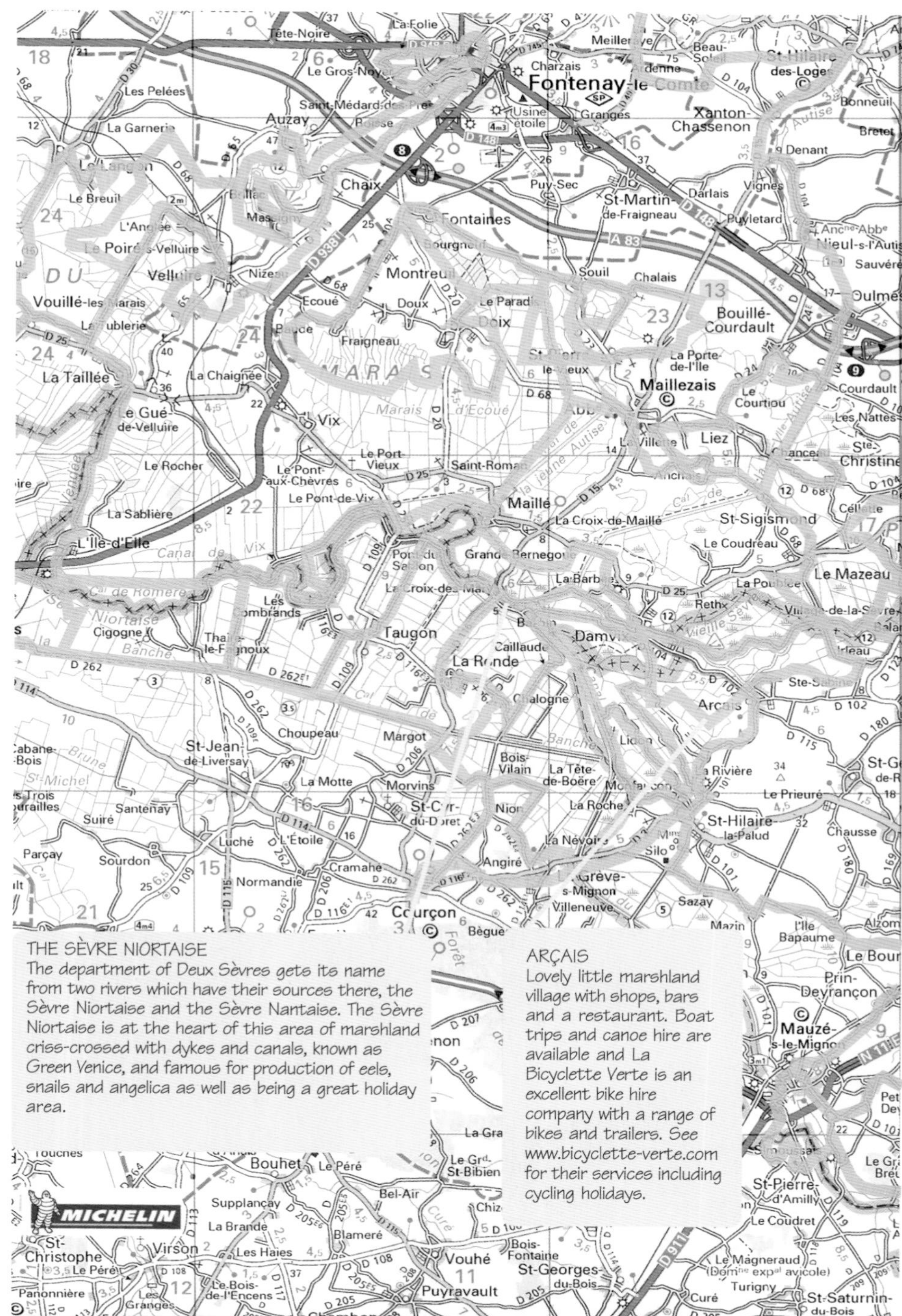

THE SÈVRE NIORTAISE

The department of Deux Sèvres gets its name from two rivers which have their sources there, the Sèvre Niortaise and the Sèvre Nantaise. The Sèvre Niortaise is at the heart of this area of marshland criss-crossed with dykes and canals, known as Green Venice, and famous for production of eels, snails and angelica as well as being a great holiday area.

ARÇAIS

Lovely little marshland village with shops, bars and a restaurant. Boat trips and canoe hire are available and La Bicyclette Verte is an excellent bike hire company with a range of bikes and trailers. See www.bicyclette-verte.com for their services including cycling holidays.

COULON

Lovely little town on the Sèvre where you can hire a flat-bottomed boat, with or without a guide, and have a peaceful scull around. A guide may be able to set the water on fire for you! (There's methane from the rotting leaves under the water.) To find out about life on the marshes, the eel-fishing, the boats etc., visit La Maison des Marais Mouillés.

NIORT

A town built on two hills, Niort has lively shopping areas and a good market. There are medieval houses and town hall and the massive towers of an ancient castle contain one of the town's several museums. Riverside (Sèvre Niortaise) gardens are great for relaxing.

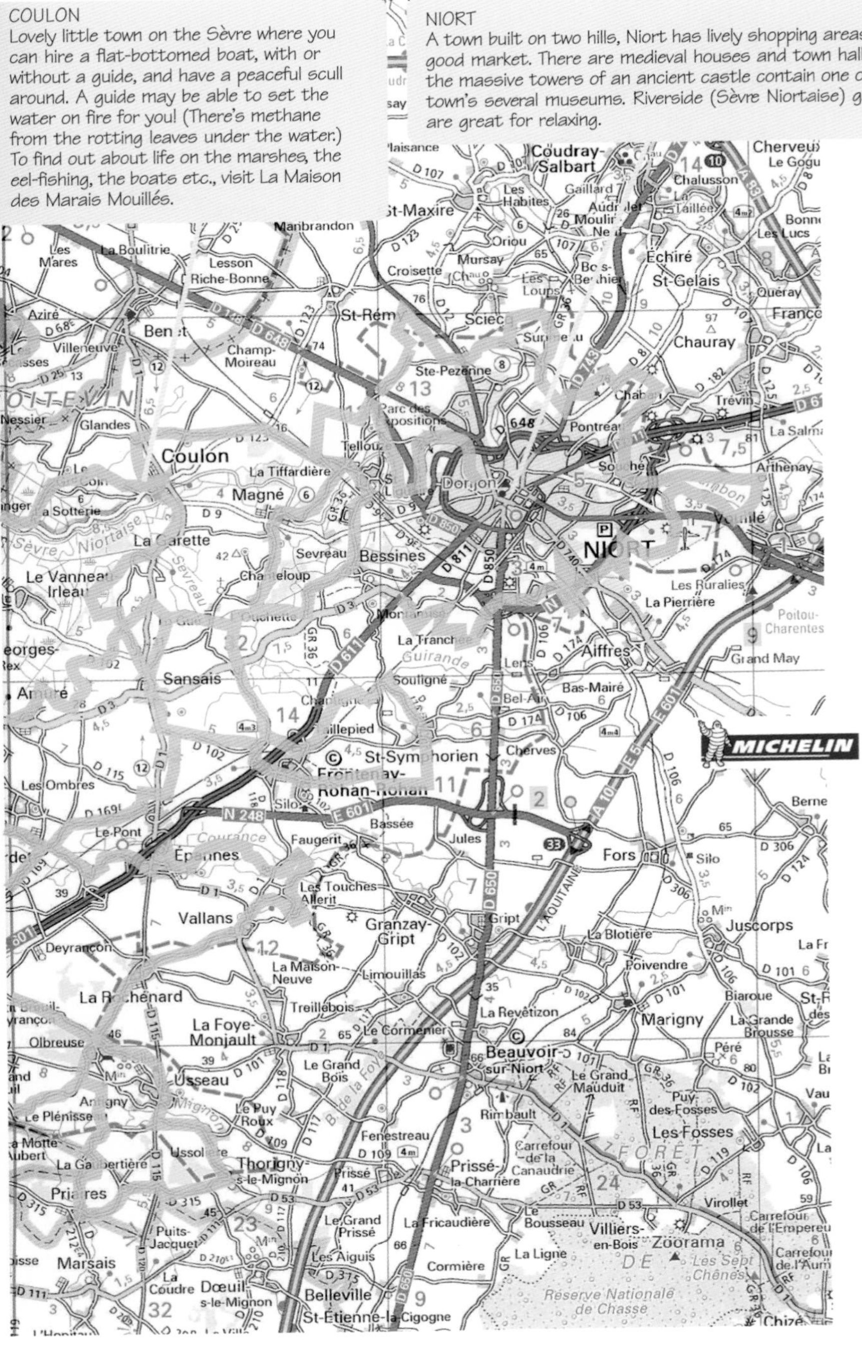

Arçais is a good stop off point if touring the Marais

La Sèvre Niortaise is the main river through the Marais and cycle routes run alongside much of its length

Coastal Routes - Poitou-Charentes & Pays de la Loire

Route Info

Coastal routes Poitou-Charentes and Pays de la Loire
A magnificent sweep of Atlantic coast from the mouth of the Loire in the north to the Gironde estuary in the south offers some truly beautiful rides. Sample wild, untamed coastline with crashing waves, big beaches and big skies. Amble through distinctive landscapes formed by generations of salt production. Go for a promenade promenade. Some very nice but busy holiday resorts and areas contrast with many quieter yet still attractive spots.

Grade EASY

Start / finish
A route network - of sorts - stretches all the way between Royan and the northern limit of the Vendee department (actually in the Pays de la Loire region)

Route length Cycling the length of the coast from Royan and through Vendee would mean covering 170 miles / 273km. However, as the the network is somewhat intermittent - especially in connecting between areas - this chapter selects the best route sections for day rides as set out in Route Advice. Add the many miles of island cycle route (Oléron, Ré and Noirmoutier) and you have countless cycling opportunities on this lovely stretch of coast.

Route advice
Traffic-free trail follows much of the coast. There's an 18 mile / 29 km tarmac greenway from St. Palais-sur-Mer north of Royan round to Ronce-les-Bains, opposite the Île d'Oléron. South of the Île de Noirmoutier, a massive 78 mile / 125 km stretch of cyclepaths goes down to Talmont-St-Hilaire. There are many miles of paths and quiet tracks on the islands.

Train access TGVs to St. Nazaire, La Rochelle and Angoulême (soon to Les Sables-d'Olonne). Only carry folding or demounted and bagged bikes, so perhaps consider local bike-carrying trains. Lines to St. Gilles-Croix-de-Vie, Les Sables-d'Olonne, Rochefort and Royan. Nantes - Noirmoutier SNCF coach service has cycle racks.

Nearby routes
The Loire (pg48) and the Marais Poitevin network (pg104) are very nearby. The northern section of the Atlantic Coast route (pg40) is just a short boat trip from Royan.

Maps, guides and websites
www.vendee.fr Excellent cycle maps between Noirmoutier and the Marais P. The free e-book "Vendée Vélo" has detailed maps (French version only).
www.iledere.fr (English version) for info and downloadable cycle path map. Paper maps from tourist offices.
www.oleron.org has a map of the network. For other information see *www.ile-oleron-marennes.com*
La Rochelle has a map of the area's cycle network available at tourist offices.
www.poitou-charentes-vacances.com has info on cycling around Royan, Rochefort, La Rochelle, Île d'Oléron and Île de Ré and an orderable booklet on cycling in the region.
www.ile-noirmoutier.com (has English version) or get IGN 's "Carte de Loisirs de Plein Air. Île de Noirmoutier à vélo et à pied"
www.westernloire.com Good maps of the Vélocéan network (pg 117)

Whilst different areas use different types of sign all the routes detailed here are well signed. The left picture shows the signing system around La Rochelle and far left that on the on Ile-de-Ré

Cycling for all ages at St-Martin-de-Ré, the attractive 'capital' of Ile de Ré

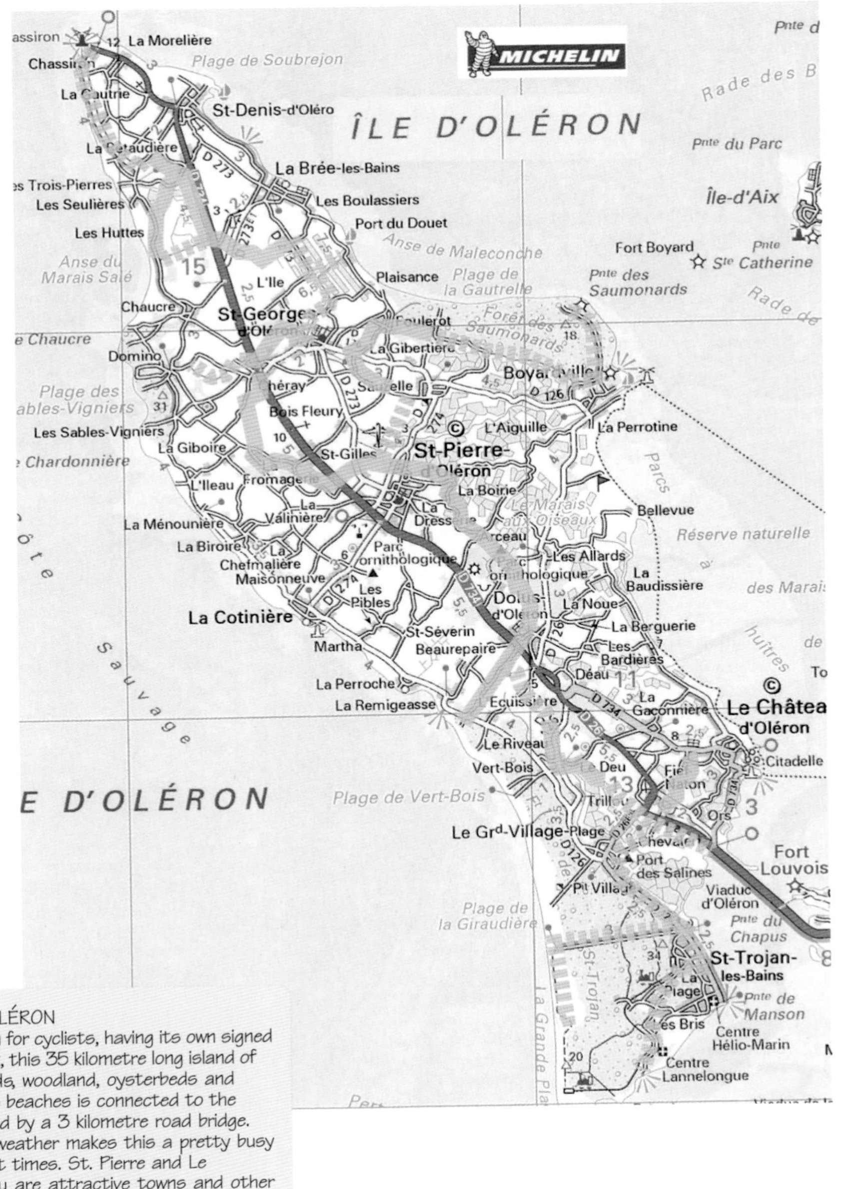

ÎLE D'OLÉRON

A haven for cyclists, having its own signed network, this 35 kilometre long island of vineyards, woodland, oysterbeds and glorious beaches is connected to the mainland by a 3 kilometre road bridge. Great weather makes this a pretty busy place at times. St. Pierre and Le Château are attractive towns and other attractions include a bird park and Fort Boyard, a fort in the sea off the north coast of the island which is quite a dramatic sight.

THE CÔTE SAUVAGE

The mainland coast south of the Île d'Oléron between the island channel and Bonne Anse bay (there's a well-known zoo at the nearby resort of La Palmyre) is known as the Côte Sauvage. Several kilometres of sea and sand offer glorious beaches and crashing waves which attract many surfers. In the forests behind the bank of sand dunes, some of which are very substantial, paths and cycle tracks wend their way through the pine forests.

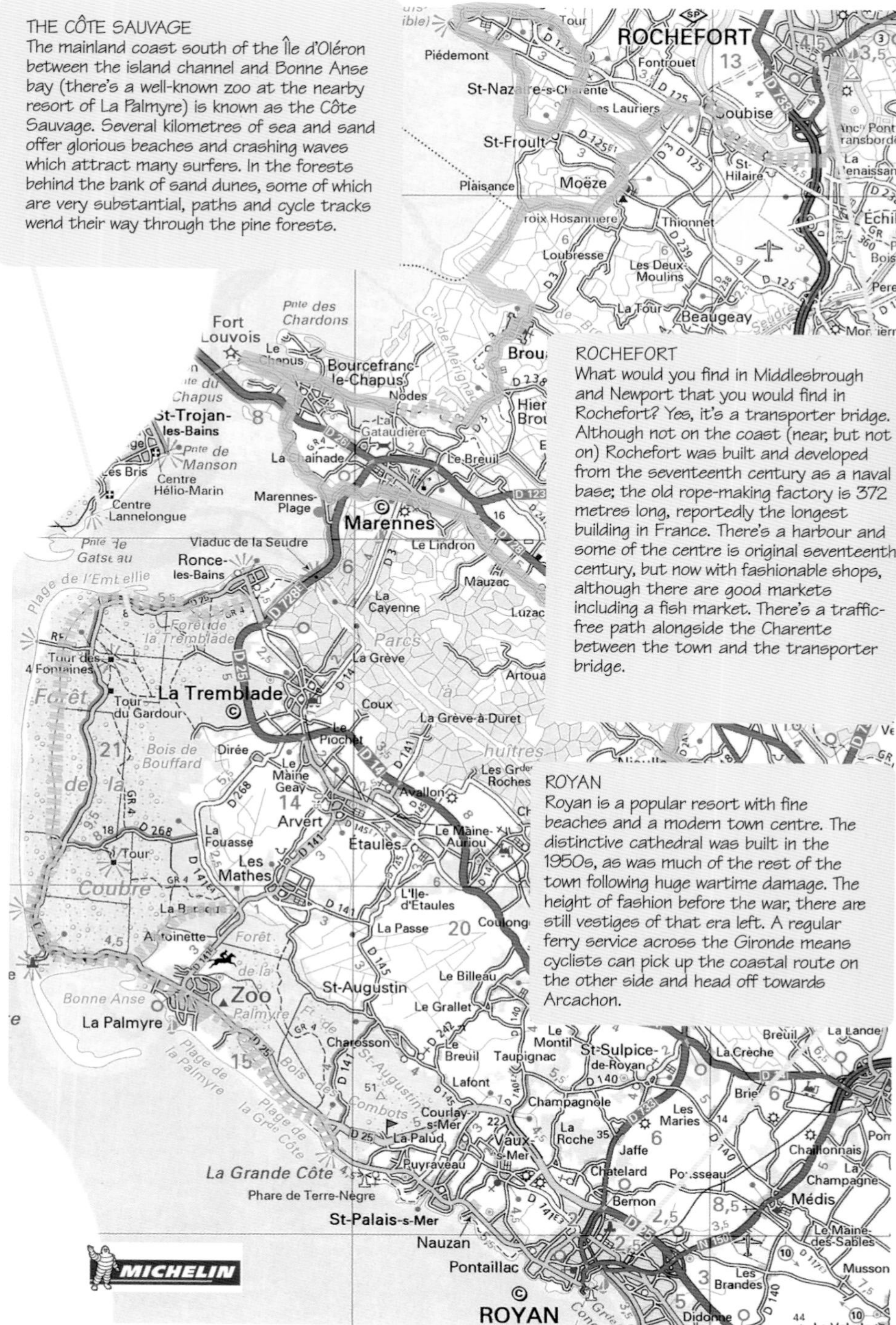

ROCHEFORT

What would you find in Middlesbrough and Newport that you would find in Rochefort? Yes, it's a transporter bridge. Although not on the coast (near, but not on) Rochefort was built and developed from the seventeenth century as a naval base; the old rope-making factory is 372 metres long, reportedly the longest building in France. There's a harbour and some of the centre is original seventeenth century, but now with fashionable shops, although there are good markets including a fish market. There's a traffic-free path alongside the Charente between the town and the transporter bridge.

ROYAN

Royan is a popular resort with fine beaches and a modern town centre. The distinctive cathedral was built in the 1950s, as was much of the rest of the town following huge wartime damage. The height of fashion before the war, there are still vestiges of that era left. A regular ferry service across the Gironde means cyclists can pick up the coastal route on the other side and head off towards Arcachon.

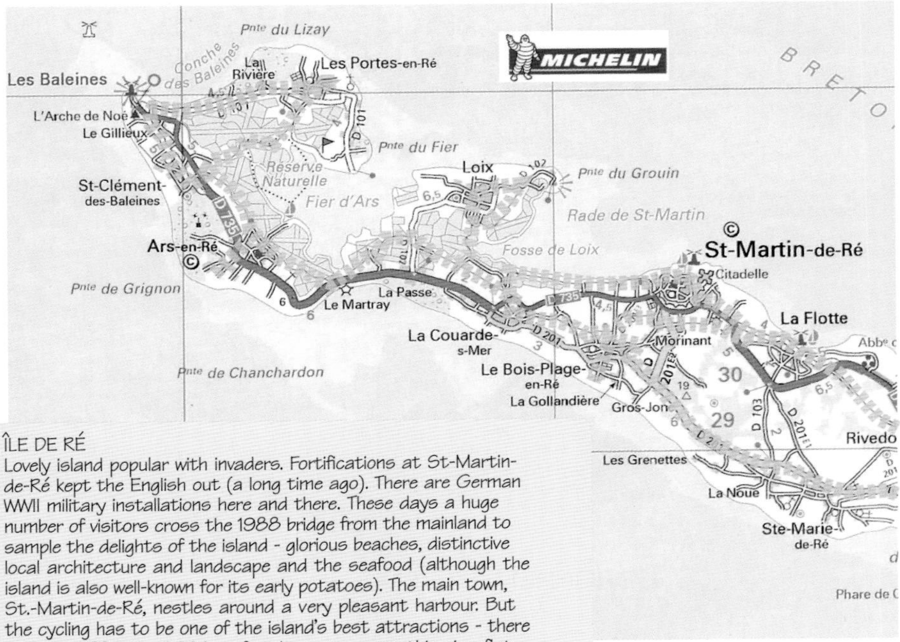

ÎLE DE RÉ

Lovely island popular with invaders. Fortifications at St-Martin-de-Ré kept the English out (a long time ago). There are German WWII military installations here and there. These days a huge number of visitors cross the 1988 bridge from the mainland to sample the delights of the island - glorious beaches, distinctive local architecture and landscape and the seafood (although the island is also well-known for its early potatoes). The main town, St.-Martin-de-Ré, nestles around a very pleasant harbour. But the cycling has to be one of the island's best attractions - there are some 56 miles / 90 km of cycle route across this nice, flat island (and the bridge has a cycle lane) with plenty of bike shops and hirers.

Once over the bridge and onto Ile de Ré you are straight onto high quality cyclepath to the pretty village of Rivedoux Plage

LA ROCHELLE

A busy resort served by TGVs. Superb old town centre and port well-known for its medieval seafront towers. There's a large marina south of the centre and plenty of very good beaches. La Rochelle is good for cycling - Yellow Bikes is a low cost hire scheme - with a long coastal path being developed to the north and other long tourist/commuter paths also planned. Map of area cycling network, which is good but maybe a little lacking in signs, available at tourist offices.

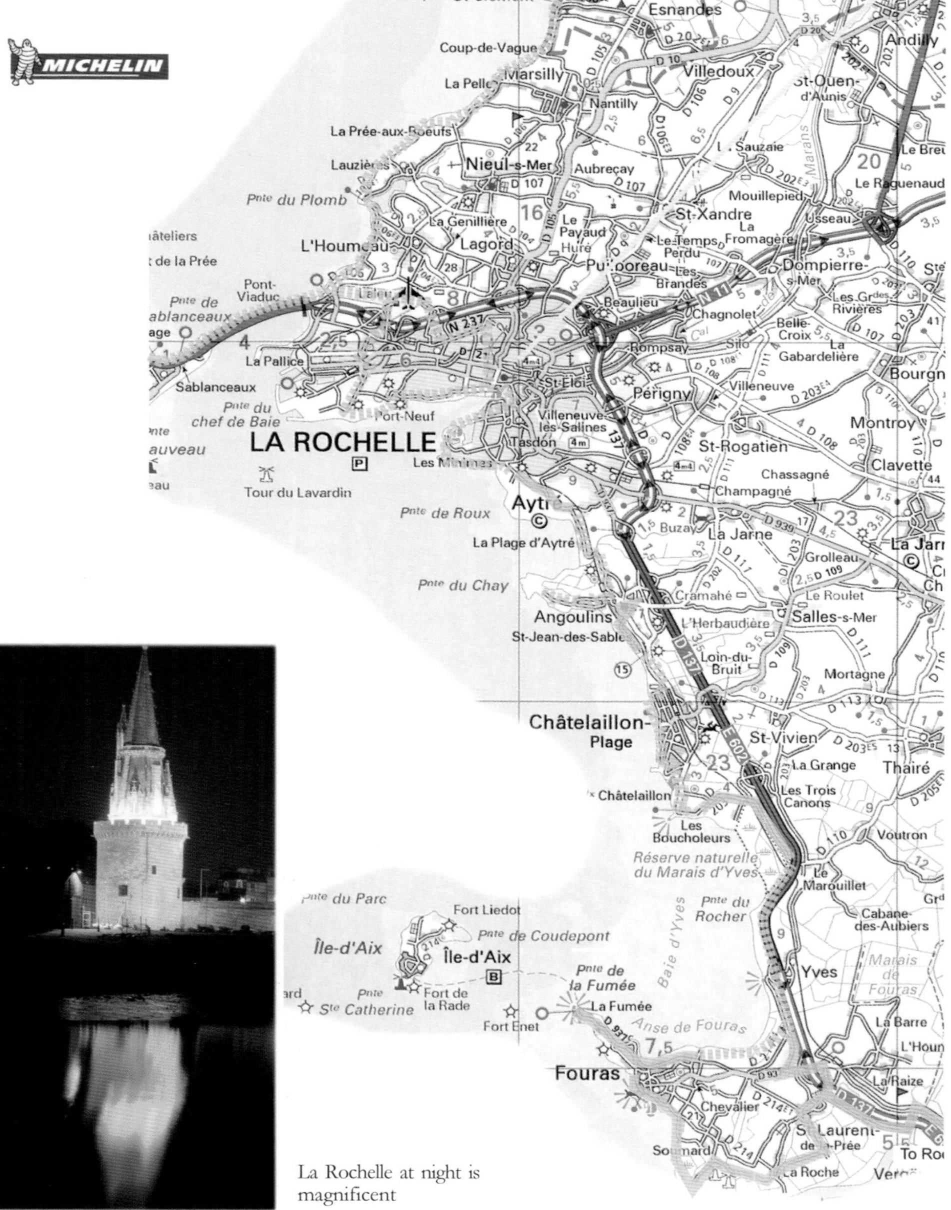

La Rochelle at night is magnificent

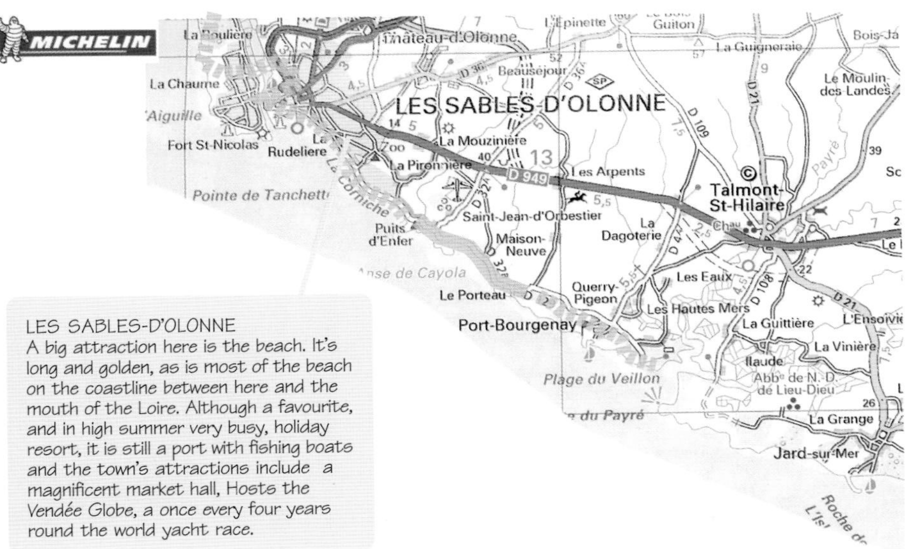

LES SABLES-D'OLONNE
A big attraction here is the beach. It's long and golden, as is most of the beach on the coastline between here and the mouth of the Loire. Although a favourite, and in high summer very busy, holiday resort, it is still a port with fishing boats and the town's attractions include a magnificent market hall, Hosts the Vendée Globe, a once every four years round the world yacht race.

La Rochelle's elegant harbour front

ÎLE DE NOIRMOUTIER

This twenty kilometre long island linked to the mainland by bridge and causeway is a land of saltpans, woodland and beaches. The main town, Noirmoutier-en-l'Île, is a homely-looking place with an ancient castle, a church and a small harbour. The island has well-mapped cycle routes.

VÉLOCÉAN NETWORK 24 miles / 39km - St Michel-Chef-Chef to Le Port du Collet via Pornic - more under development

INLAND VENDÉE

When added to Vendée's coastal network, the département boasts miles 336 miles/ 540km of path - this will be doubled in coming years.

OTHER ROUTES IN THE AREA

The Charente (following chapter) is prime Cognac country - here is Courvoisier's warehouse right on the river cycle route at Jarnac

Charente

Route Info

The Charente
Much of the Charente area is rich green countryside and the River Charente, one of many rivers hereabouts, is something of an attraction with cruises and other activities. Towns and cities range from quiet and unassuming to clearly well-heeled and the area's best-known product is probably the Cognac from western Charente. Cycling is good, mainly on quiet country roads but with a developing greenway system.

Grade See Route advice below for section gradings

Route length 91 miles / 146km

Route advice
A lovely ride from Saintes (actually just outside Charente but a lovely ancient town at which to start) to the lakes of the upper Charente, deep in rural France, is detailed on pgs 120-122. **(Grade EASY between Saintes and Marthon and Grade MEDIUM thereafter).**
Le Grand Huit is around 311 miles / 500 km of signed route around the department laid out on existing cycle routes and greenways. Also, there is a large number of smaller circular rides (which can be ridden as short family rides or longer discovery or exploration rides) but only a couple of these are signed at present, experimentally - circuits 27 at Rouillac (up to 44 miles / 71km) and 8 at Barbezieux (up to 29 miles / 46 km). **Grade MEDIUM**
A couple of good stretches of greenway in the *département* are the Galope Chopine from Barbezieux to Chantillac (14 miles / 23 km) and the Coulée d'Oc between Marthon and Chazelles with more to follow. Just a short hop to the south is the Chevanceaux to Clérac greenway in the *département* of Charente-Maritime.

Train access
TGVs (only folding and demounted and bagged bikes) serve Angoulême from Paris and go on to Bordeaux. Local lines from Angoulême through Cognac to Saintes and the coast and to Limoges

Nearby routes
Poitou-Charente Coast (pgs 109-117, the Marais Poitevin (pgs 104-108) and Périgord (pgs 155-157).

Maps, guides and websites
www.lacharente.com Has a map of Le Grand Huit and further information
www.poitou-charentes-vacances.com Contains info on cycling in and around Angoulême and describes a booklet available locally on "La Coulée Verte", 20 kilometres of greenway on the riverbank across Angoulême. There is also an orderable booklet on cycling in the region.

Signage

'Le Grand Huit' and Cognac to Angoulême are well-signed

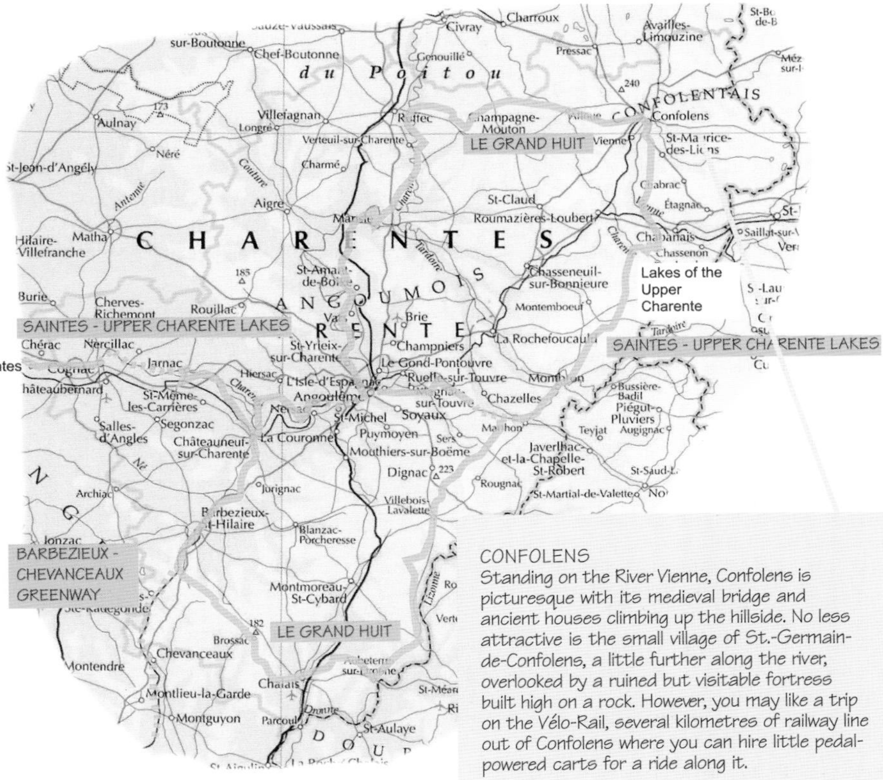
LE GRAND HUIT
SAINTES - UPPER CHARENTE LAKES
Saintes
Lakes of the Upper Charente
SAINTES - UPPER CHARENTE LAKES
BARBEZIEUX - CHEVANCEAUX GREENWAY
LE GRAND HUIT
C H A R E N T E S
A N G O U M O I S
du Poitou
CONFOLENTAIS
Confolens
Angoulême
Cognac
Jarnac
Civray
Charroux
Ruffec
Aigre
Matha
La Rochefoucauld
Chabanais
Barbezieux-St-Hilaire
Montmoreau-St-Cybard
Chalais
Montguyon
Chevanceaux
Montendre
Soyaux
Dignac

CONFOLENS

Standing on the River Vienne, Confolens is picturesque with its medieval bridge and ancient houses climbing up the hillside. No less attractive is the small village of St.-Germain-de-Confolens, a little further along the river, overlooked by a ruined but visitable fortress built high on a rock. However, you may like a trip on the Vélo-Rail, several kilometres of railway line out of Confolens where you can hire little pedal-powered carts for a ride along it.

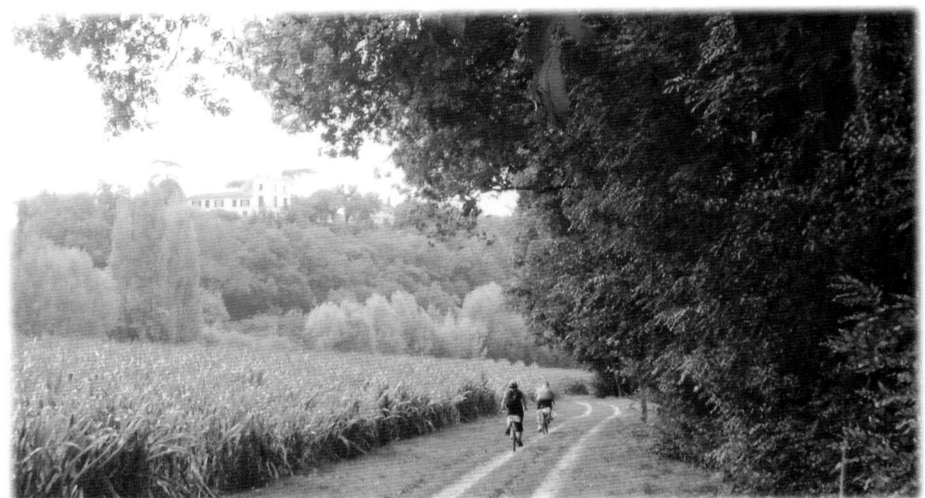

The alternative towpath route between Cognac and Jarnac

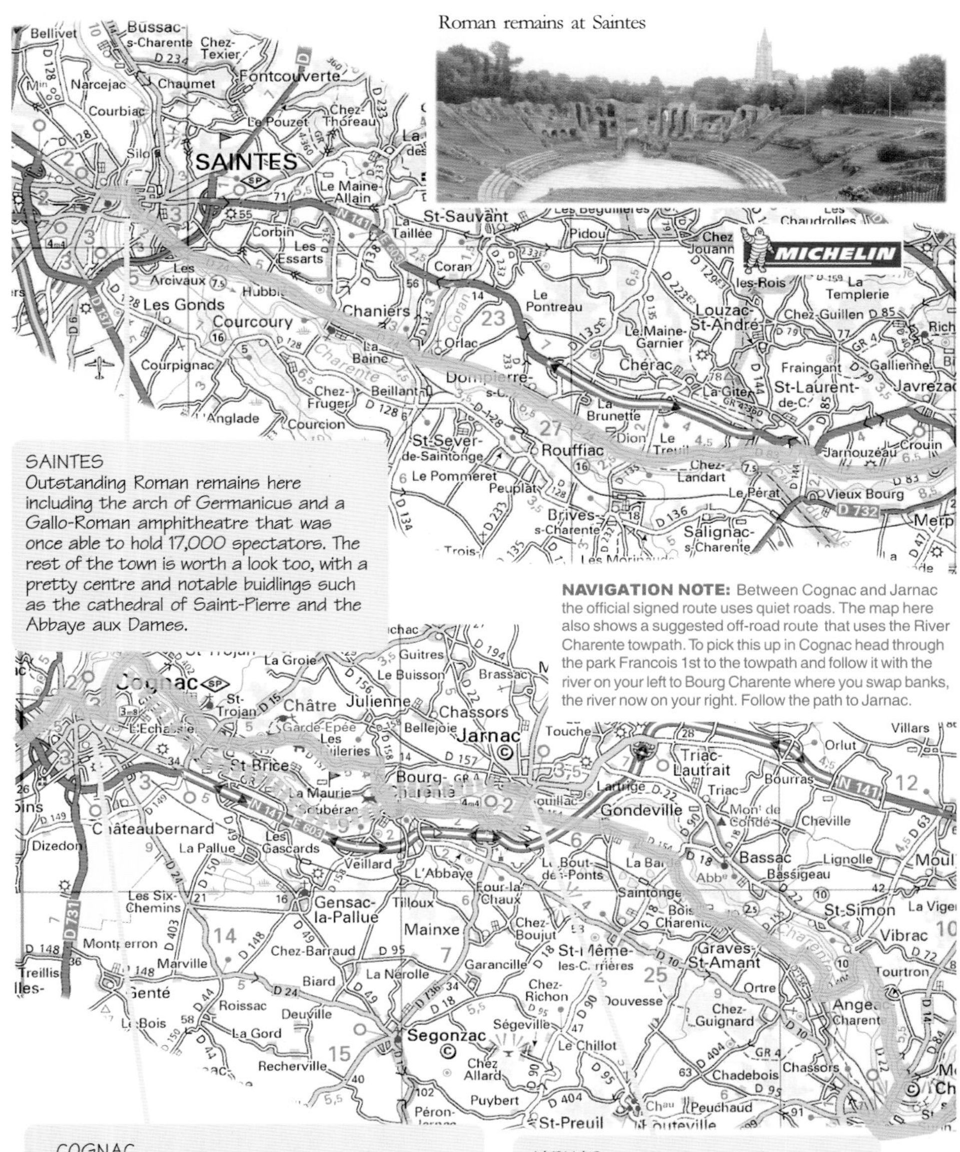

Roman remains at Saintes

SAINTES

Outstanding Roman remains here including the arch of Germanicus and a Gallo-Roman amphitheatre that was once able to hold 17,000 spectators. The rest of the town is worth a look too, with a pretty centre and notable buildings such as the cathedral of Saint-Pierre and the Abbaye aux Dames.

NAVIGATION NOTE: Between Cognac and Jarnac the official signed route uses quiet roads. The map here also shows a suggested off-road route that uses the River Charente towpath. To pick this up in Cognac head through the park Francois 1st to the towpath and follow it with the river on your left to Bourg Charente where you swap banks, the river now on your right. Follow the path to Jarnac.

COGNAC

A rather nice little town with some medieval buildings and castle remains, but it's the omnipresence of the golden nectar that strikes you. Its odours are everywhere and every second building seems to bear the plate of one or other of the great Cognac producers. The surrounding countryside is devoted fervently to its production and there are plenty of opportunities to visit, taste and buy.

JARNAC

Its Charente riverside setting is what really makes Jarnac; the stretch of river from here to Cognac is excellent for boat trips. House of Courvoisier based here in the local rather magnificent château. Birthplace and last resting place of President Mitterand.

The sumptuous architecture of Angoulême lies at the heart of the Charente

ANGOULÊME

Capital of the Charente, Angoulême is dominated visually by its cathedral and its impressive town hall. Between these two buildings a warren of small streets houses a great choice of small restaurants, bars and shops. There are good views over the surrounding countryside from the edges of the city.

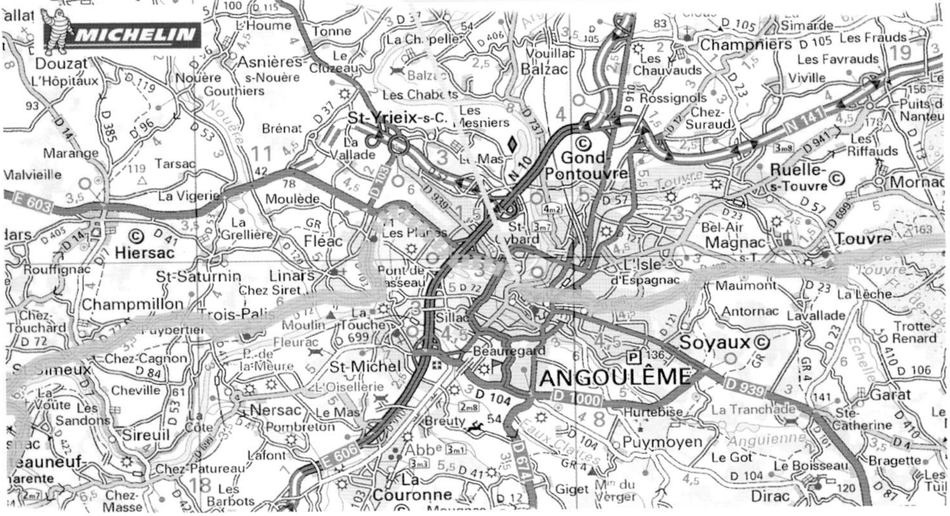

LAKES OF THE UPPER CHARENTE

Not far from the source of the Charente is an immense area of gentle hills coated in chestnut and oak woods and containing the largest stretch of water in the Poitou-Charentes region in the form of lakes Lavaud and Mas-Chaban. There is a huge range of signed trails for mountain bikers and children will enjoy the rope bridges and commando nets at Adventure Parc. Lovers of watersports will enjoy sailing, windsurfing or canoeing on the lakes.

The route follows the river Charente for much of its length - here is a lovely navigable stretch just downstream from Angoulême, on a towpath section of route

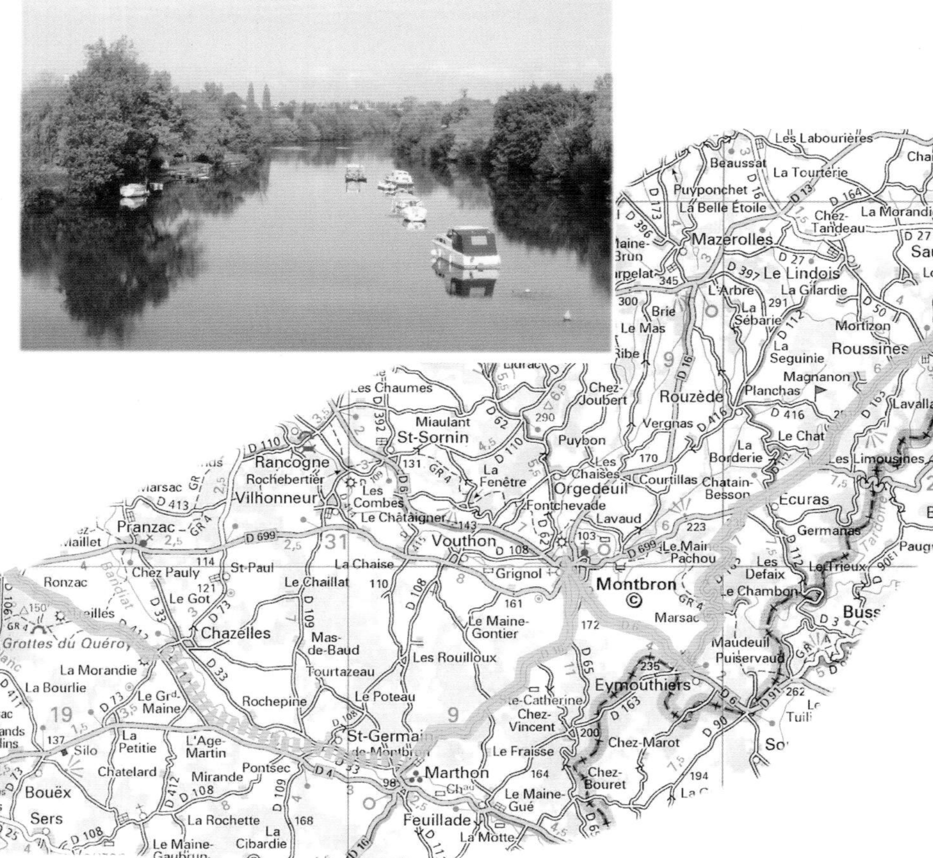

Family Rides in the Corrèze

Route Info

The Corrèze
Some short and easy family rides in lovely Limousin countryside which always seem to offer something worth seeing along the way, be it a pretty medieval village or a piece of dramatic modern engineering. The Corrèze landscape is known for its limestone plateau and waterfalls.

Grade EASY

Route length 7 miles / 11 km to 20 miles /32 km

Route advice
Fifteen well-signed family routes. Four have sections where a mountain or all-terrain bike might help.
Each ride has a designated start point in a town or village with decent facilities and an information board at the start.

Train access
Railway stations serving the area are at Ussel, Meymac, Tulle, Brive-la-Gaillarde and a number of other places along the line. Many services are by bus and some trains may not carry bicycles - care needed.

Nearby routes Across Volcano Country (pgs 21-24), Périgord (pgs 155-157), the Massif Central (pgs 130-137) and the Lot Valley (pgs 138-143).

Maps, guides and websites
www.vacances-en-correze.net offers basic information and contacts. *Itinéraires Touristiques Cyclables de la Corrèze* is a little booklet available locally for 1,5 euros describing these15 family rides in Corrèze. The route maps are reasonably practical and the basic information is there.

Signage

The start and finish point of each route couldn't be more obvious

And signing along the way is excellent

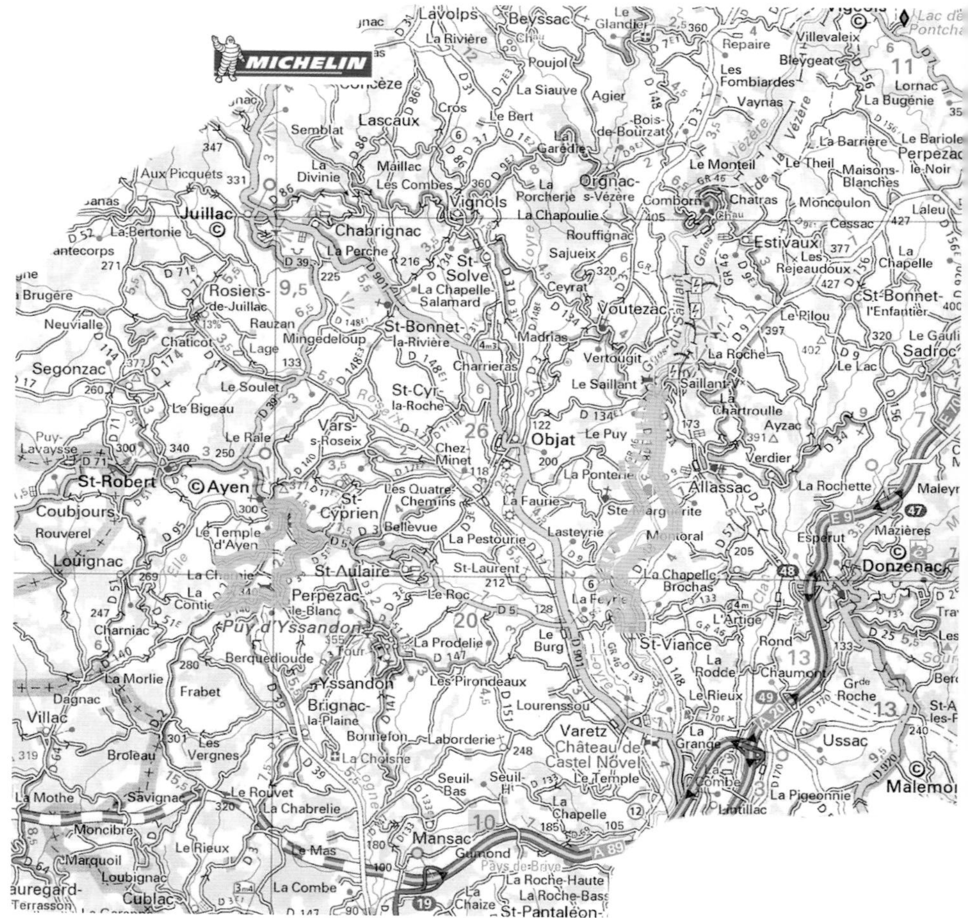

Exploring Off-Road in France

Several of these family routes in the Corrèze use very easy-going off-road tracks. Whilst this guide is aimed at leisure users who want tarmacked or at least very good off-road surfaces you might also want the option to explore further off-road if you have a mountain bike with you.

Probably the best starting point is IGN map 906 *France VTT & Randonnées Cyclos* (Mountain Bike & Cycle Touring in France). The *Fédération Française de Cyclisme* (FFC) has established a network of off-road centres across the country, eash with at least 100km of off-road riding. The routes are signed and graded in with 4 levels - gree, blue, red and black - in order of increasing difficulty. Some easy routes may be suitable for families and the IGN map shows the name and location of each centre, the signing system used (based on a triangle and 2 circles) and the number of circuits in each difficulty grade.

The map also shows longer road touring routes, but not in sufficient detail for you to navigate from. Generally these routes are not signed and you will need to be reasonably fluent in French and get more details on how to ride them. More info available from *Fédération Française de Cyclotourisme* (FFCT) on www.ffct.org (French only).

Collonges la Rouge
Photo: Frédéric Magnoux / CDT Corrèze

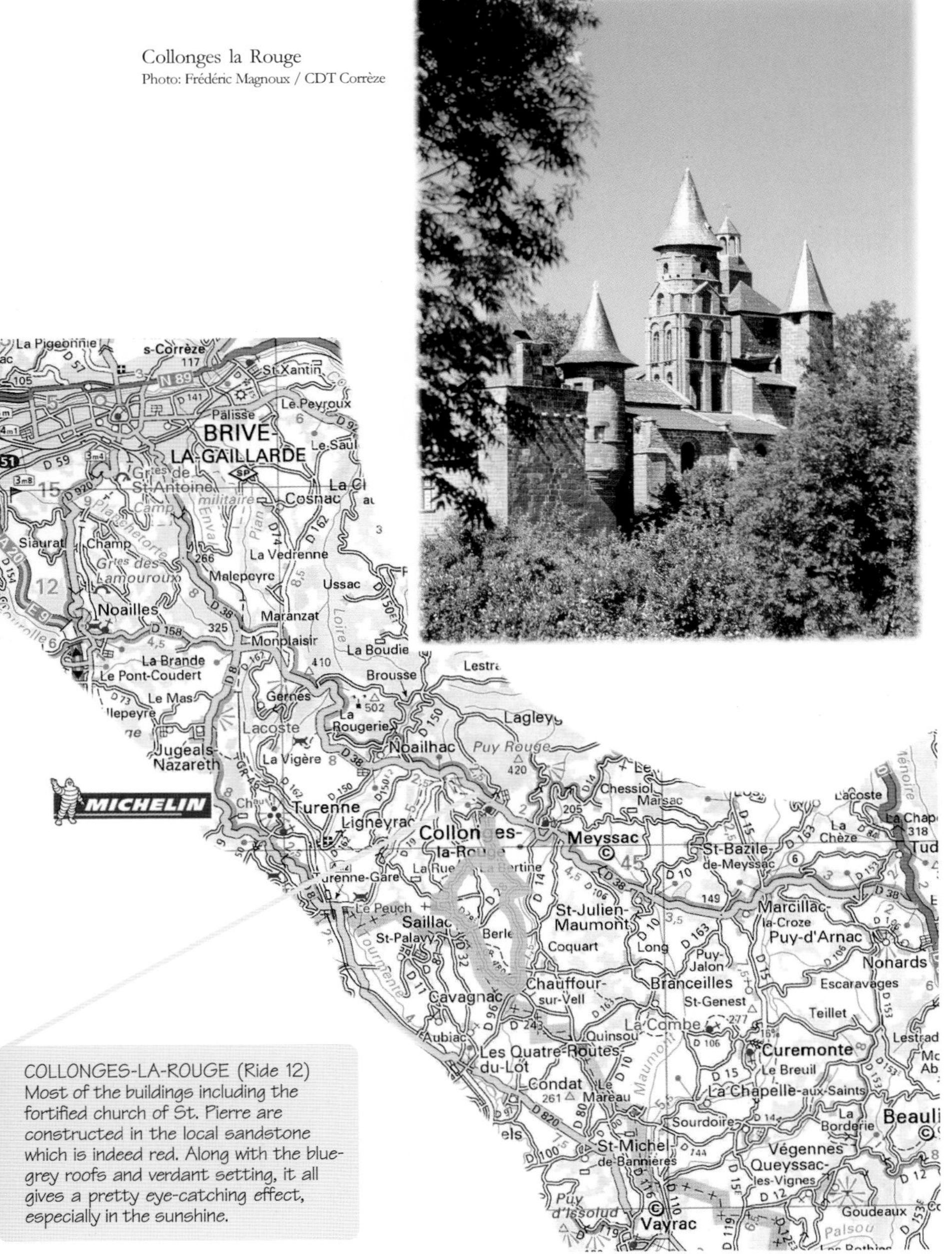

COLLONGES-LA-ROUGE (Ride 12)
Most of the buildings including the fortified church of St. Pierre are constructed in the local sandstone which is indeed red. Along with the blue-grey roofs and verdant setting, it all gives a pretty eye-catching effect, especially in the sunshine.

Argentat

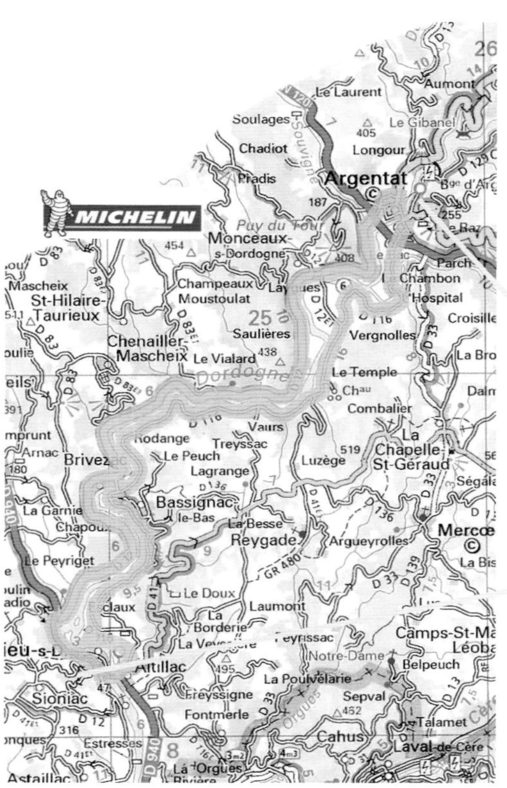

ARGENTAT and BEAULIEU-SUR-DORDOGNE (Rides 10 and 11)
Two delightful towns sitting right on the Dordogne. Argentat was the highest point on the navigable river used as a port. It's a good place for shopping and eating and the old town area has ancient buildings and quiet, wandering streets. Beaulieu occupies a most lovely setting on a great wide bend in the river and its medieval buildings and riverside walks make for a lovely visit.

TREIGNAC (Ride 3)
Pretty medieval village of slate-roofed stone buildings standing on the fast-flowing River Vézère, a challenge for canoeists and rafters. Shops, bars, restaurants. Ancient bridge, market hall and chapel. Lac des Bariousses to the north and on this ride has a beach and watersports.

An ancient footbridge on the Plateau de Millevaches (an area covered by the rides from St-Merd-les-Oussines).
Photo: Pierre Soissons / CDT Corrèze

SARRAN (Ride 4)
In the heart of Corrèze, Sarran's main attraction is the purpose-built Musée du Président Jacques Chirac, home to the many gifts given to the President including a stuffed prehistoric fish and a porcelain sumo wrestler. Some exhibits are unique and valuable, others homely and entertaining. The Chiracs stayed in Sarran at times and Madame Chirac was a local councillor there. See www.museepresidentjchirac.fr

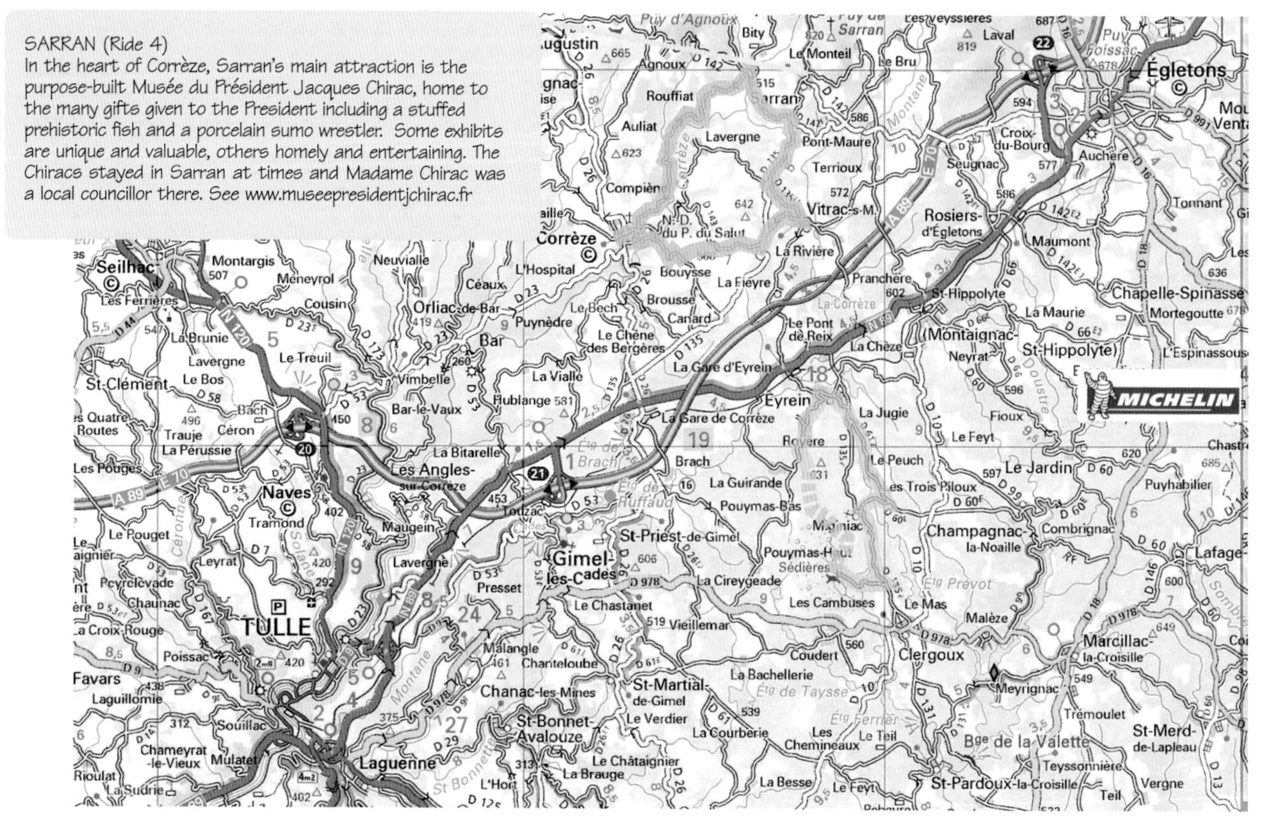

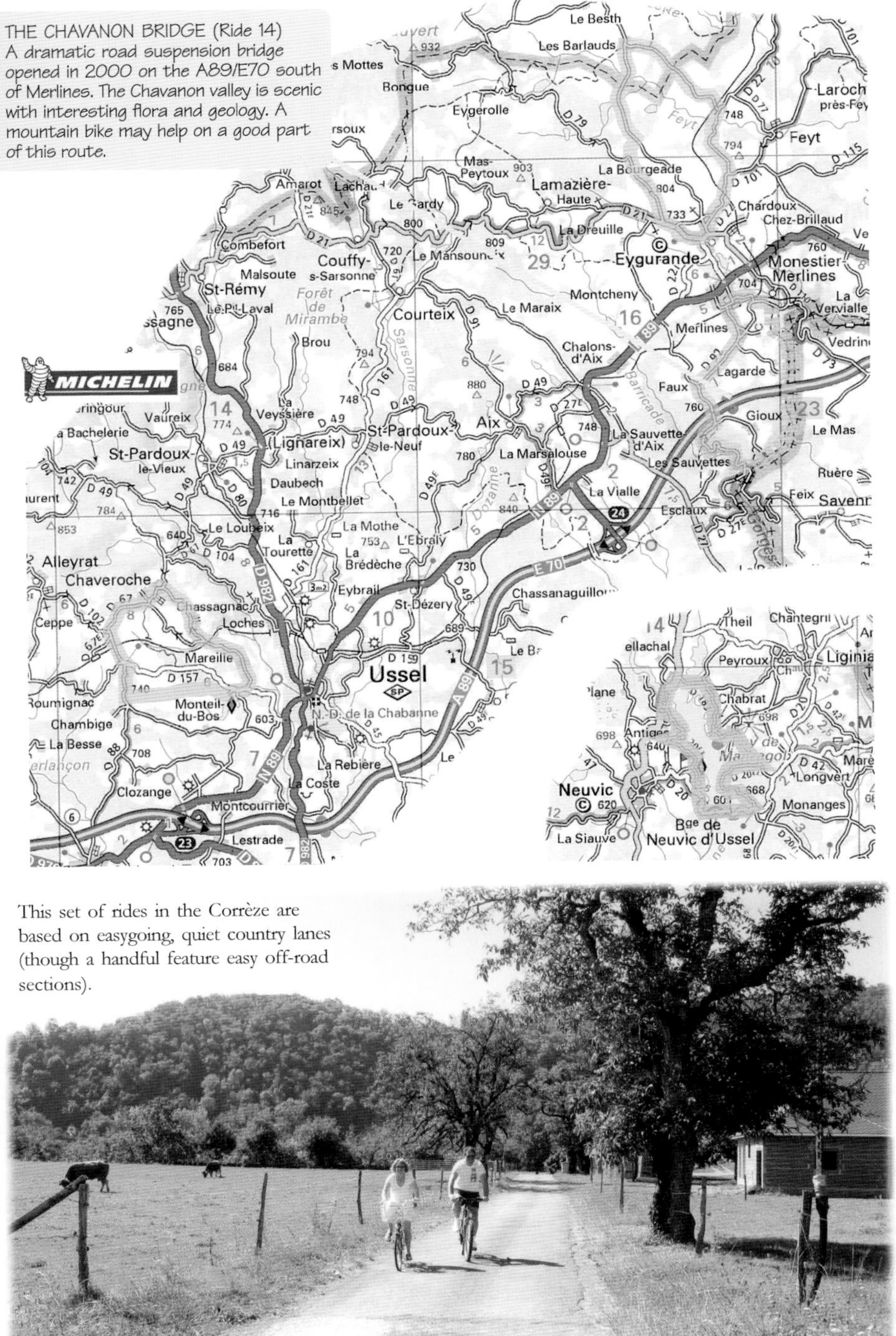

THE CHAVANON BRIDGE (Ride 14)
A dramatic road suspension bridge opened in 2000 on the A89/E70 south of Merlines. The Chavanon valley is scenic with interesting flora and geology. A mountain bike may help on a good part of this route.

This set of rides in the Corrèze are based on easygoing, quiet country lanes (though a handful feature easy off-road sections).

Massif Central

Route Info

The Massif Central
A region of spectacular landscapes and some excellent cycle routes. The volcanic area to the west of Clermont-Ferrand has some exhilarating rides, as has the hilly, sometimes mountainous Livradois area to the east. Both areas are regional nature parks, a measure offering protection against both over-development and stagnation.

Grade EASY to **DIFFICULT**

Route length 22 miles / 36 km to 50 miles / 80 km

Route advice
Twelve circular cycle routes all in the Puy de Dôme department, mainly on very quiet country roads, make good day or leisurely two or three day rides. They are signed in one direction only.

Train access
Lines radiate from Clermont-Ferrand to Le Mont-Dore, Volvic, Riom, Thiers and Issoire which puts rides 2,4,7,8, 10 and 11 on or in striking distance of trains.

Nearby routes
Corrèze (pgs 123-129),
Across Volcano Country (pgs 21-24).

Maps, guides and websites
IGN CycloGuide 63 has a map for each of the 12 routes with a chart of distances, altitudes and facilities. *www.planetepuydedome.com* has little cycling information but an order form for a cycling map and other tourist brochures. The map, also available locally, "Découverte à vélo - 12 circuits de cyclotourisme" is a good overview of the routes which gives a broad idea of facilities in towns and villages.

Volcanic scenery abounds to the west and south of Clermont Ferrand

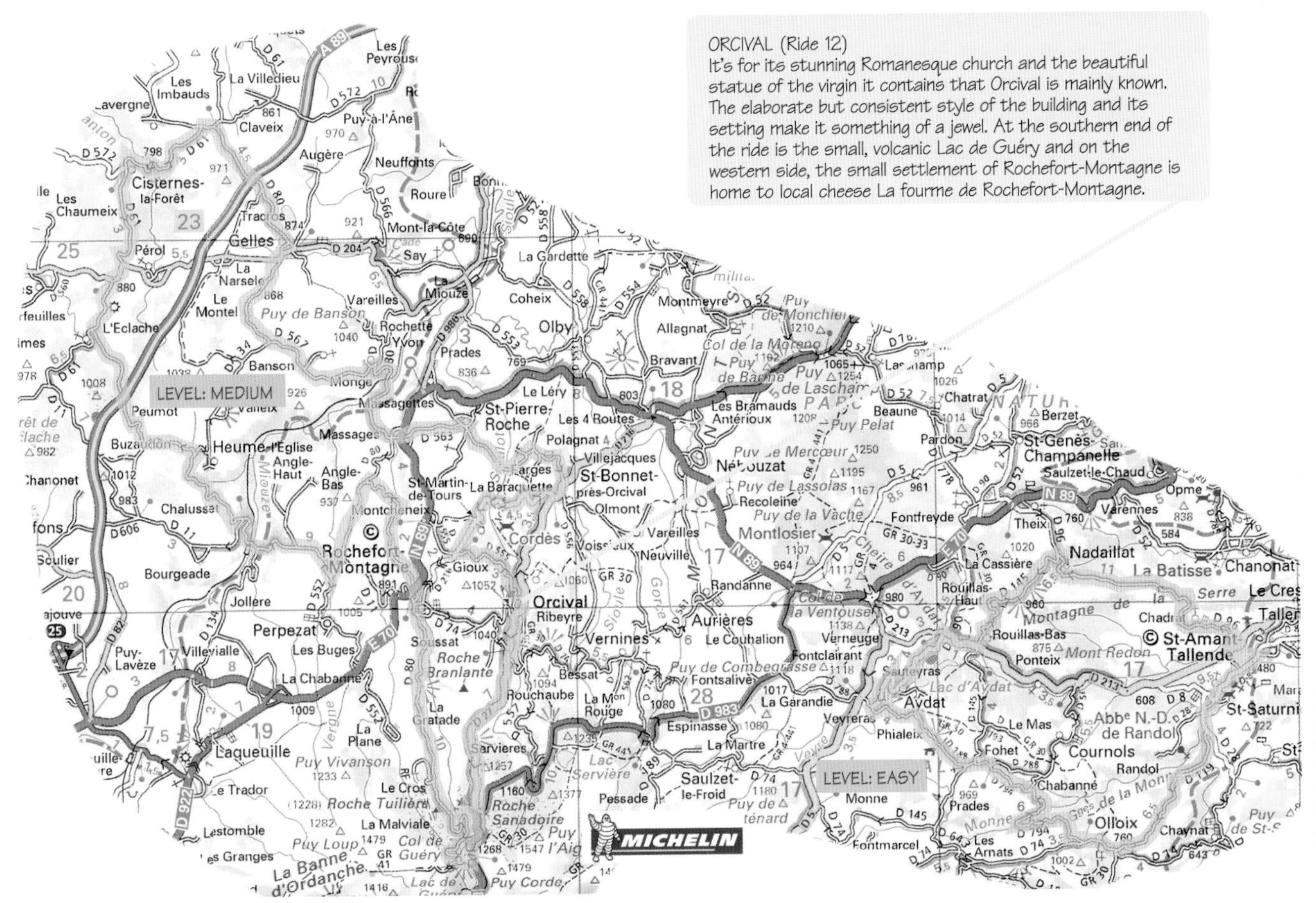

ORCIVAL (Ride 12)
It's for its stunning Romanesque church and the beautiful statue of the virgin it contains that Orcival is mainly known. The elaborate but consistent style of the building and its setting make it something of a jewel. At the southern end of the ride is the small, volcanic Lac de Guéry and on the western side, the small settlement of Rochefort-Montagne is home to local cheese La fourme de Rochefort-Montagne.

BILLOM and CHÂTEAUX (Ride 4)
Just off the ride, Billom is a small, basically medieval, market town dominated by its church in an area which has been called the Tuscany of the Auvergne. Famous for its pink garlic. Further on round the route, the Château de Mauzun, now ruins, was a huge medieval fortress with three concentric walls and many towers, absolutely dominating the surrounding countryside. At Sermentizon is the Château d'Alteribe with a collection of fine paintings, tapestries and porcelain and a furniture collection. Both châteaux are open to the public.

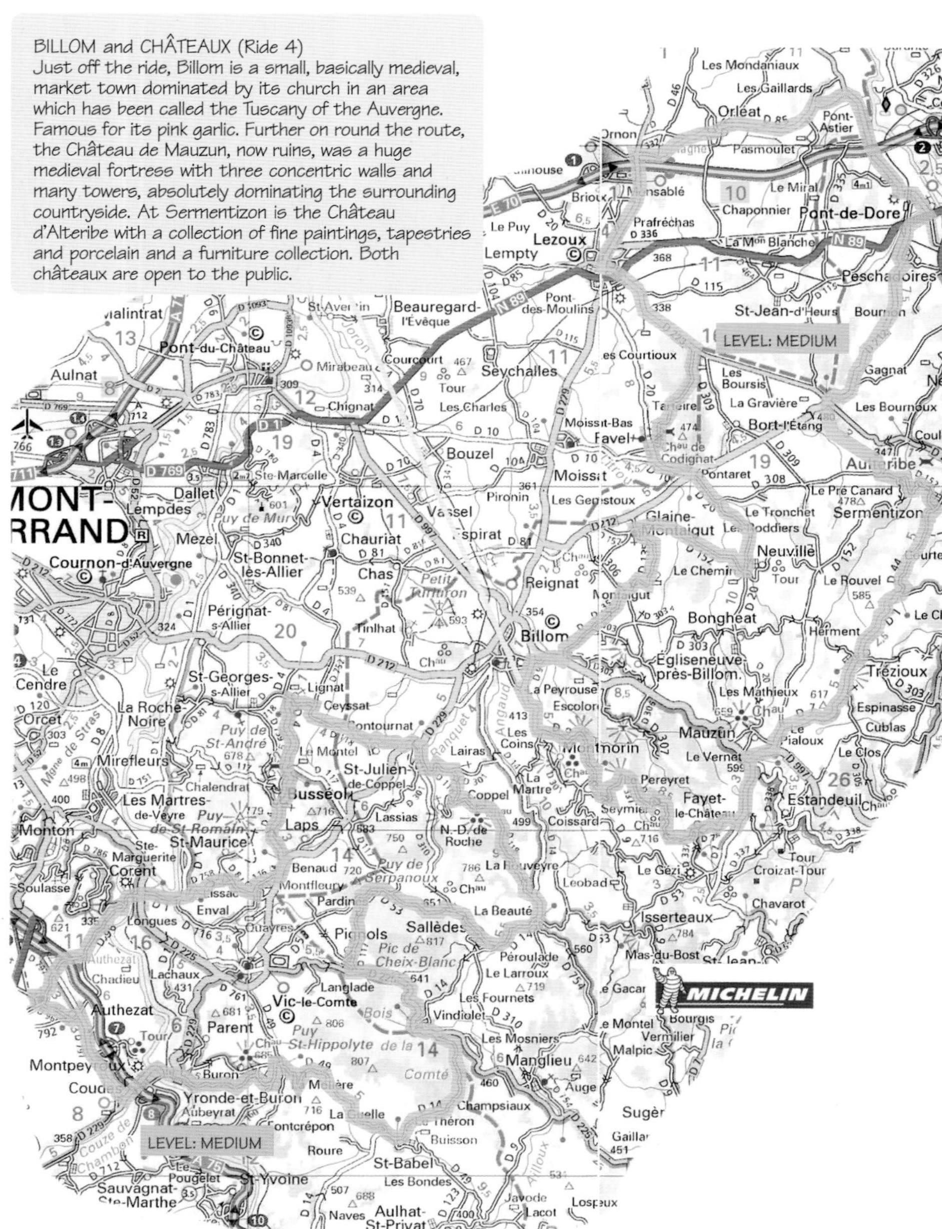

Signage

Each of the 12 circular routes in the Puy-de-Dôme *département is well-signed*

In the Tracks of the Tour de France on the Puy de Dôme

If you are a Tour de France fan and are staying in or near the 'capital' of the Puy de Dôme, Clermont-Ferrand then you'll love a trip up the extinct volcano that the *département* is named after. Home of famous tussles between legendary names such as Anquetil, Poulidor, Anglade and Gaul. Anquetil and Poulidor famously fought it out neck-a-neck in 1964 with Anquetil finally coming out ahead.

Often close to winning but never champion, Poulidor's name is now synonymous with constantly coming close to victorybut never quite acheiving it (*faire un Poulidor*).

The steadily spiralling 7km route to the summit is only open Wednesday and Sunday mornings, May to September (it's a private road) and there are strict set off and return times (check at Clermont-Ferrand tourist office to confirm details). If you want to go up without your bike you can take the *navette* (shuttle bus) service to the top or even walk it (clearly signed from the intersection of the D90 and the D68). Puy de Dôme itself is located around 7 miles / 11km west of Clermont-Ferrand.

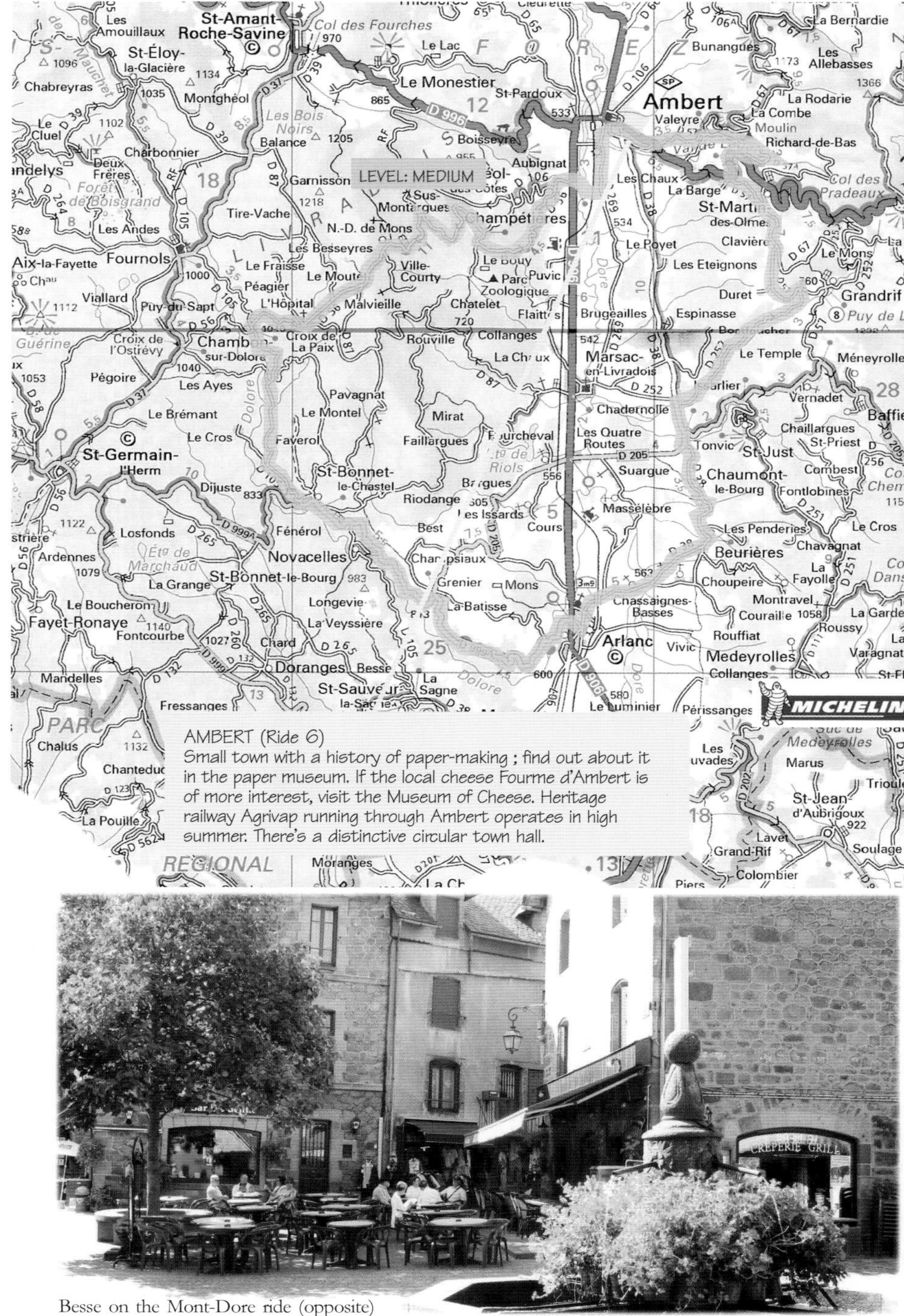

Besse on the Mont-Dore ride (opposite)

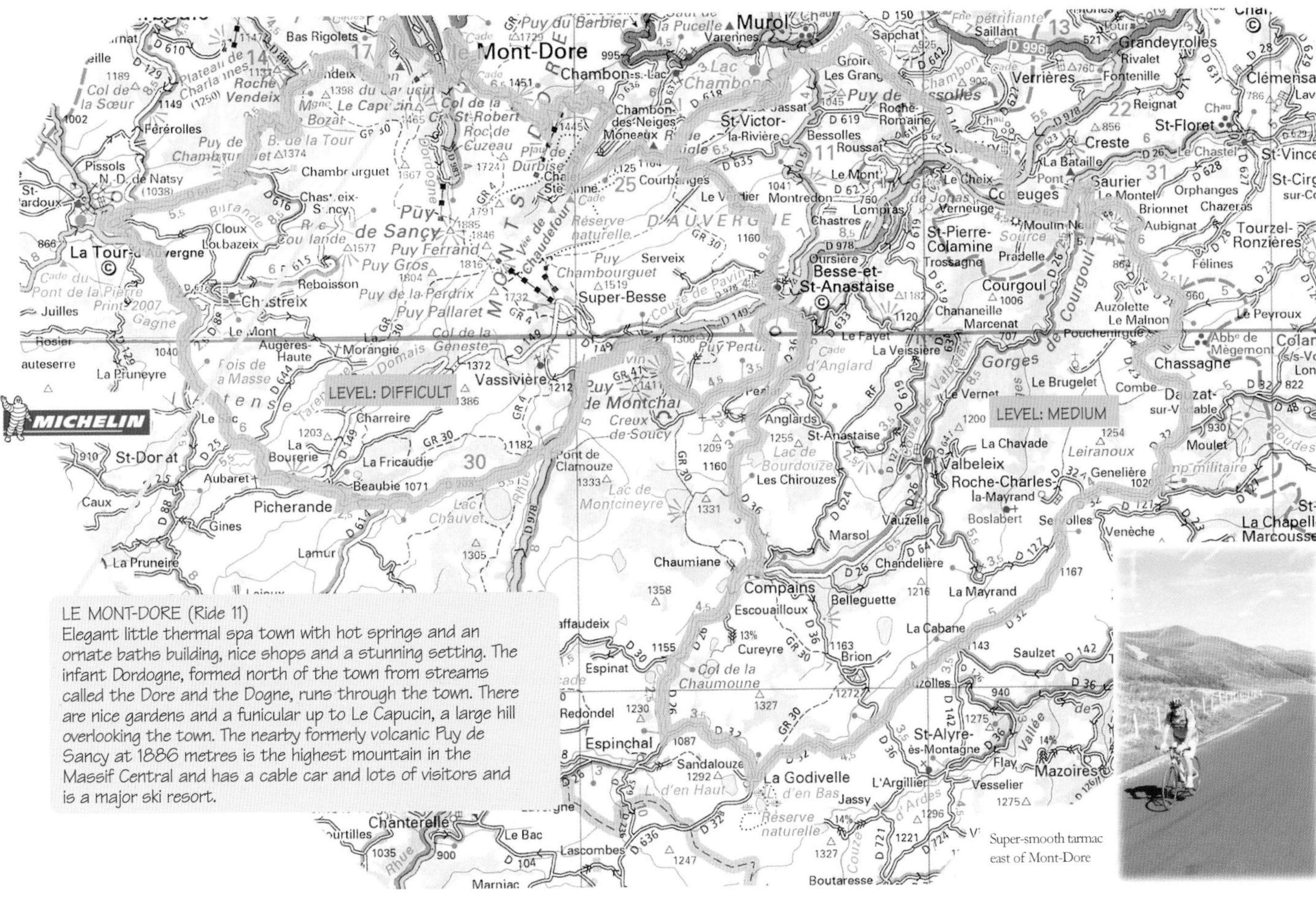

LE MONT-DORE (Ride 11)
Elegant little thermal spa town with hot springs and an ornate baths building, nice shops and a stunning setting. The infant Dordogne, formed north of the town from streams called the Dore and the Dogne, runs through the town. There are nice gardens and a funicular up to Le Capucin, a large hill overlooking the town. The nearby formerly volcanic Puy de Sancy at 1886 metres is the highest mountain in the Massif Central and has a cable car and lots of visitors and is a major ski resort.

Super-smooth tarmac east of Mont-Dore

RIOM and VOLVIC (Ride 2)
About 10 miles north of Clermont-Ferrand (with a regular train service between), Riom has some industry but also interesting museums and churches and a nineteenth century Palais de Justice built on the site of a former palace of the Dukes of Berry, not to mention an octagonal clock tower. Nearby Volvic is known for its spring water - there's a visitor centre - but locally it has also been important for its quarries - the cathedral at Clermont-Ferrand and much else have come out of the ground here. Quarry visits and museum.

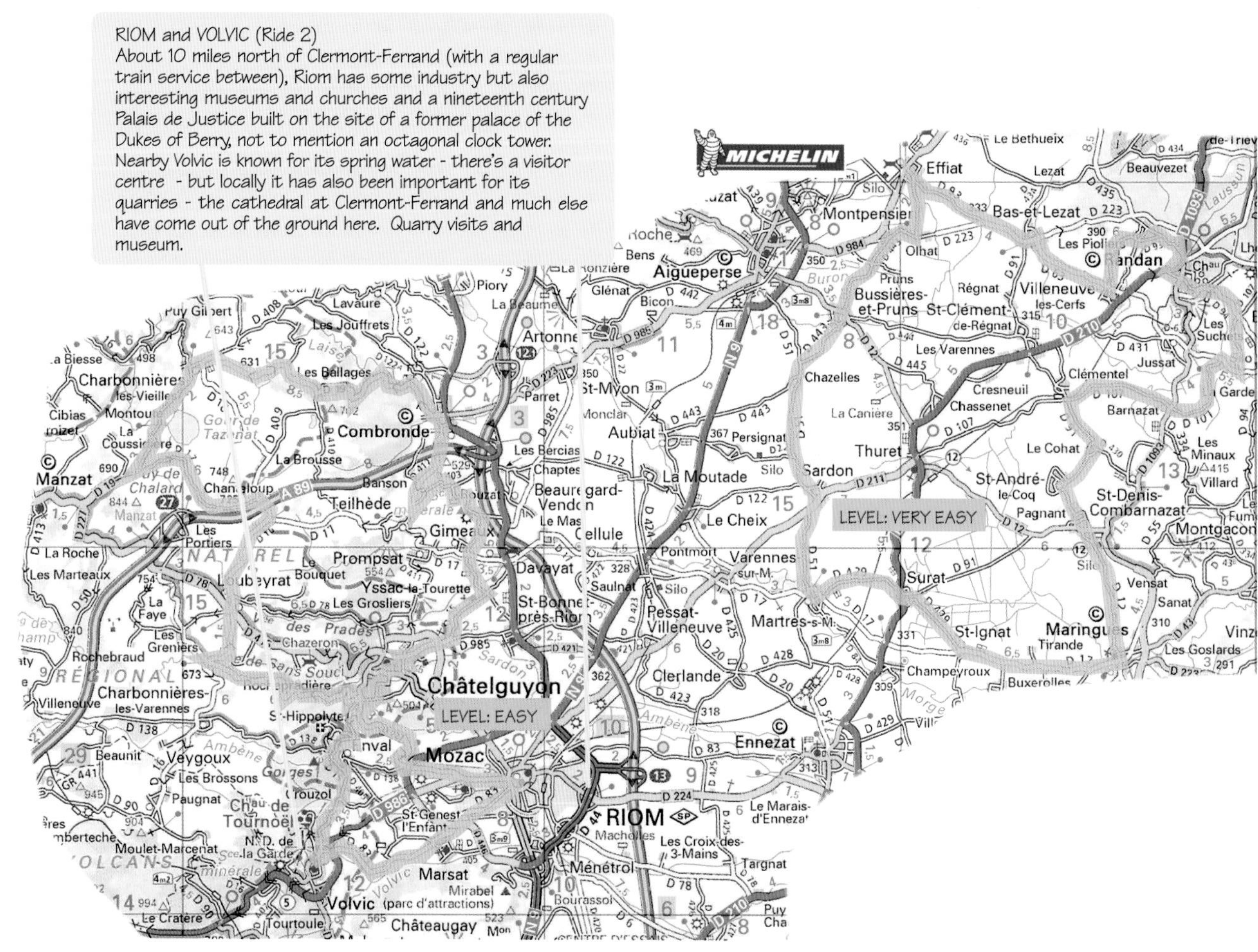

LE LAC DES FADES BESSERVE (Ride 1)
This ride runs through the area around this large lake which offers much in the way of outdoor activities and wooded scenery. The dam and the very high railway bridge at the northern end of the ride are feats of engineering. The ancient church at Miremont is in a nice setting and the rivers Sioule and Sioulet are known for their gorges.

The Lot Valley

Route Info

The Lot Valley
A nice easy ride in an area of lush agriculture and interesting towns and villages. The Véloroute de la Vallée du Lot follows the valley, not always the river, but is nonetheless rich in memorable landscapes and the circular rides in the area offer excursions to all sorts of attractions.

Grade EASY

Route length 53 miles / 85km with circular rides between 11 miles / 17km and 31 miles / 50 km. Pays du Dropt 33 miles / 53km to 64 miles / 102km, Pays d'Albret 47 miles / 75 km to 62 miles / 100km.

Start / finish Condat / Aiguillon

Route advice
Quiet, generally level roads link some lovely settlements, many of them 'bastide' towns, with remains of their ancient fortifications and often with a central square surrounded by arched walkways. Currently there is only a fifty mile section of route open between just east of Condat and just north of Aiguillon (although the best start point is probably Bonaguil Castle just north of the valley on a link route). The route is expected to be extended up to Cahors in the near future with more to follow. Ultimately, it is hoped to have a total of 310 miles between the source of the Lot and its confluence with the Garonne as signed cycle route.

The range of 23 circular rides over various terrains, some easy, some less so are off or near the Véloroute de la Vallée du Lot and add possibilities for varying the route. More and longer signed rides are available north and south of the Lot valley in the area around the River Dropt (5 circular and a link to the Garonne Voie Verte, all on quiet roads) and six in the Pays d'Albret .

Train access Stations at Monsempron Libos (next to Fumel) and Penne d'Agenais on the Agen - Limoges line and at Aiguillon, on the Toulouse - Agen - Bordeaux line.

Nearby routes The Garonne cycle Route (pgs 25-33)

Maps, guides and websites
Véloroute de la Vallée du Lot Free leaflet giving directions both ways, a list of bike hirers and shops and a plan showing the véloroute and the 23 circular rides off or near it with the attractions on them (detailed leaflets available locally). Available in tourist offices or from Comité Départemental du Tourisme. 271, rue de Péchabout BP 158 47005 Agen Tel : 05 53 66 14 14.
www.lot-et-garonne.fr/decouvrir/promenades/veloroute.htm Downloadable plan of the route with supporting information (in French).

The magnificent panorama at Penne d'Agenais

PAYS DU DROPT
These rides in the Pays du Dropt offer ancient towns with busy markets full of local produce and all manner of landscapes. For each ride there is a leaflet with map, cumulative distances and altitude shown as you go round the route, a route profile and some background. Downloadable from www.paysdudropt.com or www.cg47.org The Pays du Dropt site includes a list of cycle hire in the area.

Typical *bastide* architecture abounds

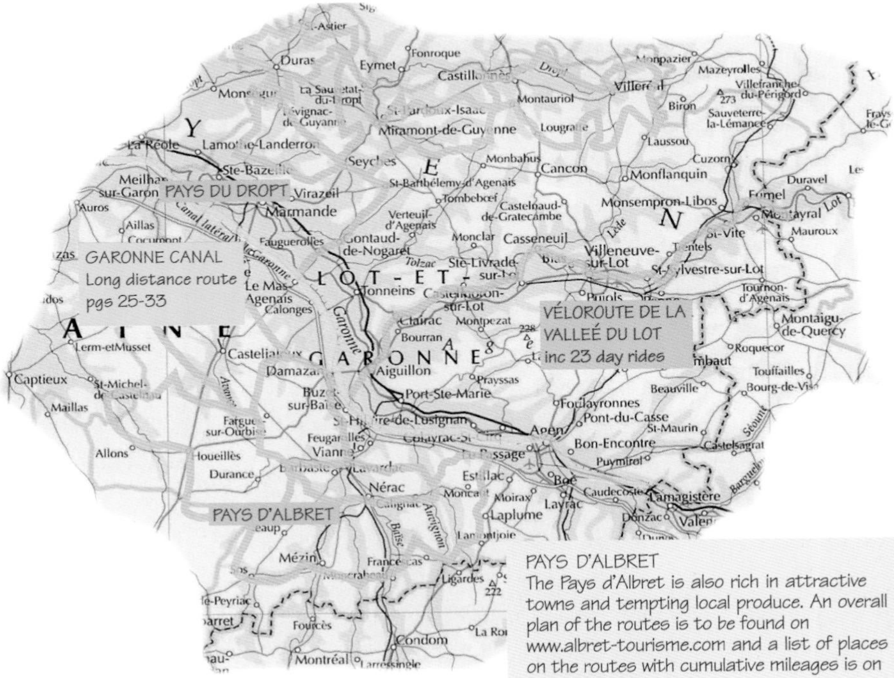

PAYS DU DROPT

GARONNE CANAL
Long distance route
pgs 25-33

VÉLOROUTE DE LA VALLEÉ DU LOT
inc 23 day rides

PAYS D'ALBRET

PAYS D'ALBRET
The Pays d'Albret is also rich in attractive towns and tempting local produce. An overall plan of the routes is to be found on www.albret-tourisme.com and a list of places on the routes with cumulative mileages is on www.cg47.org

All routes are well signed in and around the Lot Valley

Clairac village on the Lot Valley

CLAIRAC
Small, basically unspoiled riverside town with some half-timbered houses and the odd arty crafty shop amongst the normal shops and restaurants. Particularly nice around the river. Boat trips and boat hire available.

AIGUILLON
Perhaps more remarkable for its history (an influential duke and his friends lived the high life here) than what remains, although the château he built, now a college, is impressive. The town stands at the confluence of the Lot and Garonne rivers.

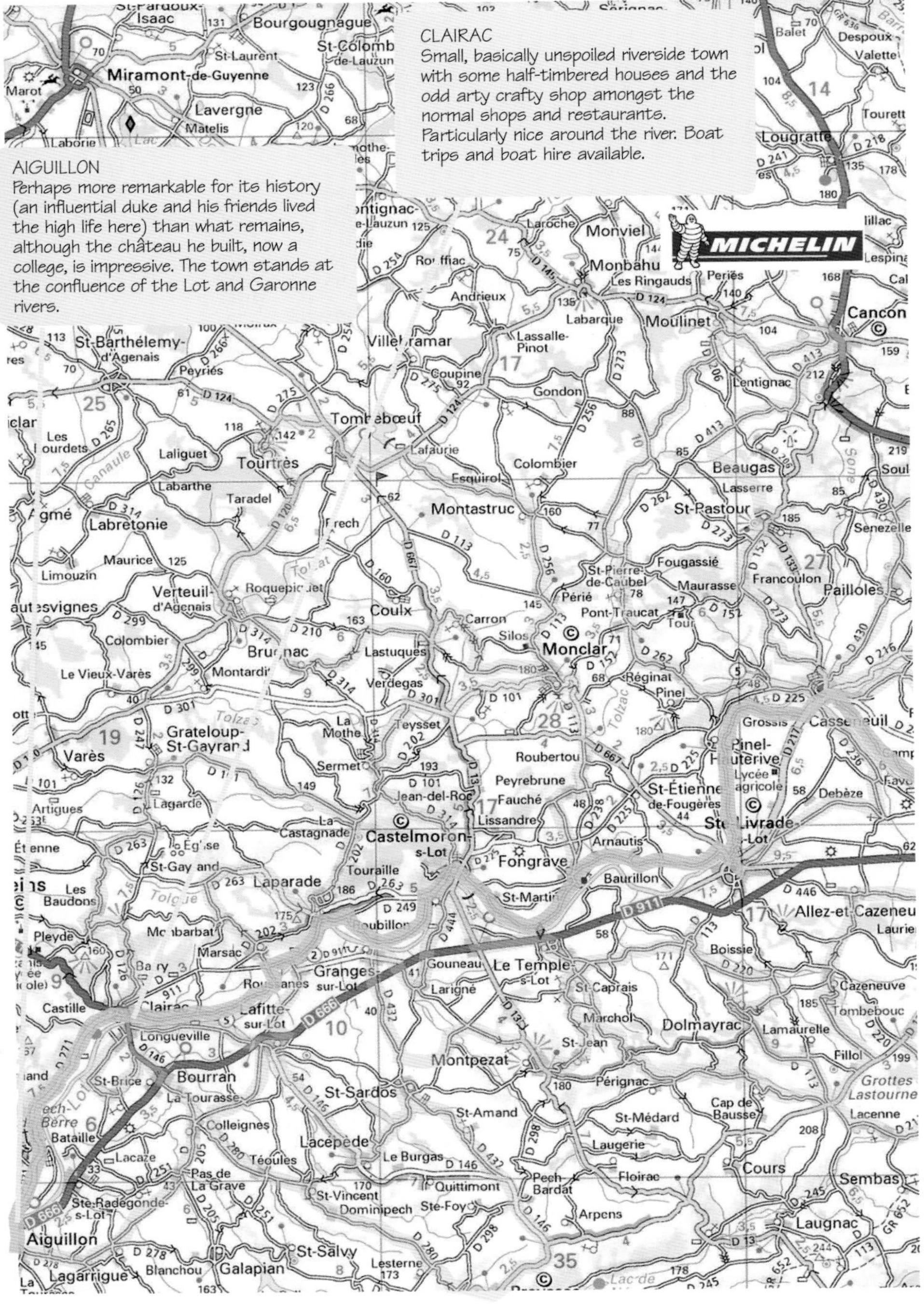

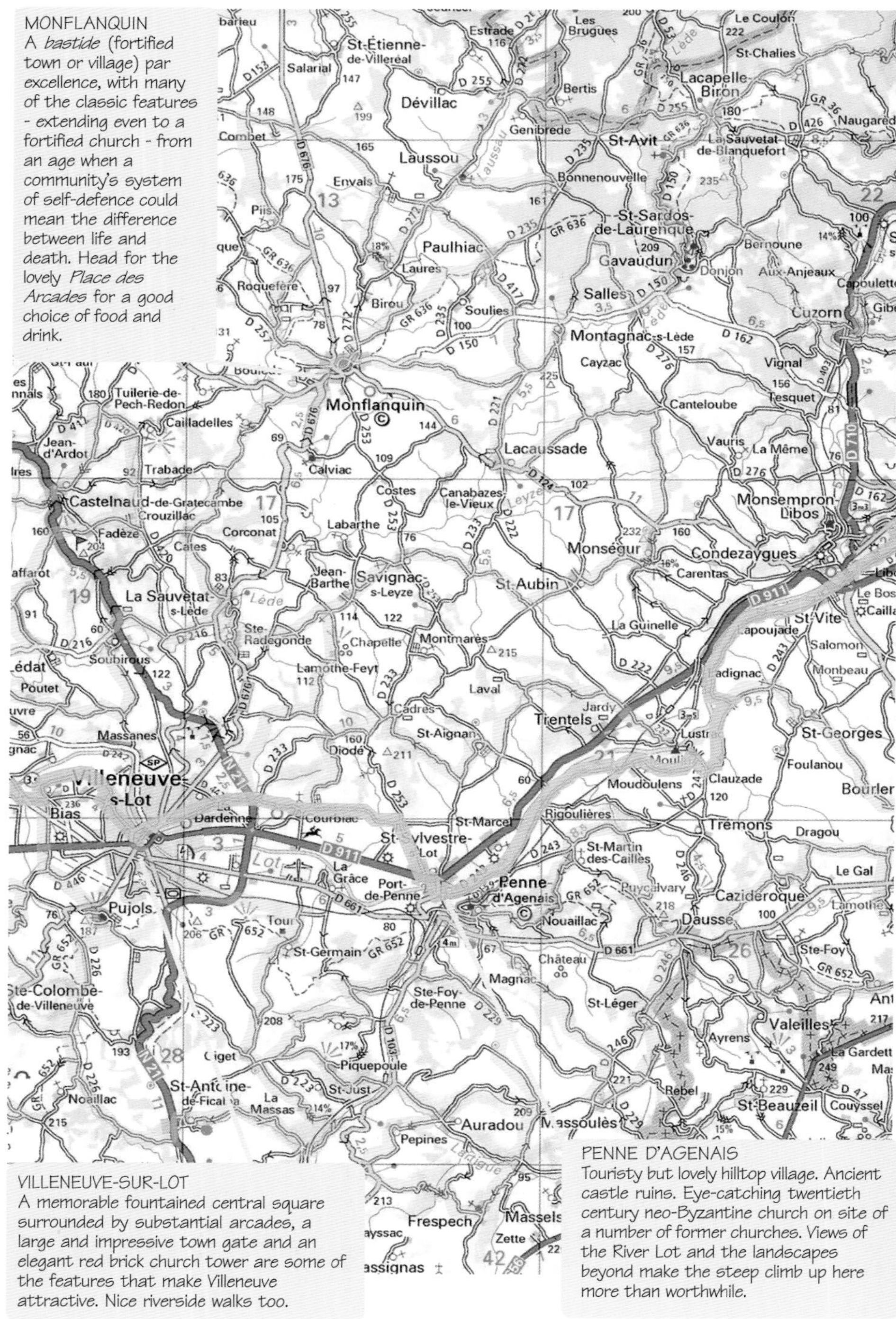

MONFLANQUIN
A *bastide* (fortified town or village) par excellence, with many of the classic features - extending even to a fortified church - from an age when a community's system of self-defence could mean the difference between life and death. Head for the lovely *Place des Arcades* for a good choice of food and drink.

VILLENEUVE-SUR-LOT
A memorable fountained central square surrounded by substantial arcades, a large and impressive town gate and an elegant red brick church tower are some of the features that make Villeneuve attractive. Nice riverside walks too.

PENNE D'AGENAIS
Touristy but lovely hilltop village. Ancient castle ruins. Eye-catching twentieth century neo-Byzantine church on site of a number of former churches. Views of the River Lot and the landscapes beyond make the steep climb up here more than worthwhile.

BONAGUIL

A link from the route near Condat takes you to what is reportedly the last medieval castle to be built in France. Although the last word in castle technology, it never saw action. It has 13 towers and is rather large, a dramatic building in a dramatic setting, all the more stunning when it's seen by the light of the annual summer firework display there.

A small gem of rural architecture adorns a domestic garden in the Lot Valley

FUMEL & MONSEMPRON LIBROS

Though these neighbouring towns are not high on the region's list of tourist attractions (they hold the immediate area's quota of industrial and out-of-town shopping development) each has its own attractions. In the case of Fumel a château whose former owner was slaughtered in his residence by the townsfolk; in Monsempron Libros' case the lovely 12th century church of St-Géraud.

From the Tarn to the Midi

Route Info

From the Tarn to the Midi
An area of mixed landscapes - wooded river valleys, undulating agricultural wolds and relics of former heavy industry now preserved or put to other uses. Albi is a busy place nestling under the iconic monolith that is its cathedral and the towns and villages of the area all have things to offer. Cycle routes are in the main well-signed and some of the quiet roads are very quiet.

Grade See Route advice sections below

Route length
Lescure to Trébas 27 miles / 44 km. Circuit des crêtes 40 miles / 64 km. Albi - Castres railpath 27 miles / 44 km. Castres - Revel 20 miles / 32 km. Revel-Canal du Midi (Rigole de la Plaine) 18 miles / 29km. Revel-Lacombe-Montagne Noir circular 35 miles / 56km.

Route advice
A route from just outside Albi follows the roads alongside the River Tarn up to Trébas through wooded valleys with some scenic hotspots along the way. **Grade** **MEDIUM**
The "Circuit des crêtes" is a circular route off a spur from Albi through rolling farmland to the dramatically-set Cordes-sur-Ciel followed by a riverside ride to Monestiés and then on to Carmaux. Not on the marked route, a greenway return from Carmaux is possible to a smaller loop at the southern end of the route running through the amazing Cap Découverte leisure centre. This is just one of the many signed cycle routes in the Tarn (though perhaps the most interesting) - to get full details of the others see Maps, guides and websites section.
Grade **MEDIUM**
From Albi to Castres there's an award-winning greenway on a former railway with excellent information boards about points of interest along the route, be they flora, fauna or local history.
Grade EASY
From Castres a quiet road route goes to Revel with a subsequent off-road link following canalwater supply channels (Rigole de la Plaine) to near Castelnaudary on the Canal du Midi. **Grade** EASY
Another more testing route along a water channel climbs into the *Montagne Noire,* the Black Mountains, to Lacombe. The suggested road return to Revel is both unsigned and extremely hilly as it climbs to the lovely viewpoint near Mont Alric. **Grade** **DIFFICULT**

Train access
The line north east out of Toulouse serves Albi and Carmaux and a line from St. Sulpice goes to Castres and Mazamet.

Nearby routes
The Lot Valley (pgs 138-143) and the Canal du Midi (pgs 34-39).

Maps, guides and websites
www.tourisme-tarn.com (has an English version) for a wide range of downloadable map leaflets for most of these routes and many others. For the routes from Revel to the canal du Midi and Lacombe the booklet "Toulouse - Séte à vélo, le long du canal du Midi" - see page 34 - has a couple of pages. The leaflet "La Haute Garonne. À vélo au fil de l'eau", available locally, has a small amount in it on the Rigole de la Plaine ride.

LESCURE D'ALBIGEOIS
Delightful village at the start of the cycle route up the Tarn to Trébas. One of everything - a baker, a grocer, a butcher (two on the days when a van comes to the market place) and a captivating tall and italianate-looking brick-built tower which was the main entrance to the medieval fortified village. Also, on the route out of Lescure, the ancient church of St. Michel.

ALBI
A rather stunning sight. The massive, monumental red brick cathedral on its hilltop setting looks over a well-preserved old city area. Bridges over the River Tarn give views of an enticing town riverscape. Birthplace of Toulouse-Lautrec, Albi is home to the Toulouse-Lautrec Museum, housed in the thirteenth century Palais de la Berbie, worth visiting for the building and views from it as well as its contents. A few miles north of Albi and in complete contrast is Cap' Découverte, a leisure cum sports centre in a truly gigantic hole in the ground, a former mine. - water sports, dry ski slopes and blood curdling rides and miles and miles of cycle path.

LAUTREC
Midway along the Albi-Castres railpath, Lautrec is a good place to break. Well-known for the ancient windmill above the town and for the pink garlic grown there, it's a nice, homely little place that wasn't built yesterday. Although Toulouse-Lautrec didn't come from there, some of his forebears did.

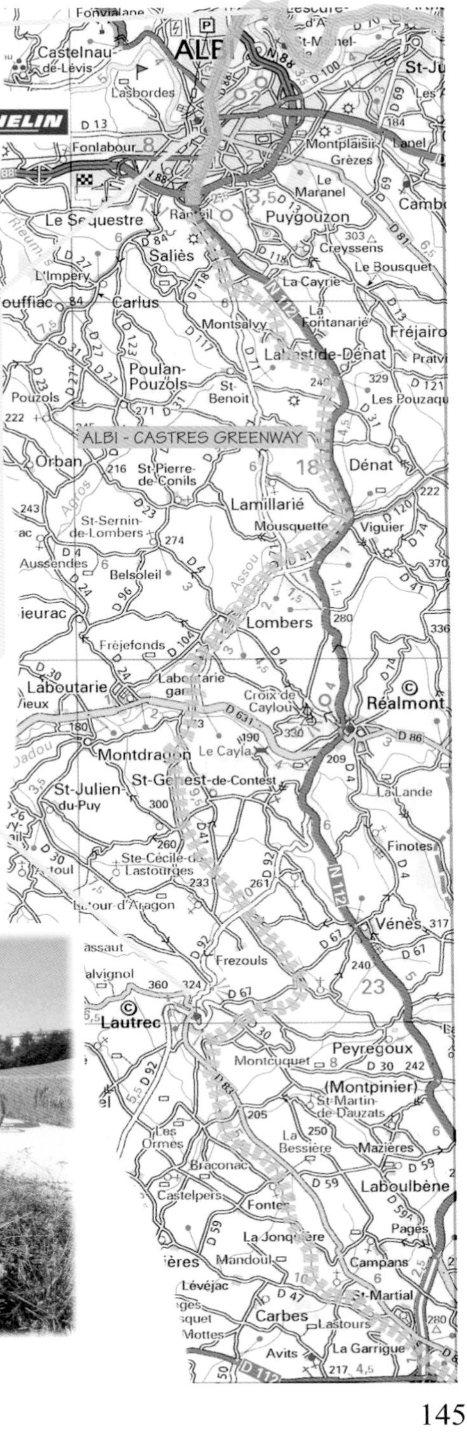

The Albi-Castres greenway is a high quality route

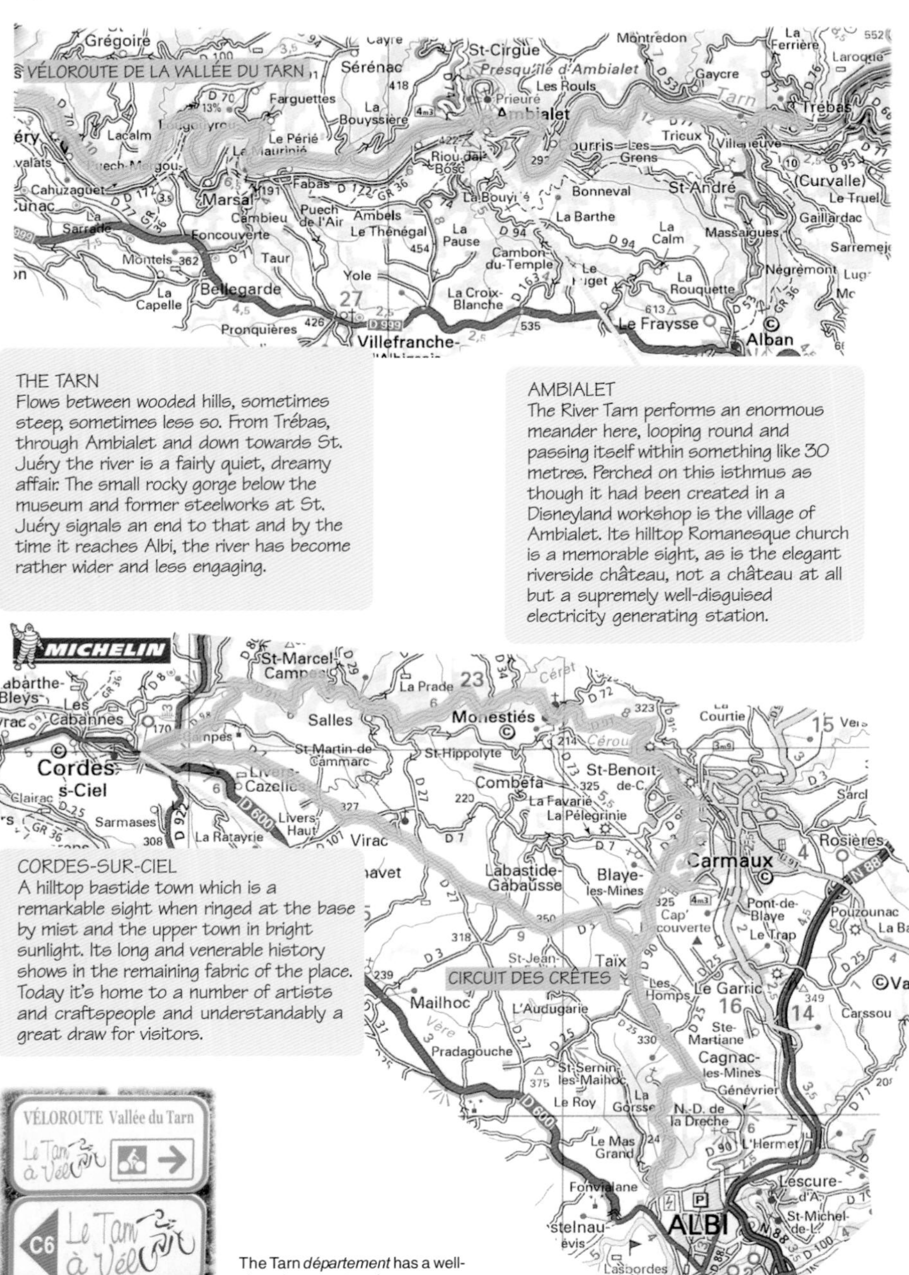

THE TARN

Flows between wooded hills, sometimes steep, sometimes less so. From Trébas, through Ambialet and down towards St. Juéry the river is a fairly quiet, dreamy affair. The small rocky gorge below the museum and former steelworks at St. Juéry signals an end to that and by the time it reaches Albi, the river has become rather wider and less engaging.

AMBIALET

The River Tarn performs an enormous meander here, looping round and passing itself within something like 30 metres. Perched on this isthmus as though it had been created in a Disneyland workshop is the village of Ambialet. Its hilltop Romanesque church is a memorable sight, as is the elegant riverside château, not a château at all but a supremely well-disguised electricity generating station.

CORDES-SUR-CIEL

A hilltop bastide town which is a remarkable sight when ringed at the base by mist and the upper town in bright sunlight. Its long and venerable history shows in the remaining fabric of the place. Today it's home to a number of artists and craftspeople and understandably a great draw for visitors.

The Tarn *département* has a well-signed route network - a véloroute along the valley and circular routes (C plus a number) as well as its high quality greenway

Between Lescure d'Albigeois and Trébas the Véloroute du Tarn hugs this little frequented river, mainly on quiet minor roads

REVEL

A town with a number of medieval houses and a huge covered market and, from the nineteenth century, a history of furniture making. A couple of miles away, the Lac de St-Ferréol, a reservoir built to supply water to the Canal du Midi and now much used as a leisure facility with swimming, boating and other activities, is on the ride to Lacombe.

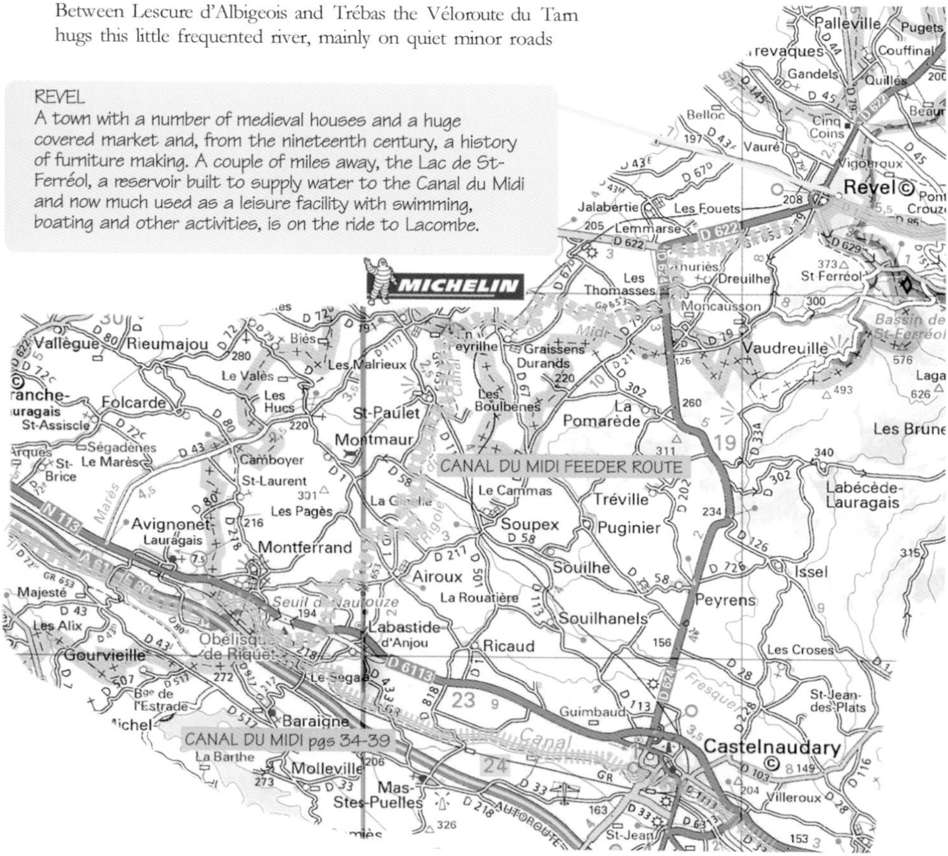

CANAL DU MIDI FEEDER ROUTE

CANAL DU MIDI pgs 34-39

CASTRES

Attractions here include the colourful old houses looking over the stretch of river in the town centre and the large collection of Spanish paintings in the Goya Museum. There are some nice gardens and the place Jean-Jaurès is spacious and quite grand. Castres is the birthplace of Jean Jaurès, the much-loved nineteenth century socialist politician and there is a museum about him.

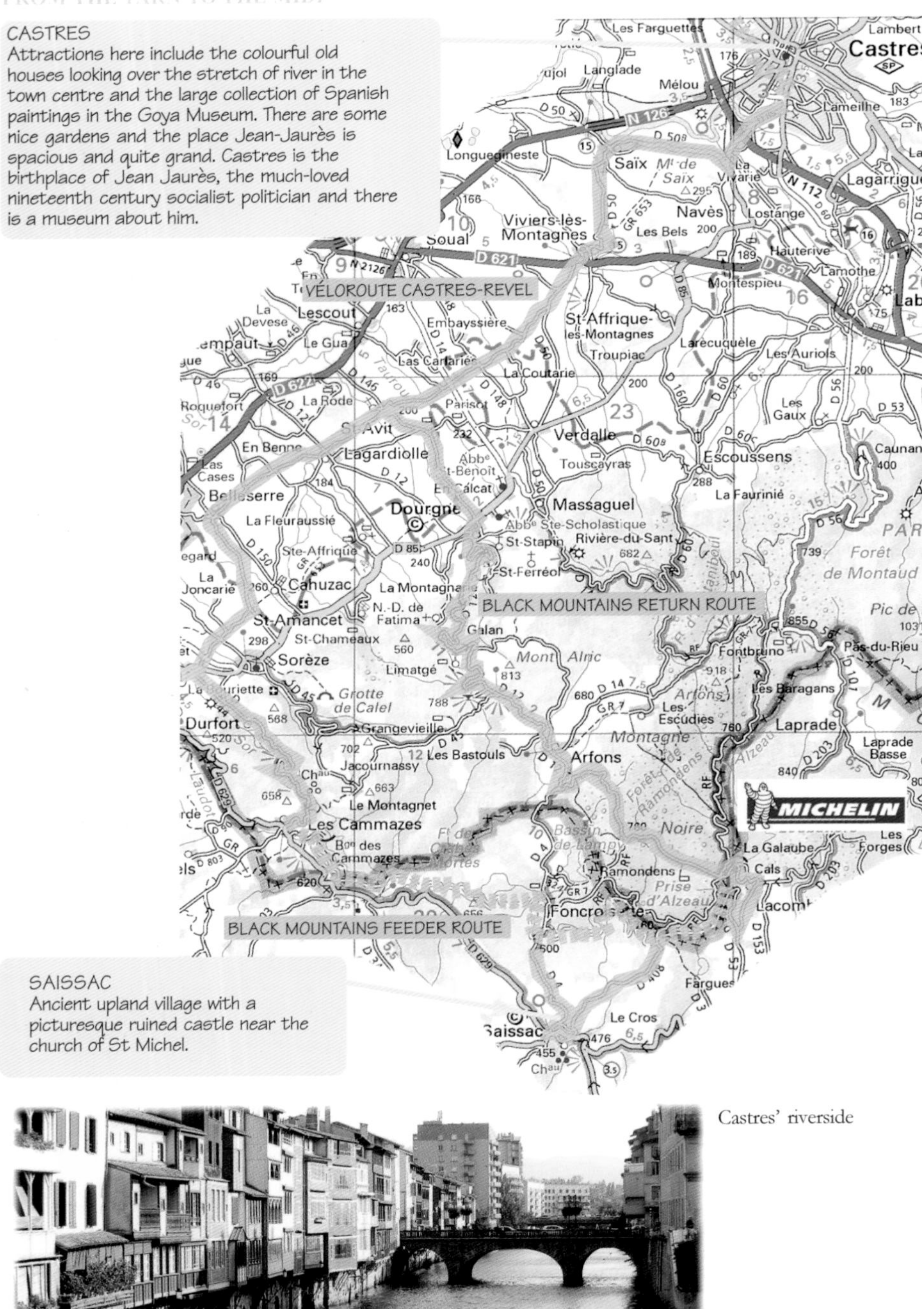

SAISSAC

Ancient upland village with a picturesque ruined castle near the church of St Michel.

Castres' riverside

Foothills of the Pyrenees

Route Info

Foothills of the Pyrenees
A selection of five easy-going rides on quiet roads and greenways in the area between the mountains and the Canal du Midi.

Grade See below

Route length Between 8 miles / 13km and 62 miles / 100km

Route advice
From the village of Saint-Bertrand-de-Comminges, 100 kilometres of well-signed Garonne Cycle Route, mainly on quiet roads, but with one or two decent lengths of traffic-free path, wends its way along the Garonne valley to Carbonne.
Grade EASY (Though it has the odd small, steep climb.)
In the area around St. Bertrand, a couple of short and easy rides on country roads with only gentle gradients in fact give some great views of the Pyrenees. These are called the Plaine de la Rivière (10 miles /16 km) and the Sites "touristiques" (8 miles / 13 km).
Grade EASY
Further west, 17 kilometres of multi-user smooth asphalt railpath, La Voie Verte des Gaves, go out from Lourdes through nice villages and countryside with sweeping views of the hills and mountains to Soulom. (There is then a further 9 kilometres on offer on a steepish gravelled path to Cauterets if you're on a mountain bike.)
Grade EASY
Over to the east there is a 23.5 mile / 38km railpath between Mirepoix and Lavelanet known as Le Chemin des Filatiers. Much of it is on stony track which needs a mountain bike or use of minor roads to avoid these. A 13 mile / 21km loop option, mainly on roads visits Montségur, the eastern leg threading back through the hills. Although the path isn't finished or properly signed, tunnels are lit and there are information boards with overall plans and distances on. The path is part of a disused railway between the château of Montségur and the canal du Midi.
Grade MEDIUM

Train access
Lourdes is on the line between the west coast and Toulouse, as is Carbonne (Barbazan near St-Bertrand-de-Comminges is on a spur line). The nearest line to the Lavelanet - Mirepoix route is about twenty kilometres west at Pamiers on the Toulouse to Perpignan line that loops through the Pyrenean foothills (to get a bike from the Perpignan end, it may be necessary to use other lines).

Nearby routes
Along the Atlantic Coast (pgs 40-47), the Garonne Valley (pgs 25-33) and the Canal du Midi (pgs 34-39).

The Garonne Cycle Route is well-signed

Several routes let you explore the Pyreneen foothills

Maps, guides and websites
La Haute-Garonne. À Vélo au fil de l'eau is a locally available leaflet on the Garonne valley ride.
www.valleesdesgaves.com has detailed info on the Voie Verte des Gaves including history, technical information and some very nice photographs. There's also a downloadable map leaflet on it in three languages including English.
www.paysdolmes.org has details of a couple of mountain bike routes out of Lavelanet. There's currently no publicity leaflet on the Chemin des Filatiers.

TOULOUSE - AN UPCOMING CYCLE CITY

Toulouse is a handy and interesting stepping off point for exploring the Pyreneen foothills. Following the lead of Paris, which introduced quality, low cost bike hire in 2007, Toulouse boasts that by April 2008 it will have the whole of the greater urban area covered by 2400 bikes at 253 automated rental stations. To encourage a quick turnaround of bikes the first half hour is free with subsequent half hours starting at only 0.5 euros.
The city also has 142 miles / 228km of segregated cycle lanes and paths (some superb, others much less so), a decent cycle map (available locally and downloadable at http://www.toulouse.fr/fr-32/transports-6/velo-toulouse-155/). Bikes are common in the city centre, no doubt helped by the city's student population - however, the local authority's efforts to promote cycling must also count for a lot. For example the city centre has a system of 'pedestrian priority' streets which are often one way for cars but where bikes are allowed in both directions. With one of the biggest pedestrian areas of any European city this looks like it could add up to a growth in cycling's popularity over the coming years.

Cycling is encouraged in many of Toulouse's pedestrian areas

ST BERTRAND-DE-COMMINGES

Utterly dominated by the hilltop hulk of its cathedral, the village of St-Bertrand-de-Comminges huddles around it, as if seeking protection from its sheer size. The cathedral is all the more unusual for its location in the green Pyreneen foothills. There are a couple of eating opportunities in St-Bertrand, but they tend to be of the tourist trap type.

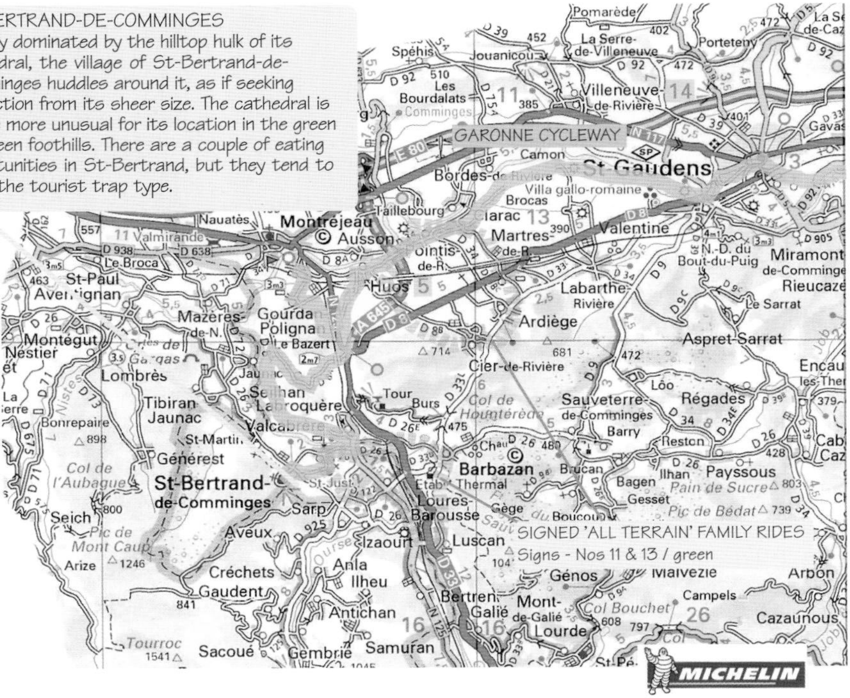

GARONNE CYCLEWAY

SIGNED 'ALL TERRAIN' FAMILY RIDES
Signs - Nos 11 & 13 / green

MICHELIN

The cathedral of St-Bertrand-de-Comminges has to be one of the most spectacularly located and isolated cathedrals in France and is on the Garonne Cycleway

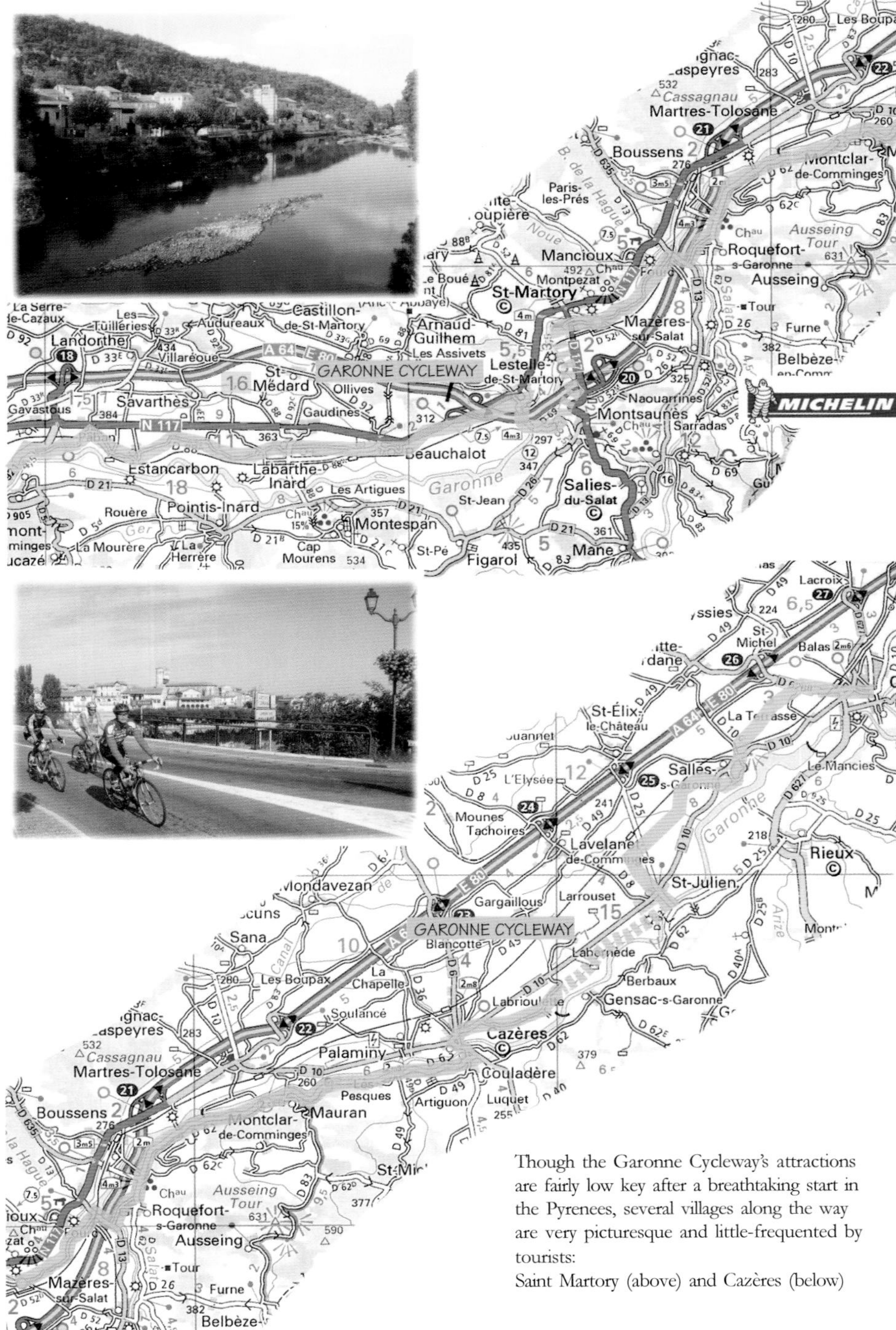

Though the Garonne Cycleway's attractions are fairly low key after a breathtaking start in the Pyrenees, several villages along the way are very picturesque and little-frequented by tourists:
Saint Martory (above) and Cazères (below)

MIREPOIX

Known for having arguably the finest arcaded market square in France - Les Couverts - it also boasts an amazing medieval town hall type building - the *Maison des Consuls* - which features a truly amazing array of carvings on its exterior, featuring animals, monsters and various medieval characters. The cathedral of St Maurice is also worth a look. There are plenty of eating and drinking opportunities around Mirepoix's centre and a tourist office.

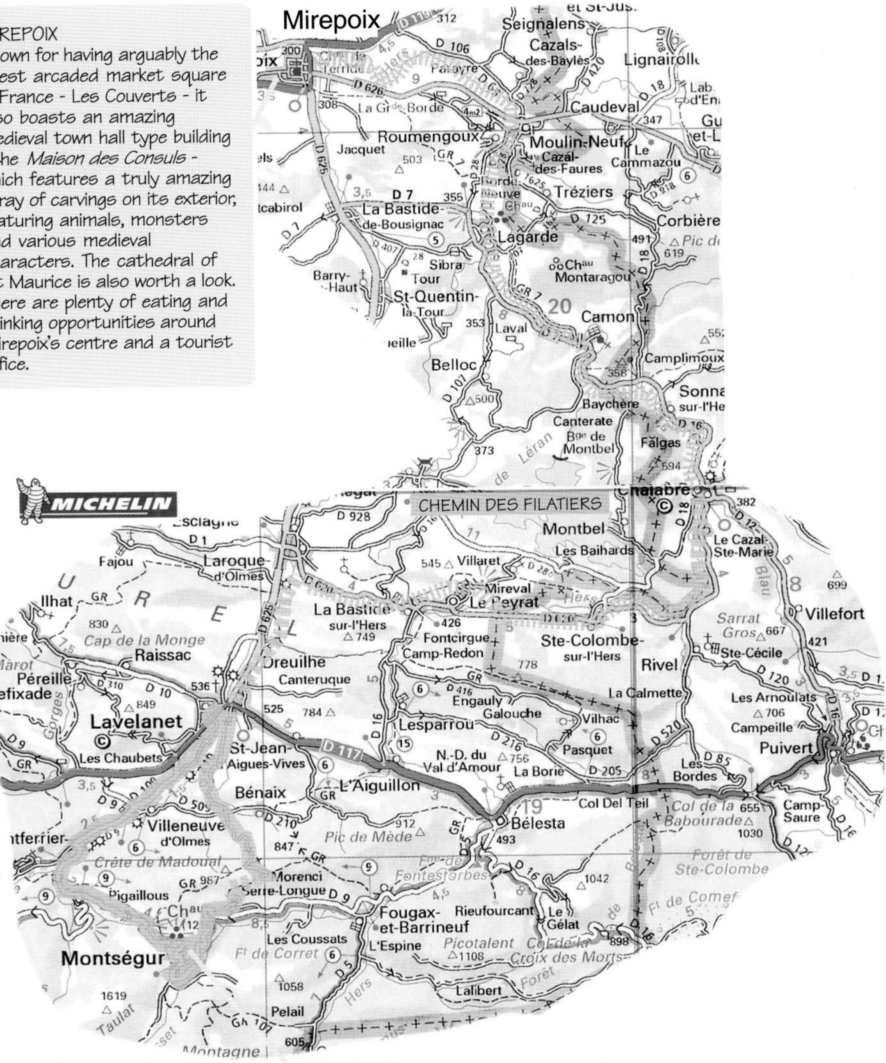

MONTSÉGUR

Housed under a cliff-top castle, the village is rather full of holiday homes but the dramatic setting still reflects its ancient Cathar history. Cathars were religious aesthetes and viewed with such suspicion that crusades against them were organised (the Albigensian crusades). Montségur Cathars were beseiged in the mid-thirteenth century which saw an effective end to Catharism in the area.
You can walk to the castle which sits above the town.

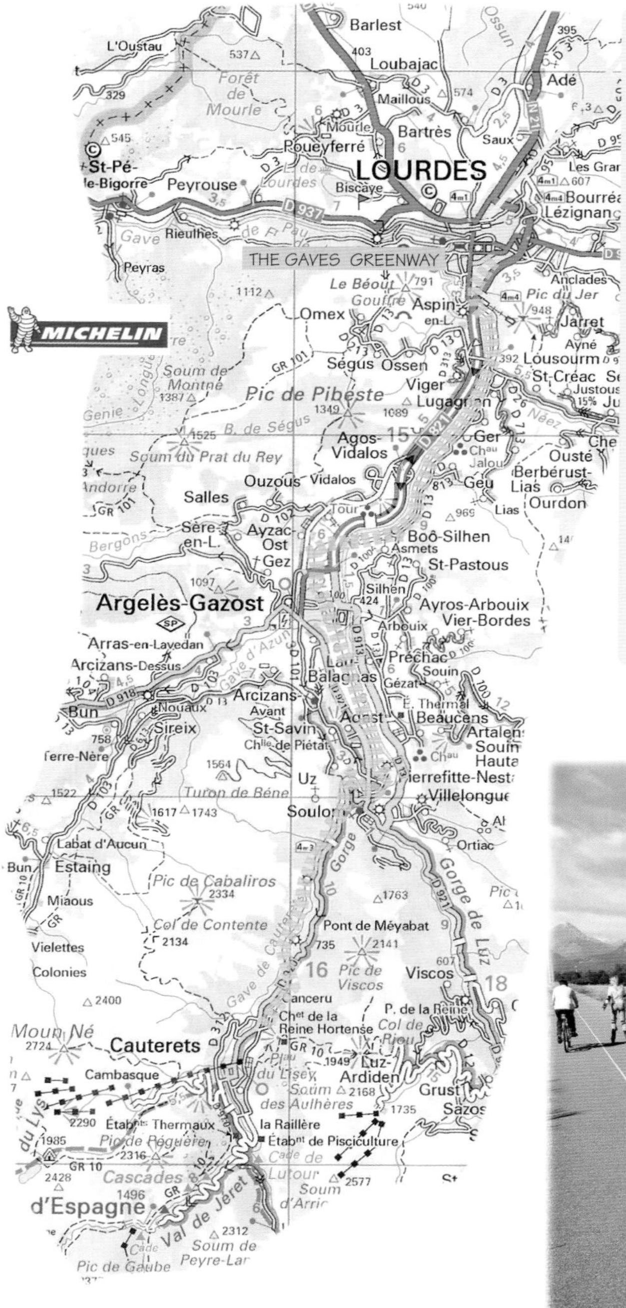

LOURDES

An incredible seven million plus pilgrims visit Lourdes each year, many seeking a miraculous cure for otherwise incurable conditions.

It all started in 1858 when Bernadette Soubirous had a vision of the Virgin Mary in the Grotte de Massabielle. The overwhelming presence of religious memorabilia here won't be to everyone's tastes but it is undeniably unique in its sheer quantity.

The grotto itself is the place where pilgrims light votive candles and take away 'holy water' from the spring and nearby are two churches. One, the undergound Basilique St-Pie-X is supposedly able to hold up to 20,000 people.

The town is pretty much devoted to pilgrims and their needs but there's an imposing château and a ride on a funicular will get you some good views from the Pic du Jer. Lourdes is journey's end on the European Bike Express Atlantic Route.

Voie Verte des Gaves

Périgueux & Around

Route Info

Périgueux and around
Three greenway rides in different parts of Périgord, an area of idyllic land and riverscapes renowned the world over for its gastronomic specialities. Its history seems to be written across every town, village and hamlet through its medieval buildings and castles. The prehistoric paintings in some of its caves are extraordinary.

Grade EASY

Route length 9 miles to 17 miles (15 to 27 km) in length.

Route advice
The Thiviers to Saint-Pardoux-la-Rivière Greenway is 10.5 miles / 17 km of railpath across wooded hills and valleys with a surface of smooth crushed stone. Sometimes the route goes through cuttings or on embankments with intermittent views of the surrounding countryside. Climbs are longer if you go from west to east. The route is normally well-shaded. There are no settlements on the route itself (and no water points) although a number of settlements are nearby including St.Romain et St. Clément, St.Jean de Côle, St. Martin de Fressengeas and Milhac-de-Nontron. Like Thiviers, St. Pardoux-la-Rivière is a good start/finish having a good number of shops, restaurants and other amenities.

In Périgueux, the prize-winning 9 mile / 15 km Voie Verte des Berges de l'Isle is a high quality smooth-surfaced track, lit at night, running between Trélissac to the east of the city and Marsac-sur-l'Isle to the west. In Périgueux it runs alongside the river and a canal then crosses and recrosses the River Isle on cycle/ pedestrian bridges.
The Sarlat to Peyrillac-et-Millac Voie Verte is 21 kilometres of smooth tarmac on a former railtrack with a further 3 kilometres of signed route on quiet roads taking you to Cazoulès, 3 kilometres from Souillac. There's a branch off across the Dordogne to Groléjac. Detailed information sheet (in French) on www.af3v.org

Train access
Périgueux is well served by bicycle-carrying trains from Bordeaux, Limoges, Brive-la-Gaillarde and Agen. Thiviers is on the Périgueux - Limoges line and Sarlat seems only to be served by coaches.

Nearby routes
La Charente (pgs 118-122), Corrèze (pgs 123-129) and the Lot Valley (pgs 138-143).

Maps, guides and websites
voiescyclables.free.fr has maps, or links to them, and basic information on all three routes in the site's Aquitaine section.
La Voie Verte. Saint-Pardoux-la-Rivière - Thiviers is a locally available map leaflet.

ST. JEAN DE CÔLE
Lovely village with the 15th and 17th century Château de Marthonie in the centre and a large and ancient church, small and ancient bridge, covered market place and half-timbered houses. There is a bakery, a grocer's, a restaurant, a hotel, a post office and arts and crafts shops.

ST PARDOUX THIVIERS GREENWAY

THIVIERS
A nice little town in Périgord Vert (named after the green landscape), Thiviers has plenty of places to eat, sleep and shop. There's a museum all about foie gras. Jean-Paul Sartre lived here as a child, miserably apparently, but still came back for holidays.

MICHELIN

BERGES DE L'ISLE GREENWAY

PÉRIGUEUX
Périgueux is the main town of Périgord Blanc, much of it built in the white stone of the area, and sports a rather distinctive five-domed cathedral. Roman remains testify to its age and some good museums will tell you about these and much more. The narrow streets and pleasant squares of the old town, and the main street, boulevard Montaigne, are attractive.

Two views of cycling the *Voie Verte des Berges de l'isle* around Périgueux
Office de Tourisme de Périgueux

CARSAC
Standing at the junction of the Dordogne and a smaller tributary, Carsac is a pretty village with a restored Romanesque church.

CHÂTEAU DE MONTFORT
A dramatic setting on a rock overlooking the Dordogne make this many times besieged castle highly photogenic.

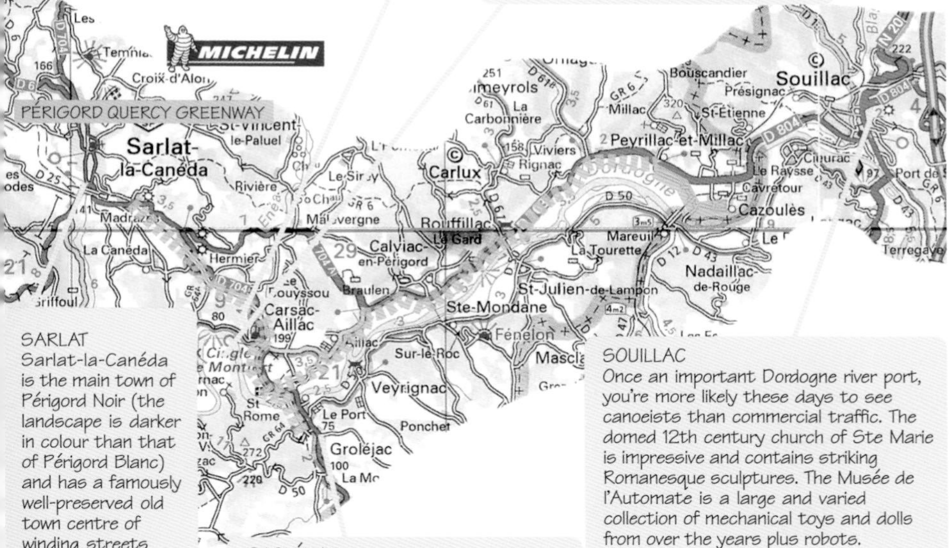

PÉRIGORD QUERCY GREENWAY

SARLAT
Sarlat-la-Canéda is the main town of Périgord Noir (the landscape is darker in colour than that of Périgord Blanc) and has a famously well-preserved old town centre of winding streets often used as a setting in films. It's known for foie gras and as the home of many artists and craftspeople.

GROLÉJAC
Nice little town by the Dordogne - swimming and canoeing there or the town's leisure lake has a sandy beach.

SOUILLAC
Once an important Dordogne river port, you're more likely these days to see canoeists than commercial traffic. The domed 12th century church of Ste Marie is impressive and contains striking Romanesque sculptures. The Musée de l'Automate is a large and varied collection of mechanical toys and dolls from over the years plus robots.

FRENCH CYCLING HEROES

Pierre Lallemont invented the first two-wheeled velocipede in 1863. Also called a boneshaker, it had pedals on the front wheel and was a precursor of the Penny Farthing.

Paul de Vivie is commonly credited with inventing the first derailleur - a two speed - for touring in the Alps. He omitted to patent the revolutionary idea and made barely any money. Henri Desgrange, organiser of the Tour de France, dismissed the radical new invention as only fit for women and invalids. Vivie was also known as Vélocio, a nom de plume, in his groundbreaking magazine *Le Cycliste*. He outlined his own 'seven commandments' of cycle touring, most of which still hold true today:
* Keep your stops short and few * Eat before you're hungry, drink before you're thirsty *
* Never get too tired to eat or sleep * Add a layer before you're cold, take one off before you're hot * Lay off wine, meat and tobacco on tour * Ride within yourself, especially in the first hour
* Never show off *

Charles Terront One of France's first sports superstars who began his career riding wooden velocipedes, then moved onto high-wheelers (penny farthing style) before moving onto modern style 'safety bicycles' as today's basic diamond frame bike design was originally called. He won countless races and rode from St. Petersburg to Paris in 14 days and 7 hours.

The Michelin Brothers Édouard and André were responsible for the mass production and mass marketing of the pneumatic tyre in France. Charles Terront used some of their tyres to race the mammoth 660 mile / 1200km Paris-Brest-Paris event of 1891. He won the race in 71 hours 18 minutes. In a race in 1892 the publicity conscious brothers surreptitiously scattered the riders' path with tacks to prove how quickly their tyres could be repaired.

OTHER ROUTES

Route Name	Département	Type	Length Miles / km	More Info
Ardèche (La Voulte sur Rhône)	Ardèche	Greenway	9 / 14	
Piste verte en Sumène-Artense	Cantal	Greenway	8 / 13	www.la-piste-verte.com
Tour du Lac Saint Point	Doubs	Greenway	12.4 / 20	www.voie-verte.com
Vaunage Greenway (Caveirac to Sommières)	Gard	Greenway	12 / 19	
Beaucaire to Pont du Gard	Gard	Greenway	Exact route being finalised at time of writing	
Mios to Bazas	Gironde	Greenway	41 / 66	
Blaye to Étauliers	Gironde	Greenway	8 / 13	
Airbus A380	Haute-Garonne	Greenway	13 / 21	
Olargues to Tunnel de la Fenille	Hérault	Greenway	22 / 35	
Mont-de-Marsan to Villeneuve-de-Marsan	Landes	Greenway	10 / 16	
Haute-Saintonge	Poitou-Charentes	Greenway	10 / 16	
Virezay - Port-Maubert	Poitou-Charentes	Greenway	10 / 16	
Perpignan to Thuir	Pyrénées-Orientales	Greenway	9 / 15	
River Agly	Pyrénées-Orientales	Greenway	9 / 15	
Beaujolais	Rhône	Greenway	7 / 11	
Le Tacot	Rhône	Greenway	4 / 6	
Voie de la Dombes	Rhône	Greenway	3 / 5	
Châtellerault - Le Bouchet	Vienne	Greenway	24 / 39	

INDEX

MAIN SETTLEMENTS AND FEATURES